The Design Puzzle:
Putting the Pieces Together

Bobbie Schwartz, APLD

Donna Marchetti & Tammi Olle
Editors

Susan Myers
Graphic Designer

© Bobbie Schwartz 2001, revised 2003 Shaker Heights, Ohio

ISBN: 0-9716317-1-9

9 780971 631717

Table of Contents

Table of Contents

Preface

In 1969, my husband and I bought our first house, which had a small garden. I knew virtually nothing about gardening but I loved flowers. On the mistaken assumption that it would be cheaper to grow my own than buy from the florist each week, I started learning about what I already had. This experience was fostered by my next door neighbor, a retired doctor who was an avid gardener. "Doc" named every perennial in my garden and taught me how to take care of them. What neither of us envisioned was that I would soon surpass him.

I became obsessed, reading everything I could get my hands on and ordering profligately from catalogs. How soon I learned that pictures and descriptions in catalogs frequently bear little relation to reality. I also learned that plants don't read the books and that experimenting with microclimates enables us to grow plants successfully that shouldn't survive.

By 1977, with my youngest child in school all day, I was searching for something to fill my time that would be satisfying. This search coincided with the knowledge that friends and neighbors had been asking me for gardening advice and that I really did know more than they did. Thus began my business. I printed business cards and bought a vendor's license. My business was very part-time at the beginning but as my children aged and I had more time, the business grew. Then I was being asked to design gardens and decided that although I thought my instincts were good, I should take some design courses. Through those courses, I sharpened my drawing skills and honed in on the principles of landscape design.

In 1984, I joined the Perennial Plant Association. One of the great benefits of belonging to that organization has been the opportunity to travel this country, hearing lectures by very knowledgeable speakers and seeing a vast array of gardens and gardening styles. I have also been able to travel to Europe to see gardens there.

Those of us who garden love to share our gardens with kindred spirits. I also love to share what I have learned about design and thus lecture around the country and write for several publications. This book is an attempt to share with you some of what I have learned over the past thirty years.

Perennially,

Bobbie

Acknowledgements

From time to time, people have asked me whether I've written a book. When I've anwered in the negative, they have urged me to do so. My rationale has always been that there no longer exists a gardening or design topic that hasn't already been written about. My husband, who recently attended one of my lectures, pointed out that I would not have to write a book from scratch but could compile the articles I've written over the years for various publications. Voila!

Thanks to those of you who've asked and thanks to my husband for the idea. Extra thanks to my husband, Niki, who has always been as supportive as any wife could desire. If I didn't have time to fix dinner, he took me out. If we were running low on clean underwear, he bought more. If I was feeling overwhelmed (you know what spring is like), he brought me a glass of wine and gave me lots of hugs and kisses.

Thanks also to all of my gardening friends: the "Garden Wenches" who install and maintain my designs and make me laugh uncontrollably, the innumerable members of the Perennial Plant Association who have become "family," and members of the Association of Professional Landscape Designers who are really good at what they do and who are working hard to bring recognition to our profession.

Special thanks go to my editors, Donna and Tammi, and to my graphic designer, Sue. I never could have done this without them.

Elements of Design

Design Principles:
Order, Unity and Rhythm

Those of us in the green industry know how important it is to educate the public, our potential customers. Most people want to save money on landscaping and, at least initially, believe they can do this by designing their own landscapes. Sadly, often only after spending a lot of money with unfortunate results do they realize that they did not know enough to translate their wants, needs and dreams into a pleasing reality that will enhance their lives. But a good landscape designer can do all of this, transforming the mundane into something truly creative and exciting while saving a client from making expensive mistakes.

Good design is based upon many components: aesthetics, function, plant knowledge, graphic presentation and, above all, design principles. A solid understanding of these principles is the foundation for professional design, the basis for problem solving in the design process.

There are a number of design principles, all of which contribute to the creation and organization of a design. The number and terms vary depending on the teacher or writer. According to Norman J. Booth and James E. Hiss, professors at Ohio State University and authors of "Residential Landscape Architecture," the three primary design principles are order, unity and rhythm. These fundamental concepts of composition provide designers with guidelines for their work, but they are not formulas.

Order provides the underlying visual structure and organization of a design. How many times have you seen a landscape with several small beds dotting the property? Sweeping bed lines that incorporate these scattered beds into one or two large beds would impart a sense of order by inclusion. Order is also abetted by progression, a logical path from one point to another within the property.

Unity provides the underlying feeling of cohesion and harmony among the elements of the composition. How many times have you seen a property with a disharmonious mix of theme, such as a combination of rectilinear and curvilinear lines arranged with no apparent rationality? This is not to say that themes can't be mixed; they certainly can, as evident in arc and tangent design, which combines the straight line with an arced line. What frequently happens is that the landscape is altered in stages, without regard for the whole. The patio is a square or rectangle, the bed against the fence is curvilinear because an old maple is in the middle of it, and the space where the play set stood is diagonal. At some point, the property needs to be re-evaluated so that a design unifying all of these areas can be implemented. In order to maintain a sense of harmony, the theme should be chosen with the architecture of the house in mind, the designer consciously deciding whether the design will complement or contrast with that architecture.

A rectilinear theme is normally used to create a formal landscape. It will have axes that divide the property into rooms and serve as paths from one area to another. The quintessential rectilinear, formal landscape is found in our Southern gardens, where beds are edged with Boxwood, and in the Italian Renaissance gardens with their long allées of Italian cypress. This formality can, however, be countered with informal planting within the hedged beds. A perfect example of this is the walled garden plantings at Sissinghurst in England, where a mixed border of shrub roses, perennials and annuals is contained within a series of hedged beds along the garden's axes.

Rectangles can be cut diagonally, thus creating triangles or diamonds or a mix of both. A design conceived in diagonals can create extra interest in an otherwise boring piece of property. The potager of Rosemary Verey is designed this way, with great attention paid to the edging plants. She used a variety of plants with interesting textures such as curly parsley, flowering kale and lavender.

A curvilinear theme tends to feel informal. Using large, sweeping curves rather than a series of wormy squiggles will give strength to the design. Remember also to mass the plantings in these beds in drifts.

The rectilinear and curvilinear themes can be combined into a third theme called arc and tangent in which straight lines are connected to arcs. This too is a formal pattern, but with a twist. An arc and tangent pool has a grace that the usual swimming pool lacks, particularly if the beds nearby echo this theme.

Rhythm creates sequential patterns and thus a feeling of motion within the composition. These patterns can be created with plants or with hardscaping. If a property is sloped, well-designed sets of steps and terraces can effectively create a sense of rhythm. One can create rhythm with plant material in several ways: by using repetition of form, species, texture or color; by varying height or width in a specific pattern; or by using a "weaver" plant, which also would contribute to a sense of unity.

A unified design, abetted by a feeling of order and rhythmic progression, will give both designer and client a great sense of satisfaction.

Design Principles:
Repetition, Variety, Balance and Interconnection

In design, there is rarely only one solution to a problem. The creation of pleasing landscapes and gardens is based on the principles of unity, order and rhythm. But when the designer plays with some of the sub-principles, such as repetition, variety, balance and interconnection, a plethora of visions becomes available.

Repetition is the use of similar elements throughout the design to further unity and create flow. One can repeat a species, a form, a texture, a size or a color. All are very effective. I was recently asked to redesign a foundation planting in which the predominant plants were *Buxus* (Boxwood), *Spiraea* (Spirea) and *Taxus* (Yew). The problem was the similarity of these shrubs; they all had fine foliage so there was very little textural contrast. My solution was to use many of the existing plants but to add *Hydrangea* species, *Hamamelis* (Witch Hazel) and ornamental grasses for new textures and leaf sizes. Some repetition is essential to good design, especially from one side of a walk to another, but too much repetition becomes boring and should be used judiciously.

Repetition also is essential in the use of hardscaping elements. If the patio is stone, the path is brick, the fence is wood, and the arbor is iron, there is no cohesion, no unity. This is not to say that every hardscaping element must be the same – two complementary materials, such as stone and brick, can work well together. Imagine designing a patio in stone with a brick edging or brick design element within it; then connect the patio to a walk made of stone with brick edging, brick with stone edging or just brick. Next, erect an arbor through which one enters the patio from the walk. The arbor could have brick or stone pillars connected by wood or iron. The fence could be made from either wood or iron to match the arbor, perhaps with brick or stone pillars instead of wooden posts.

Elements of Design

While repetition is important, too much is monotonous. Therefore, try to incorporate the element of surprise as a deterrent to design boredom. A tall plant that is either dense or has large, bold foliage can be placed at the edge of a curving path to prevent the stroller from seeing the entire landscape in one glance. Or a tall but airy plant can provide a veil through which the stroller is enticed to move farther into the landscape.

Variety is the use of dissimilar elements to create interest. Start by utilizing the full palette of plant materials: trees, shrubs, perennials, annuals, vines, herbs and bulbs. Then within those categories, vary the heights, widths, textures, colors, time of bloom, berries and seedheads, colors of bark, and deciduous and evergreen material. Remember, however, that too much variety is unsettling. Make judicious choices and then mass them, repeating some of them periodically.

Balance is the impression of equilibrium. It can be symmetrical or asymmetrical. Your choice will affect the emotional perception of the design. Symmetrical balance tends to convey a formal feeling, while asymmetrical balance seems more relaxed. If you look at rectilinear design with strong axes, usually the backbone of formal designs, you will find that such design can be softened if the plantings within the borders or hedges are somewhat wild, or if the beds, normally edged with Boxwood, are edged instead with perennials that flow over the bed lines onto the walkways. One of the best examples of asymmetrical balance I have ever seen was a large island bed with one very tall Spruce at one end. The rest of the bed, the length of which was equal to the spruce's height, was filled with Heather. While Heather does not fare very well in our climate, one type of low, evergreen perennial such as *Arctostaphylos uva-ursi* (Bearberry), planted *en masse*, would balance the Spruce.

Interconnection is usually a physical linking of elements within the landscape. Many landscapes are nothing but a collection of fragments of plantings and beds (a small grouping of Azaleas here, one large *Rhododendron* over there, a vine on the fence or the house) rather than a cohesive composition. Bed lines can be extended to include several fragments. Then the plantings within them can be composed and massed to call attention to the distinctiveness of the plants, both their individuality and the way they relate to each other in terms of height, color, texture and form.

One island bed is frequently a fragment. A series of island beds that reflect the shapes of the others is a cohesive design interconnected by echoing lines and hopefully some repeated plant material. When seen from a distance, such a series usually looks like one huge bed, the paths between them indiscernible until the viewer comes closer. When the element of interconnection is used effectively, the viewer feels comfortable in the landscape. When the landscape is merely a series of fragments, the viewer's eye bounces from place to place instead of moving serenely through the landscape.

Hardscaping elements as well as plantings should be connected. If the landscape contains a patio, an ornamental pool, an arbor, a fence and a path, they should not seem to be disparate elements in the landscape but should be connected in some way so that they function as part of a larger composition. This is why a master plan is much more desirable than designing in bits and pieces, which may never be coherent. It is unquestionably more expensive in the short run to have a property designed this way, but it saves a lot of future expense to correct problems that arise after bit-and-piece design.

Establishing a balance between repetition and variety as well as incorporating interconnection between design elements is not easy, but it is essential to the production of a good design.

Design Principles:
Massing, Emphasis and Scale

Massing, emphasis and scale are design elements that allow designers to manipulate the principles of unity, order and rhythm.

Massing is merely grouping plants together. Although this seems to be a very simple concept, it is amazing to me how rarely it is used in landscapes. All too often, a landscape appears to be a collection of ones and twos, which has the effect of bouncing the eye hither and yon instead of letting it rest. Massing provides emphasis to the character of the plant and then lets the eye wander to the next mass in a leisurely manner. The massing will become even stronger if some of the masses of plant material are repeated throughout the landscape. In creating a mass, try to avoid placing the plants in straight lines unless you are designing a very formal landscape. If you look at masses in the wild, plants are closer together toward the center but taper out gradually. So think about the look you are trying to create when planning spacing of your masses.

The size of the mass may and should vary depending on the amount of space to be landscaped and the size of the plant to be massed. Large conifers can be a mass of one as can a very large plant such as *Crambe cordifolia* (Sea Kale) because it is six feet tall and wide when in bloom. This would also be true of *Salix integra* '*Hakuru Nishiki*' (Hakuru Nishiki Willow), whose distinctive foliage draws attention even though it will only grow to five feet by five feet. Smaller woody material is usually massed in groupings of three to seven. Plants such as perennials will benefit from being massed in groupings of three to eleven or more because many perennials look lost if only one is planted. A small landscape presents a different challenge: Even three of anything is a mass in a small space.

Keep in mind that massing does not mean that all of the plants within the mass must be the same size. Think about the way plants grow in the wild. They do not all seed or mature at the same time and rate.

Therefore, a grouping in the wild has plants of varying heights and diameters. When you buy material, try to vary the sizes within the mass for a more natural look.

Not all plants should be massed. The antithesis of massing is the use of specimen plants. By their very nature, specimen plants become focal points. These should be plants so special that only one is needed. It could be a tree with very unusual bark, such as *Acer tegmentosum* 'White Tigress' (White Tigress Maple), which has striking white vertical stripes on its green bark. Or it could be a large ornamental grass such as *Miscanthus sinensis* 'Cabaret' with its wide-striped and slightly stiff but graceful foliage.

Emphasis, also referred to as dominance, means that the eye will go toward certain elements within the landscape, specifically focal points. All other elements in the design should complement the focal point, which can be single or multiple, small or large. A large, artistically designed patio could be a focal point from which all other elements take their cues. For instance, if the patio is composed of brick, the plantings might be chosen to echo the color of the brick, e.g. *Achillea* 'Terra Cotta' or 'Feuerland', one of the orange cultivars of *Crocosmia* such as 'Emily McKenzie' and one of the *Hamamelis* (Witch Hazel) cultivars with reddish-orange flowers such as 'Jelena'. Additional plantings could be chosen to complement the brick-red color. Then, in some beds away from the patio but within sight of them, one could place a few rusted iron obelisks to echo the red and, additionally, add height to the design with an ornament rather than a plant. The obelisks would thus become additional, secondary focal points.

Achillea

In a more serene setting, a weathered gray bench sited at the top of stone steps would become a focal point that is framed and softened with plantings of a pastel perennial such as *Anemone hybrida* or a shrub such as *Hydrangea macrophylla* 'Dooley'.

While a landscape can have multiple focal points, one must be careful to coordinate them and limit the number. Too many focal points will make the landscape seem cluttered instead of designed. I'll never forget seeing a Kentucky front yard that probably had over a hundred wire ornaments in it. This wasn't even a collection – it was a haywire bedlam.

Scale is the relationship between elements in the landscape. If any one element is so large that it does not seem to belong in the landscape, it is out of scale. I once visited a perennial garden that was enclosed by a ten-foot hedge. The plants varied in height from six inches to eight feet with the exception of one, an *Arundo donax* that was at least fifteen feet high. It towered over everything else in the garden and seemed to have no relationship to the rest of the garden. If there had been a progression of heights leading up to that grass – for example, a six-foot *Verbascum bombicyferum* next to a nine-foot *Viburnum* in front of the *Arundo donax* and a *Miscanthus floridulus* next to it – there would have been a relationship, which would have been further reinforced if there were tall trees behind the hedge.

The same problem existed in another perennial garden where white lilies towered over the rest of the plants. Just as an interior designer endeavors to create a sense of comfort within the home, the landscape designer endeavors to create that sense of comfort within the landscape. This feeling is not to be equated with boredom or lack of excitement and is easily negated by a poorly scaled landscape.

A corollary of scale is proportion, which refers to the sizes of the parts within the design. When a designer chooses trees for a residential property, the size of the house and the lot must be considered. A tree that matures at eighty to a hundred feet would dwarf a ranch house on a small suburban lot but would help diminish the elephantine dimensions of some of the massive homes being built in small-lot subdivisions. When designing bed lines around a residence, think proportion. Too many contractors create skimpy, narrow beds inside skimpy, narrow sidewalks that not only give little room for beautiful plantings, but also are just too small to complement the home. Bed depth is crucial to the establishment of good planting composition as well as ingenious and comfortable approaches to the entrance.

Thoughtful designers will use specimen plants or hardscaping elements for emphasis and counter with massed plantings for contrast while keeping all of the design elements in scale to produce a harmonious design.

Design Principles:
Color

All of the principles and sub-principles of landscape design – order, unity, rhythm, repetition, variety, balance, interconnection, massing, emphasis and scale – can be manipulated by the use of color, line, form and texture.

Let's start with color to see how this works. To create order, one could take a specific color such as pink and design a garden that goes from pale shades up to the deepest and brightest and perhaps back down again. Or one could use the Gertrude Jekyll model, which goes from pale blues and purples supplemented with silver, then to pinks, on to peach, orange, red and yellow and then gradating down again.

To create unity, one could choose any color and use it periodically throughout the landscape. This repetition of color should not be limited to flowers but should include foliage as well, where possible, and might even extend to the color of some of the hardscaping. If the intervals between color repetitions seem to be patterned, a rhythm will be created. That rhythm can vary if the interval changes as one moves through the landscape.

Color can be used to create interconnection as well as repetition. These sub-principles are related but not identical. Employing different elements, such as perennials, woodies, hardscaping and accents, of the same color in the landscape connects them and helps create the unity that was discussed above. Some of the world's famous gardens have separate "rooms" for different colors; these are interconnected by a series of hedges that form the walls of the "rooms."

Color can also create balance through careful repetition. The use of a color only twice could evoke either symmetrical or asymmetrical balance, depending on the diameter and height of the plants and where they are placed. At this point, one becomes a stage designer, mindful that on the outdoor stage spaces are larger than they seem. For instance, a black six-foot obelisk sounds tall but will appear relatively small because of the retiring nature of black. A rusty six-foot obelisk, on the other hand, will seem large because orange is an in-your-face color. If all the plants, accents or hardscaping of a particular color are installed on one side of a landscape, that landscape will seem very unbalanced, leading most people to feel uncomfortable without understanding why. The color must be distributed throughout the landscape to avoid this problem.

To create variety, one could naturally assume that at least one more color should be added but this is not necessarily the case. All pale shades, even of different colors, would have some variety but probably also be incredibly boring. Better variety could be achieved with the use of pale against bright shades of one color or, of course, the use of more than one color. One must decide whether the scheme will call for analogous colors or contrasting colors. That decision frequently depends on the mood or emotion that one wishes to create. Either will supply variety but a contrasting color scheme will be stronger.

Determining the amount of a color to use in a particular place is like deciding whether to have an appetizer or an entrée. A little bit will stimulate the appetite, but a lot will satisfy it. Then perhaps there is room for dessert, another bit of the color. Using bits of color is like grazing, which will eventually fill you up, while massing will satisfy much faster.

Color is a very logical method of creating emphasis or focal point. *Salix integra 'Hakuru Nishiki'* creates a focal point with its stunning white/green/pink variegated foliage. Bright colors, especially red, orange and yellow, always attract attention. (That's why the advertising man who created the McDonald's logo is a genius.) Think about metal sculptures in the landscape. If fabricated out of steel or bronze, the color is, of course, metallic, but also somewhat unobtrusive. The viewer must really pay attention to the subject. If, however, the sculpture is a simple abstract spiral but painted chrome yellow, it will create a spectacular focal point.

Lastly, color is a great influence on scale. Size feels different with varying colors. Imagine a long rectangular annuals bed filled with alternating blocks of yellow Marigolds and purple Heliotrope. These blocks are the same size, but what the eye will register is yellow. The only way to feel that the colors are present in equal or at least similar amounts is to increase the Heliotrope by one and a half or twice the amount of Marigolds. Color also influences scale because of the relationship between color and distance. Bright colors come forward. Used in the front of a bed, they make the bed seem shallow. Used in the back of a bed or at a distance, they create the illusion of great depth. Conversely, pastels, particularly blue and purple, fade. Used in a shallow bed, they create the illusion of depth and used at a distance, they cannot be seen.

In the arena of landscape design, color is a tool that one cannot do without; it is also a tool that gives the designer great latitude to create something special.

Design Principles:
Line

Just as color can be used to manipulate design principles, so too can line. Frequently referred to as the theme, line is what defines shape in the landscape design. It can be straight, curved or a combination of the two.

A rectilinear theme will result in a landscape of straight lines connected to one another in a series of squares and rectangles, or other angular geometric shapes, which are usually further connected by axes. Such a theme frequently produces a very formal landscape – often with hedges that serve as the lines – because designs employing this theme tend to be symmetrically balanced. This is not to say that a creative designer could not use this theme in an asymmetrically balanced design. Such formality can always be blurred with informal plantings within the shaped beds. A sense of interconnection is easily achieved with a rectilinear theme because one area will naturally lead to another.

A diagonal theme is very similar but the shapes are set at an angle. The resulting diamonds and triangles often are combined with squares and rectangles.

A curvilinear theme is created when a series of curves, circles and arcs are used. One must be bold and produce strong curves that are large and sweeping rather than a series of squiggles. Balance, whether symmetrical or asymmetrical, will not be as immediately evident in this type of design, but it is essential. Designers face two other challenges when using a curvilinear theme: creating a feeling of interconnection and avoiding acute angled, difficult-to-mow corners of lawn that abut curvilinear beds.

The fourth theme is arc and tangent. Here straight and curvilinear lines are combined to create a very formal but beautiful design. The herb garden of Joanna Reed, a Philadelphia designer, uses this theme very effectively. A large square is divided by axial stone paths that intersect in a circular stone path. That path forms and surrounds a circular bed filled with *Stachys byzantina* (Lamb's Ears). In the center of the bed is a round urn. Thus four outer beds are formed, each of which has two long rectilinear sides plus two shorter rectilinear sides that are connected by an arc.

While we usually think of line as the arrangement of the ground plane, remember that line also applies vertically. If you are designing an arbor, will it be rectilinear – straight support beams crossed on top by more straight bars? Or will the supports be columns of round stone? In the latter case you will have combined rectilinear and curvilinear shapes. If the crossing bars are curved upward on the ends, they will echo the shape of the columns.

Line also refers to plant heights and branching structure. With the vast array of choices offered by the plant palette, the designer has unlimited opportunity to vary vertical and horizontal lines in both height and width but also in thickness. Some trees and shrubs, such as *Quercus robur* 'Fastigiata' (Fastigiate English Oak) and *Ilex crenata* 'Schworbel's Upright' (Schworbel's Upright Japanese Holly), are quite narrowly upright while others, such as *Aesculus parviflora* (Bottlebrush Buckeye) or *Hydrangea arborescens* 'Annabelle' (Annabelle Smooth Hydrangea), are dense and spreading. It is crucial that one keep scale in mind when planning vertically so that the rest of the design is neither overwhelmed nor minimized. A fourteen-foot ornamental grass in a mixed border where no other plant is more than seven feet is totally out of scale, but so is a one-foot conifer in a mixed border of plants five feet and over.

Line can also refer to the manner in which one plans the planting. Earlier in the book, I discussed massing of plants. But there are occasions when one deliberately designs and plants in rows. One of these occasions is the creation of a hedge. Another is the creation of an allée. Walking through an allée is a wonderful experience; it is both romantic and cooling, particularly in the heat of summer, and is a green alternative to an overhead structure. The branches above evoke impressions of woodland glades or European cities.

So how does line relate to unity? Basically, it determines whether a landscape seems cohesive. It is possible to combine themes, but it must be done very carefully, or the landscape will appear to be a hodgepodge. This frequently happens when a series of designers work on different sections over the years with little regard to the existing landscape. If a landscape needs to be unified, repetition of line will help considerably. To avoid boredom, however, some variety in line theme, size and shape of rooms, and the pace should be integrated into the design.

Line contributes to order by letting the designer create a logical progression from one space to another in an interconnected way. Assume, for instance, that one has been presented with a Georgian house that has dormer windows. This means that there are both rectilinear and diagonal lines in the architecture of the house. The present walkway is a narrow concrete path from the driveway, which then angles ninety degrees to a small stoop at the front door. A good designer could devise a much more attractive and interesting entrance to the house by adding a five-foot-wide stone or brick walk from the public sidewalk to the front door. Halfway up the walk, there could be a square set on the diagonal, which might be surrounded by small diagonal beds planted with shrubs or perennials or both, depending on the rest of the design. The stoop could be enhanced by adding one or two wider steps, the second being wider than the first.

Line also can be used to manipulate rhythm in a number of ways. The width of a walkway will determine how quickly and comfortably people can move from one place to another. A curving path of stepping stones will require more care and an even slower pace than a curving path of brick and certainly more than a rectilinear path of almost any width. The size of the rooms and the manner in which they are appended to one another also will be a determining factor in how quickly one moves from one area to another. A designer attempts to use line in this way so that the viewer is forced to slow down, thus noticing plants or other elements in the landscape that might otherwise be missed.

It is easy to create emphasis or focal points in rectilinear, diagonal, or arc and tangent designs because such designs usually have at least one axis that is a natural location for a garden accent. Siting is more difficult for a curvilinear design, although the center of a circle is also a natural location for a focal point, particularly if there are spokes radiating from the center. If, however, the curvilinear design is more abstract, the best site may actually lie within a bed rather than outside it.

One cannot create a design without the use and manipulation of line. Isn't it fun to think about the infinite number of ways to use it?

Design Principles:
Form

In our discussion of design principles, we have touched on the use of color and line. Now we come to the use of form, which is just another word for the shape of an object. Think quickly now: How many plant shapes can you name in one minute? Among natural forms, at the very least, there are upright, oval, columnar, spreading, weeping, conical, pyramidal, round, irregular and distorted. Then there are the manipulated forms: espaliered (training of branches against a wall for a relatively flat look), pollarded (severe architectural shaping of branches close to the trunk to create a dense form), pleached (interweaving of overhead branches into a thick canopy) and topiary (special shaping, usually for containers or lawn specimens).

The shapes mentioned above refer to plant outlines. Let us not forget that there are also a seemingly infinite array of leaf shapes (lanceolate, oblong, elliptical, ovate, orbicular, oval and sagittate), leaf margins (entire, serrate, crenate, dentate, sinuate, incised and lobed) and leaf venations (pinnate, palmate and parallel) as well as simple and compound leaves (pinnate, bipinnate, palmate), and that the leaves have various arrangements (alternate, opposite, whorled and basal). It doesn't matter whether you know what each of these words mean, only that you are sufficiently cognizant of an array of plant material that you can choose plants for their variation of foliage.

Through repetition, form can contribute enormously to the unity, order and rhythm of a design. For instance, a formal setting at Levens Hall in Wales used two-foot conical *Taxus* at each end of low Boxwood hedges. The hedges formed the border of arc and tangent beds and then repeated the *Taxus* as a taller cone within a circular, low-hedged bed full of annuals.

In a less formal setting, one could alternate two different forms at the front of a perennial bed or mixed border. For early summer color, one could alternate the verticality of *Digitalis grandiflora* (Yellow Foxglove) with the rounded form of *Alchemilla mollis* (Lady's Mantle). If one desires to span seasons, the verticality of *Digitalis grandiflora* could be interspersed with the rounded and slightly spreading form of *Aster divaricatus* (White Wood Aster), which blooms in the fall.

Alternating the same plant form with different leaf shapes is less common but also effective. Try choosing two complementary perennials and grasses, such as *Solidago 'Golden Fleece'* (Dwarf Goldenrod) and *Sporobolus heterolepsis* (Prairie Dropseed), which bloom simultaneously in late summer and fall. While their leaf shapes differ, their mounding form is the same. Or, to have something eye-catching for at least two seasons, consider plants that bloom at different times, such as *Geranium sanguineum* (Bloody Cranesbill) and *Sporobolus heterolepsis*. In either instance, both repetition and variety will have been manipulated with form.

Balance must be ever-present in one's mind when working with form. Just imagine how bizarre a landscape would look if all the round shapes were on one side of the lawn and all the fastigiate shapes were on the other. Rhythmic repetition of form will keep the design balanced.

Geranium sanguineum

Using weeping forms can be tricky because their uniqueness makes them become focal points. Too many weepers look like a collection of plants rather than a designed landscape. Thus they need to be limited. Weeping Japanese Maples are so beautiful that clients often want several, and it is all too easy to be so entranced with them that one adds too many. In this case, let's hope that there is a large piece of land so that the maples can be distributed. An occasional upright Maple could also be included.

Though distinctive forms such as weepers should not be massed, this is not the case with fountaining forms. They tend to be rounded but with somewhat pendulous habit. For example, *Pennisetum alopecuroides* (Fountain Grass) and *Viburnum carlcephalum* (Snowball Viburnum) both look very good in masses. When Fountain Grass is massed and the wind blows, it gives the impression of waves on the ocean.

Rounded forms also mass very well. Picture the ubiquitous *Spiraea japonica* 'Goldflame' that brightens the landscape in early spring with its yellow foliage and later with its pink flowers. This is a plant that begs to be massed in order to produce maximum impact.

Some upright forms also mass well. *Hydrangea quercifolia* (Oakleaf Hydrangea), an upright form with slightly arching branches, draws attention to its foliage, flowers and bark. One is interesting but several are stunning.

Any form can be chosen as a focal point, but the choice should be based on location as well as the specimen itself. Tall, variegated ornamental grasses are natural choices because of their height but are especially effective in a location where foliage can whip in the wind. A weeping Japanese Maple becomes an echo of an oriental landscape if it is sited next to a pond where one can see its reflection. A deciduous tree with a large, spreading canopy conjures up images of picnics and a comfortable chair for reading or some other form of relaxation.

As always, scale must be kept in mind. That large, spreading deciduous tree may only be seven feet high when planted but may grow to fifty feet. How close will it be to the building? Will it be in scale at maturity or will it be too big for the space? Would a columnar or oval tree be more in keeping with the shape of the building?

So, when designing, try to visualize all the different forms that can be utilized and then start moving them around the drawing board.

Design Principles:
Texture

Last, but not least, is the use of texture to manipulate the design principles. Color, line and form are all very useful, but texture adds a totally different dimension. Texture is what stimulates the sense of tactility. Watch a child eye *Stachys byzantina* (Lamb's Ears) and then be unable to resist touching it and brushing it, almost petting it. Conversely, watch any child or adult encountering *Acanthus spinosus* (Spiny Bear's Breeches), which looks and is dangerous. He will not only refrain from touching it, but will also pull his body away from it.

The textures most familiar to us are those of broadleaf evergreen, coniferous evergreen and deciduous plants. Within those broad categories, there are many subdivisions.

Textures are directly related to the physiology of plants. For instance, woolly plants like *Stachys* have developed their texture as a survival technique to slow water evaporation and reflect sunlight from the leaf. Shiny foliage, typical of *Magnolia virginiana*, repels rain and permits fast drying, thus preventing fungi from growing on the leaves. The fleshy foliage of succulents such as *Sedum* allows these plants to survive high temperatures and little precipitation.

Sedum

The physiology of plants is, of course, related to the sites in which they naturally grow. For example, those plants that have woolly texture will usually be found on hot, dry sites, while those with very large leaves are usually found in damp locations. If these natural environments are disregarded, the design will fail. *Stachys* will rot in damp soil, and *Ligularia* will shrivel up in dry soil.

Most landscapes are composed of several environments in which different types of plants can be used. Thus one would instinctively vary the textures to fit the environment. Repeating and varying textures in the landscape will contribute greatly to the feeling of unity and order, and should engender a sense of rhythm, balance and interconnection as well.

It is easier to appreciate textural differences in the landscape if the plants of a particular texture are massed. Picture a shady site with one *Leucothoe axillaris* and one fern, perhaps an *Athyrium niponicum* 'Pictum' (Japanese Painted Fern) – very unsatisfying. Now imagine a grouping of five *Leucothoe* with their shiny leaves and in front of them, a mass of the silvery, pinnate-leaved, painted ferns.

Sometimes, if the plant is very large and the texture unusual, a single specimen is sufficient for both emphasis and scale. Christopher Lloyd, the eccentric English designer, has a long, mixed border containing one *Onopordum acanthium* (Scotch Thistle). It is eight feet tall with branched, silvery, felted but spiny foliage. Planted near the front of the border, it definitely attracts attention, but it is not out of scale despite its height because the border includes other plants that are even larger.

In my garden, I have one six-foot *Crambe cordifolia* (Sea Kale) set among other perennials that are one to two feet tall. The texture of the leaves is large and coarse, while the texture of the flowers is delicate, like a *Gysophila* (Baby's Breath) on steroids. The folial texture stands out among the other perennials, which have small, linear foliage. The plant itself is not out of scale because of the delicacy of the flowers above the foliage, which grows only eighteen inches high.

Let us not forget that texture is also an integral part of the hardscaping. What materials will be used for the sidewalks, the patio, the entrance arch? The material chosen for walks will affect the rhythm of those who use them. Concrete and stone are smooth and easy to walk on; brick can be smooth but often heaves or shifts if not laid on a well-prepared bed and then edged. Pavers are frequently slightly mounded so footing is not quite as smooth as brick. A designer should consider the textures of walkways in light of the age and steadiness of the clients and their guests.

Textures, as well as colors and forms, can greatly enhance a patio design. Keep in mind that the perception of color will be affected by the texture of the material. A glossy color will be brighter than one with a matte finish. As for an entrance arch, the sense of place and the formality factor will be markedly affected by the texture of the material. A bentwood arch imparts an air of country informality, the perfect entrance to a vegetable garden. A teak arch with a curved crossbar creates an Oriental atmosphere, while a stone arch implies antiquity.

Our emotions and experiences in the landscape are colored by textures. Take advantage of that effect in your designs. Site an ornamental grass such as *Miscanthus* (Maiden Grass) next to a path so that the stroller will swish against it as though in the jungle. Site a *Morus alba* 'Chaparral' (Weeping Seedless Mulberry) close enough to the house for a child to feel comfortable hiding under its weeping branches of large leaves while imagining he is a caveman or a cowboy evading a tribe of Indians.

I want to leave you with one last thought about design principles. They are guidelines, not laws etched in granite. If you are a new designer, use them as a checklist to critique your design. If you've been practicing for a while, you already do this instinctively. Remember too that the principles are merely a framework for your creativity.

The Perennial Garden as a Jigsaw Puzzle

I am frequently asked, "How do you put it all together?" meaning, of course, how does one design a perennial garden? The best way to start is by drawing the bed lines. This is not as simple as it sounds because the bed should appear to be an integral part of the landscape. If all other beds have a particular theme (rectilinear, curvilinear, diagonal or arc and tangent), then this one should match them. One must be very careful when using curvilinear lines to make the curves large enough; otherwise the end result is a bunch of squiggles.

Siting a perennial bed involves assessing the available light and soil. Is the bed out in the open or is it shaded by trees? How much shade will they cast and at what time of day? Morning shade but afternoon sun will be preferable for sun-loving perennials. On the other hand, morning sun but afternoon shade would be perfect for red daylilies, which tend to fade in the sun. How close to the bed are the roots of other plants and how deep or shallow are they? Remember that tree roots steal moisture that the perennials will need. What is the soil like – dry, average, moist or wet? Is the soil a crumbly loam (don't we wish) or heavy clay that needs lots of organic amendments?

Knowing the characteristics of particular perennials isn't enough but it certainly is a necessity. How tall does it get? How wide? Is it a clumper or a runner? What color blossom does it have? What type of blossom does it have (too many of the same kind become boring)? When does it bloom? What does the foliage look like (size, shape and texture), taking into consideration the realization that the foliage is what one sees for the preponderance of the growing season and perhaps, even into the winter? Is it fragrant (too much can be overwhelming; consider any sensitivities or allergies)?

The next step is understanding why certain perennials look good together. The basic principle of combining plants is using ones that complement each other. This can be done by planting, side by side, perennials with contrasting types of foliage but complementarily colored blossoms. For example, try *Echinacea purpurea* 'Bright Star' with its medium-sized, ovate foliage and pink, daisy-type blossom beside *Coreopsis verticillata* 'Moonbeam', which has wiry foliage and lemon yellow small daisy-type blossoms. This could also be done by using analogous colors such as pink and purple. Try using *Geranium cantabrigenese* 'Biokovo Karmina' with its small, rounded foliage and bright pink blossoms in front of or beside *Iris siberica* 'Caesar's Brother', which has strappy foliage and dark purple blooms. One can also use perennials with colored foliage to pick up the color of a neighboring blossom. *Hosta* 'Frances Williams', which has cream-edged foliage, paired with *Alchemilla mollis*, which has chartreuse yellow blossoms, is one such combination. As it happens, the two foliages also create quite a contrast; that of the *Hosta* is large and quilted while that of the *Alchemilla* is small and scalloped. One can also combine a single specimen plant (usually large and striking) with several smaller plants. An example of this would be a grouping of *Salvia officianalis* 'Purpurea' (Purple Sage), which has purple tinged foliage, fronting a *Buddleia* (Butterfly Bush) with purple blossoms.

Alchemilla

It helps to have an artistic eye when working with color because color is a very tricky element. Each basic color has many shades and tints. Take red, for instance. There is wine, maroon, ruby, cherry, crimson, scarlet, brick and rust, just to name a few shades. But suppose combining some red with some pink is desirable. Which shades of pink (blush, salmon, coral, clear, rose, fuchsia) will be compatible with, rather than clash with, the desired shades of red? It takes a practiced eye to discern these subtle differences. My husband is a good example. A few years ago, we decided to buy an oriental rug. I knew that I wanted the basic color to be pink, not the brick red that is the usual dominant color. We looked at several rugs. Many times he would point out one that was pink only to have it rejected by me because it had orange undertones which made it salmon. The good news is that we finally found one with purple undertones that made it rose. As I say, not everyone sees the difference.

Combining perennials also involves mixing their heights and forms but not in a rigid short/medium/tall order. The front of the border should have varying heights, even going so far as to plant something tall in the front as long as one can see behind it. This means using either a see-through plant such as the ornamental grass, *Molinia caerulea 'Skyracer'*, which has two-foot foliage and seven- to eight-foot wispy inflorescences, or a three- to four-foot *Caryopteris* (Blue Mist Plant) with taller plants behind. Perennials take various forms: creeping, erect, weeping (also known as droopy), mounding, open, compact, etc. It is just as important to vary the forms as it is the heights.

The next piece of the puzzle is finding a method of unifying the garden. This can be effected by repetition of color, form or species. For instance, spotting ornamental grasses throughout a garden, not necessarily or even desirably all the same, comfortably leads the eye from one end to the other while still taking in everything else that is there. This could also be achieved by repeating a specific perennial in a specific color at intervals throughout the garden. Another option is to use mounding dwarf conifers at intervals throughout the garden.

A perennial garden need not be limited only to perennials but will benefit from judicious use of annuals, vines and woodies as well.

One of the most challenging aspects of designing a perennial garden is providing a satisfying sequence of bloom. To do this, one must create a series of vignettes. Each vignette is composed of perennials that bloom at the same time but then the vignettes must be positioned beside one another so as to harmonize with each other and thus create a garden. Each vignette takes into account all of the factors mentioned above but sometimes it doesn't quite work. Perhaps the foliage is too similar. Then when that plant is changed, it means that others must be changed. One of the best checks is a perusal of the plan, by category, all done on trace so that it can be easily erased (of course!). First, time of bloom: Are all the months covered? This is crucial because the essence of a perennial garden is constant change. Then foliage: Is there enough contrast and will it always look good, particularly if it is in the foreground? Then height: Is there enough variety? Then repetition: Is it there in some form? If all of these questions are answered satisfactorily, a lovely garden has evolved.

I am sure that it is now apparent how many pieces it takes to compose a successful garden puzzle. It also requires much time and thought but the final result is incredibly satisfying.

The Whole Can Be Greater Than the Sum of the Parts

What makes a landscape look like all the pieces are part of the whole instead of a hodge-podge of beds? One contributing factor is timing. Rarely does a homeowner invest in a master plan for the landscape while the house is being built. Instead, foundation beds are drawn and a few trees are placed in the lawn. In fact, the foundation beds are usually created by the developer, who has no concept of the size of mature plants. Thus, the beds are never deep enough and the sidewalks are too narrow. Little regard is given to the style of the house to provide an appropriate landscape.

Another factor is the lack of artistry. A landscape designer is an artist of the outdoors, using both hardscaping and plant material to create a beautiful picture. But many people do not have the ability to see in the mind's eye what will be created until it is actually done or what immature plants will look like in five to ten to twenty years.

The most important element of a unified landscape is a single theme by which I mean the same type of bed lines everywhere. These lines can be:

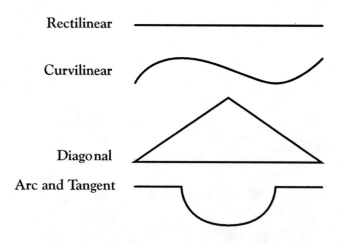

Rectilinear

Curvilinear

Diagonal

Arc and Tangent

They could also be a disciplined combination of:

Rectilinear and Diagonal

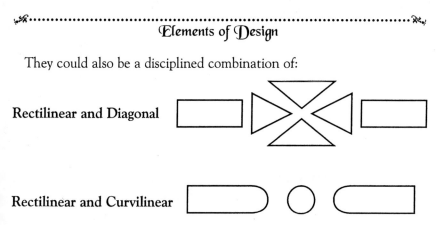

Rectilinear and Curvilinear

In each instance, regardless of the chosen theme, the lines of the planting beds and hardscaping should mirror each other. Sometimes, the choice of theme is easy because the house has window, roof or gable lines that cry out to be echoed on the ground plane. More frequently, the question is whether to reinforce the lines of the house or whether to soften them with curvilinear lines. A partial answer may be gained through conversation with the owner. Is a formal or informal air desired? If informal curvilinear lines are used, they should be large sweeping curves instead of a series of squiggles.

Although rectilinear lines appear to create very formal settings, this is not necessarily the case. One of the best examples of this contradiction is the garden at Sissinghurst in England. There are a series of rectilinear gardens all connected by rectilinear long walks or large lawns. But within these gardens, which contain many beds, is a sense of informality and ease that results from the careful use of plant material that weaves within the beds and overflows at the edges.

One of the most common uses of curvilinear lines is the island bed. As used today, it frequently looks out of place in the landscape, either because it is too small or because it is the only one. Island beds were popularized by Alan Bloom at his garden at Bressingham. When first entering the garden, we see what looks like one giant bed but upon closer inspection, we see a series of large island beds, separated by grass paths, which echo each other. A local garden has replicated this idea on a very small scale by creating two beds that form an arc the width of the back yard. The beds are separated only by a swath of grass large enough to accommodate a lawn mower.

Arc and tangent lines almost always create formality. I have seen several in Savannah gardens of the 1800s that are edged in Boxwood, a material which creates formality all by itself. If a plant of different habit such as *Nepeta* (Catmint) were used, the edges would be partially hidden and thus softened.

Another important element of a unified landscape is careful use of repetition. Too much repetition is extremely boring while not enough will leave a garden looking more like a collection of plants instead of a well-designed landscape. Repetition can be achieved through the use of color, form or botanical grouping.

Color can be repeated either with foliage, flowers or both, depending on the taste and desires of the client. For example, to incorporate red in a landscape through the use of foliage, you would find it in the emerging foliage of *Acer palmatum dissectum* 'Viridis' as well as the permanent color of many other Japanese Maples. You could also use *Imperata cylindrica* 'Red Baron' (Japanese Blood Grass), or *Panicum virgatum* 'Rotstralbusch' (Red Switch Grass) with tinges of red that intensify in the fall. To bring red bloom into a landscape, use perennials such as *Monarda* (Beebalm), *Dianthus* (Pinks), *Astilbe* and *Hemerocallis* (Daylily), among others. The foliage of several trees and shrubs brightens the fall landscape with its red hues: *Cornus florida* (Dogwood), *Viburnum*, *Euonymus alata* (Burning Bush) and *Vaccinium* (Blueberry), to name a few.

Form can best be repeated in the landscape with woody ornamentals – globular, conical, mounding, and vase-shaped – take your pick. I would not use the weeping form too much since it is so strong. Too many weepers can make the landscape resemble a nursery.

A landscape that utilizes several different ornamental grasses repeats a botanical grouping as does one that uses several different conifers. Within such groupings you will find an enormous array of sizes. Grasses can range from six inches to twelve feet. Conifers start at a few inches and extend up to one hundred feet.

Another element of unification is rhythm, which can be created through a progression of color, form, texture or a combination of all three. A good example is the combination of *Arundo donax* (Giant Reed), *Miscanthus sinensis* 'Malepartus', *Boltonia* and *Aster novae-angliae* 'Alma Potschke'. There is a progression of height from the three-foot Aster to the ten-foot *Arundo donax*. There is a progression of textures from the fine leaves of *Boltonia* up to the coarse leaves of the cornstalk-looking *Arundo*. There is a progression of color from the soft pink inflorescence of the *Miscanthus* to the hot pink of the Aster.

The easiest setting for a progression of color alone is a perennial or annuals bed. Longwood Gardens specializes in this type of bed. One year, it combined *Eupatorium coelestinum* (Hardy Ageratum), *Verbena bonariensis*, *Verbena* 'Homestead Purple' and *Salvia farinacea* 'Victoria' to create a virtual progression of blues and purples.

In a general landscape, progression of texture is easy and fun to devise. Intersperse plants that have large entire foliage such as *Hydrangea*, *Hosta* and *Hamamelis* (Witch-hazel) with plants that have dissected foliage such as Japanese Maples, ferns and *Sumac*.

If the three elements discussed are employed, the landscape will flow from one part to another, giving the people in it a sense of comfort and security. Thus the whole will be greater than the sum of the parts. And you will get praise for creating a landscape that makes the client happy.

Paris Gardens:
Another Perspective on Design

Traveling around the corner or around the world gives us an opportunity to discover new ideas and perhaps, find inspiration. I'd like to share with you my impressions of some of the gardens of Paris that I visited on subsequent trips a few years ago. Paris, one of the largest cities in the world, has at least 400 public gardens, some tiny, some huge, but it is difficult to live in Paris without having a green space nearby. All parks are designed for people and especially for children. Even coming into the city from the airport, one can't help but notice the landscaping along the freeways. Parisian gardens demonstrate a heritage of different styles: 17th century – very formal and symmetrical with clipped hedges, allées and topiary as epitomized by Versailles; late 18th century with its structured informality, which has an English touch; and 19th century seen in the Haussman parks and boulevards with elaborate beds. Today you find varying degrees of exquisite detail and firm control co-existing with more informal, natural plantings as well.

The first place a visitor to Paris goes is the Champs-Elysées. Midway between the Arc de Triomphe and the Place de la Concorde is a traffic circle called the Rond-Point. Six arced, banked beds, all alike, rim the circle with beauty. In the spring, the beds are filled with peachy orange Tulips, yellow *Narcissus*, yellow and white Pansies and blue Primrose as well as silvery *Santolina*. In summer, the beds are replanted with pink, purple, white and silver annuals in triangular masses on the inner side and with orange New Guinea *Impatiens* and Nasturtiums on the backside.

If you continue down the Champs-Elysées toward the Place de la Concorde, you will stroll under an allée of European Horsechestnut, which gives blessed relief from the sun during the summer. Just to the side of the broad walks on the north side of the Champs, is the Jardins (Gardens) des Champs-Elysées, which continues all the way down to the Place de la Concorde. In April there is a bed of roses that greets the eye with red foliage that is seen against the bloom of pink *Magnolia*, a bed of yellow *Forsythia* edged with yellow Primrose plus numerous beds of shrubs and perennials, which will bloom later. In the summer, there are beds of *Hydrangea* in addition to several beds full of brightly colored annuals and perennials.

Parisians create inviting settings with generous use of flowers tucked in many spaces. Almost all hotels, restaurants and cafes skirt their entrances and windows with containers that are planted with evergreens and seasonal flowers. You can see this at the Hotel Crillon on the Place de la Concorde as well as at numerous other hotels and cafes throughout the city.

I'd like to take you on a walking tour of the gardens I visited over the course of four trips. I could hardly wait to visit La Bagatelle in the Bois de Boulogne, located in the 16th arrondissement. To get there, I took the Métro to the Porte de Maillot. Upon emerging to the street, I immediately saw the gardens in the middle of the traffic circle. They encompassed many of the elements of Parisian gardens: pleached allées, roses and beds of annuals.

From there, I took a bus that travels through the Bois and got off at La Bagatelle. At the entrance, I paid a small fee of ten francs (approximately two dollars in 1998). Once inside, I started walking and before long came to an area that took my breath away. Masses of bulbs were planted like rivers in the grass. It was quite obvious that most of the people there, including pre-school classes and lots of families with small children, had come just to see these beautiful plantings. When I returned in July, I went to where the bulbs had been, but if I hadn't seen them in April, I wouldn't have known anything had been there.

Then I headed to the Roseraie, which I had skipped in April on the assumption that nothing would be happening there. Along the way, I stopped at the Orangerie, a large former conservatory which is now used for concerts, and the Parterre Française situated in front of it. The Parterre is a large, formal, very symmetrical bed filled with colorful annuals in loose patterns of repeated plants and colors. The urns on pedestals, placed at precise intervals, gradually bring your eye down to the ground plane from the height of the trees which serve as a backdrop.

When the word Bagatelle is mentioned, knowledgeable gardeners think automatically of rose gardens. The Roseraie at Bagatelle is the epitome of a large formal rose garden with low trimmed Boxwood hedges and grass within each bed as a groundcover. I would hate to be the person responsible for mowing those beds. This is formality carried to an extreme. Even the roses themselves are placed within the beds in very rigid lines. Many rose gardens are boring because the plants within them are all approximately the same height. Effective use of rose-covered obelisks and conical evergreens provides interest as it directs the eye to varying heights. The Roseraie has a very open feeling until you walk through the pergola, which not only provides a wonderful sense of enclosure but also periodically acts as a director, focusing your eye on the bench at the end at the path. If you walk up the slope to the kiosk, you have a wonderful overall view of the Roseraie and can fully appreciate all of the elements of its formal design.

Because of its "rose reputation," not everyone realizes that Bagatelle encompasses much more. Another area of Bagatelle is marked on the map as Jardins des Présentateurs, in other words, demonstration gardens. Vine-covered arches raise your eye while arc and tangent hedges divide a wide rectilinear bed so that totally different vignettes can be presented within very close proximity. Another aspect of the demonstration gardens is an area of edible plants. Espaliering of fruit trees is quite common in European gardens and the art is more easily learned from a newly planted one than an established one. Such a one had been installed at one end of a vegetable garden.

The French make great use of colored foliage in flowerbeds. In one bed, purple *Perilla*, blood-red *Iresine* and silver *Santolina* were interwoven, then highlighted with dots of orange Dahlias. Variegated foliage such as that of *Salvia officianalis 'Tricolor'* was used to emphasize and echo the white of *Gaura* blossoms planted within it. I have come to the conclusion that the French hate bare walls and that they regard them as opportunities to be creative and imaginative. Low walls that create garden "rooms" serve as a background for plants but also do double duty as a plinth for decorative pots filled with blooming plants. In this garden, metal rods have been attached to a tall wall at the back of a narrow bed so that clematis and climbing roses can scramble up. They then act as a beautiful backdrop to the perennials at their base.

After leaving the demonstration gardens, I passed through an area of lovely formal beds including a large parterre which incorporates Rose standards, Fuchsias and Marguerites in its border. Beyond those beds are the chateau, a small house built in the 1700s just before the revolution which is now used for special exhibits, and le Trianon, which was not built until the late 1900s but looks older because it is modeled on the Trianon at Versailles. The walled garden beside the chateau is an excellent example of a French garden: formal lines created by a low Boxwood hedge but somewhat wild within.

Beyond this area is one that reminded me of the English school of gardening thought called the landscape style, exemplified by the work of Capability Brown, which emphasized large expanses of lawn trees and water. This lovely little lake and grotto, however, uses more flowering plants than Capability would have, which is why some believe it was probably designed by an Englishman named Thomas Blaikie

Leaving this area and turning right, going past the Rhododendron collection, one arrives at the collection of shrub roses called "les rosiers du paysage." In addition, there are numerous roses which are identified by number only; these are test roses which could become the next collector's item.

Leaving Bagatelle and crossing the Allée de Longchamp, I came to the Pré-Catalan which is, for the most part, large expanses of lawn and trees bordered near the paths with small flower beds. A stream runs through it and, in the spring, the masses of *Narcissus*, Tulips and *Hyacinth* planted along its banks are a vision of loveliness. Across the walk, tiny bulbs and wildflowers with their yellow, white and dark red flowers enliven the unmown grass.

The bed lines of Parisian gardens, if not rectilinear, are typically very baroque, very curvilinear. One such bed in the Pré-Catalan, backed by a tall evergreen hedge, lines a pathway with repeated groupings of annuals, including many not usually seen in American gardens such as *Iresine*,

Salvia coccinea 'Coral Nymph', Amaranthus caudatum and *Abutilon variegatum.*

Few Parisians have the luxury of any land, so they utilize the parks as their connection with nature as well as a place for their children to play. The Parc Monceau, in the 8th arrondissement, is a large park with wide expanses of lawn, undulating flower beds and play areas. In the spring, *Scilla sibirica* (Squill) are massed in the grass and mixed Pansies are massed in some of the baroquely designed beds. In summer, the Pansies are replaced with fibrous Begonias. Other beds are filled with masses of Petunias, which are punctuated with *Canna* and *Gaura,* or masses of Begonias punctuated with *Canna* and *Fatsia.*

This park was designed just before the Revolution by Carmontelle for the Duc de Chartres as a picturesque garden that could serve as the backdrop for parties and fun. He created focal points, streams and original "buildings" such as the ruins, a minaret, a windmill and a pyramid. There is also a pond surrounded by an old specimen of Weeping Willow, a Weeping Beech and Roses. The park was redesigned in 1793 by Blaikie, which gives it an English touch, but the park remains very French.

The Palais du Luxembourg and its surrounding gardens, in the 6th arrondissement, were commissioned by Marie de Medici in 1612. She took possession in 1625 and the grounds, designed to remind her of Tuscany, her birthplace, remain much as they were then. Today the Palais is where the French Senate meets. A rectangular pond and fountain can be seen as one approaches the Palais. It is bordered with urns and ivy that has been trained to grow on metal rope swags that connect wooden posts.

In spring, the fenced flower beds in front of and beside the Palais are aglow with color. These are the only beds at the Luxembourg to which the public does not have access, but the guards can't keep you from admiring them. The front beds are full of red and yellow Tulips, interwoven with orange Primula and bordered with Boxwood. In summer these beds have been transformed into a tapestry of coral Geraniums and dark blue *Salvia farinacea 'Victoria'.*

Beside the Palais are two beds, one rectilinear and one curvilinear. The rectilinear bed is filled with interwoven red Tulips, white *Bellis perennis*, and pink Primrose, while the adjoining curvilinear bed is ablaze with yellow Pansies. The same beds in summer are colorful mixtures of yellow, orange, white and blue annuals in the rectilinear bed and yellow, coral and scarlet in the curvilinear bed. Outside the iron fence, directly in front of the Palais, is the "jardin à la française," a large rectangle of lawn bordered in summer with a variety of annuals in a white/yellow/blue scheme. This area is framed by two raised terraces, the balustrades of which are enhanced with classic urns filled with Petunias, Geraniums and Oleander.

Once you go beyond the formal gardens, you come to a park-like area that has lots of trees and areas for children to play plus a marionette theater, two restaurants and tennis courts. This area also has flower beds that tend to be circular, often surrounding a statue. One bed I saw in April consisted of white Tulips with white and yellow Primrose. A similar bed in July was filled with yellow, orange and purple annuals. Another spring bed was full of alternating pink Hyacinths and white *Bellis perennis*, later filled with yellow, orange, red and maroon annuals and vegetables such as Ruby Chard. All of these beds are filled in a tapestry design.

The Jardin des Plantes, in the 5th arrondissement, is unquestionably the most utilitarian garden in Paris because it is used as a laboratory garden for students at the Botanical School. It contains plants from every corner of the earth. The plantings in the vast parterre in front of the Gallery of Evolution change from season to season. In the spring, they are filled with Pansies and several cultivars of *Narcissus*, all of which are labeled. In the summer they are filled with a particular genus of annual. In 1996, it was *Nicotiana*, the Flowering Tobacco, and again, every species and cultivar was labeled. I understand that in August the beds are filled with Dahlias.

Unfortunately, some gardens are not always accessible, having to recover from conditions with which we are all too familiar. Due to severe drought in the summers of 1994 and 1995, the Alpine Garden was still closed to the public in 1996 but the little I could see from the fence was enticing. The Iris Garden has nearly four hundred varieties and is at its best in May and June. It also has several species of perennials that bloom in summer. The Botanical School garden was still closed to the public in April 1996 but by July had been opened for several hours a day. This garden is arranged by plant family to facilitate the study of perennials and ornamental grasses. In the middle of this garden is an artfully designed pool for the display of water-loving plants.

The Parc André-Citroën, in the 5th arrondissement, opened in 1992 on the grounds of the old Citroën factories and is surrounded by new factories, apartment houses and office buildings. The design was a collaboration between an architectural team headed by Patrick Berger and a designer team headed by Giles Clément. The site is divided into three main areas: the White Garden, the Black Garden and the Central Park. All of the design is based on the physical elements of the earth and their transmutations. I saw it for the first and only time in July and wish I could see what these gardens look like in spring.

The White Garden is filled with white blooming perennials and vines, but it also has plants that bloom in other colors, reminding us that white is a blend of every color. It is a terraced garden and has several partially enclosed areas such as the Clos des Épis (Spires) and the Clos des Géraniums. In July, the Clos des Épis is a wonder to behold. In bloom are *Digitalis, Verbascum, Lythrum, Eremurus, Kniphofia, Cimicifuga, Ligularia, Penstemon, Acanthus* and *Hosta*, all backed by cloud-layered Pines and *Gleditsia 'Sunburst'*, a yellow-foliaged Honey Locust.

When I emerged from the White Garden, I walked into a huge plaza. It has orange trees in individual square containers that frame a water feature of multiple vertical jets. Proceeding through this plaza, I approached a canal that is bordered on the left by a garden the length of the canal called Metamorphosis. It has a very formal composition made up of layers of dwarf Bamboo, sheared *Cornus* (one of the shrubby ones) and a shrub Willow, punctuated periodically with darker green columnar Oaks, also tightly sheared. This bed acts as a visual wall from the building just behind it. At the far end of the canal are two waterfalls, which face each other. One is a series of cascades; the other is a sheet of falling water – very unusual. Just beyond them are railroad tracks and then the Seine. To the right of the canal is a vast expanse of lawn called the Parterre, but it is a modernistic version since it is not bordered with flowers.

Farther to the right, and looking down on the Parterre, is a series of themed gardens. Each one bears a color name that relates to a specific mineral. They are separated by canals that become waterfalls when seen from the Parterre. This area of the park, plus the Movement Garden, was designed by Giles Clément. Naturally, the golden garden represents gold and uses yellow-foliaged shrubs and trees as well as yellow-blooming plants such as Rosa 'Golden Wings'. The silver garden is filled with gray-leaved plants like Willow, *Artemesia* and *Santolina*. The orange garden, representing the rusty oxidation of steel, uses *Parrotia persica* whose leaves turn orange in the fall and *Kniphofia*, among others. The red garden, symbolic of bauxite, was colorful with a small-flowered red *Salvia* and magenta *Lychnis coronaria* as well as espaliered Crabapple, which would have bloomed in May.

The green garden is associated with the oxidation of copper and uses the multiplicity of textures, sizes and shapes of foliage to emphasize that green has many shades. Particularly arresting were the leaves of *Peltiphyllum*, giant *Heracleum* and *Angelica*. The blue garden is supposed to evoke the coldness of mercury. I didn't feel cold but I was entranced. This was the loosest garden and was mostly composed of perennials, both hardy and tender. I counted at least fifteen genera in bloom and there were obviously others, like Bearded Iris, which had bloomed earlier. Each of these serial gardens can be seen from above but should also be entered to give you a totally different perspective. Most of them are purposefully designed so that you cannot see everything at once.

To the left of the serial gardens is the Movement Garden. This garden is extraordinary. Monsieur Clément told me that there is no maintenance here except grass cutting. It took him quite a while to convince the maintenance staff that he really didn't want them to do any pruning, dividing, thinning or weeding. His aim was to imitate nature by installing plants that would seed or run and it is, therefore, quite wild looking. Even the grass looks wild – as though it had been trampled down by someone walking through a meadow. The main plants were giant *Inula*, Bamboo, Sweetpeas and *Adenophora*.

As you leave these gardens and re-cross the plaza, you come to the Black Garden, which is similar to the White Garden in its structure but quite different in its planting. There is more emphasis on trees and shrubs of darker colors. It is divided into several small gardens called "clos," which means an enclosure. The Clos du Hémérocalles (Daylilies) has only the orange daylilies for color, and most of its other plants have foliage which ranges in color from medium to very dark green.

Another clos is lovely in summer with *Lavandula* and lining a path and red-fruited Cutleaf Sumac leaning over them. Then, turning the path, one encounters a red-blooming *Campsis*. It must be spectacular in the fall when the Sumac leaves turn red. The only somber color in a third clos is the dark red foliage of Cutleaf Japanese Maples. This is offset with green lawn, hedges and a series of yellow-foliaged shrubs that I could not identify (the sprinkler was on and I wasn't willing to get soaked). This park is still evolving. Some parts of the original plan have not yet been realized and others have had to be changed, but it is well worth the effort to get there.

The last garden I visited in July was the Parc Floral, which is situated in the Bois de Vincennes on the eastern outskirts of the city. It was created in 1960 as a pleasure garden and as an exhibit of an extraordinary number of plants. It fulfills these aspirations but is unsatisfying because it lacks cohesion. A small but lovely area that I saw shortly after entering the park was an hourglass pond with lush plantings of *Hosta* and ferns under a deciduous canopy. Most of the park is wide open with few trees to provide shade from the sun, but this area is a refuge. The herb gardens, which are collections of culinary and medicinal plants, are well designed but they have no grace. Walking farther into the park, I came to the water lilies in a series of ponds divided by modernistic, swirling concrete and surrounded on its far edges by several flower beds full of color but inartistically arranged. However, the beds are full of interesting ideas. One diagonal bed had lattice fencing, about three feet high, which serves as a support for espaliered Willows, weaving through several of the beds. Vegetables, such as a blue Kale *(Brassica lacinato)*, are used for their unusual texture and color.

Some of the beds combine annuals and perennials. One that featured a combination of white, yellow, pink and purple included *Lobelia*, Petunias,

Gaura, Heliopsis, Salvia farinacea and *Eupatorium fistulosum*. A nearby bed had swaths of yellow, orange and purple flowers and ornamental grasses. I recognized all except one, which was planted twice: one yellow grouping and one orange. As I questioned passersby, the only answer I could get was "soucis." Later I was able to translate this as *Calendula*. Although many plants in the park are labeled, those in the annual beds are not. This park should take a lesson from the Jardin des Plantes. All of these annual beds feature masses, unlike the elaborate tapestry designs of the baroque gardens elsewhere in Paris. One curvilinear bed masses all of its plants in triangular groupings. It is made more interesting with Willow arches which lift the eye above the ground plane.

At the back of the park is a beautiful shaded woodland that hosts collections of *Hosta, Astilbe* and *Hydrangea*, both mopheads and lacecaps. These collections are labeled so that one can really compare plants that are similar in form but vary in color and height.

Browsing the aisles of any bookstore will reveal that multitudes of volumes are written on the historic and emerging gardens of Paris. I have discussed only a few of the hundreds of public gardens in Paris, but I guarantee that you will delight in any of them.

Get Your Dirt Ready:
The Art of Soil Preparation

You have a plan and now want to translate it to reality. An important first step is preparing the soil. Eighty percent of plant problems are related to poor soil. If you stint on soil preparation, you might as well throw your money away. The best plants will either die or merely survive if you have not provided a good environment for them to grow in. Preparing the soil involves an investment of both time and money. Fortunately, there is a very organized process to preparing soil.

Step One:

Have your soil tested to determine what the soil has and needs. A soil test will indicate several key elements, such as the ph level (which indicates the availability of essential elements in the soil for plant growth), the level of crucial mineral elements and the Cation Exchange Capacity (which measures the capacity of the soil to absorb nutrients). The C.E.C. depends largely on the amount and type of clay present and the organic matter content of the soil. Soil tests are relatively inexpensive and are performed by independent companies. A few weeks after you mail in your sample, you should receive an analysis of your soil with recommendations for its improvement.

Step Two:

Lay out your bed lines. Start with a garden hose since it's easy to move. Lay it out as closely as possible to the plan you have, then step back to assess it from several angles as well as from inside, outside and above. Make sure you have sufficient room to accommodate a lawn mower. Once you are sure of your lines, you can either spray paint them or mark them with flags.

Step Three:

Convert what probably was lawn to planting beds. The thing to decide now is how much time and money you have. The most inexpensive but longest method (six to twelve months) is to cover the grass with several layers of newspaper, wet them down and then keep them moist so they don't blow away. This method will kill the grass underneath and have the added benefit of adding organic matter to the soil (newspaper is processed wood, i.e. nitrogen). If you don't want to wait that long, you might use the alternative method of killing the grass with an herbicide such as Roundup, which is biodegradable (and therefore does not harm the environment). Wait two weeks for the herbicide to be effective, then remove the grass with a grass cutter and turn it upside down. A third alternative is not to kill the grass but just to remove it with a sod cutter and put it on the compost pile.

Step Four:

Assess the type of plants that will be going in the bed. If the plants are shallow-rooted, such as groundcovers, add an inch or two of humus and plant. If, however, you are adding perennials or shrubs, you should rototill the base soil and then add at least four to six inches of soil amendments. These amendments will vary with the type of soil you have (clay or sand) and the soil analysis. You will definitely want to add a large percentage of organic material such as compost, leaf humus or composted sewage sludge plus large-particled sand (never play sand) to increase the drainage capacity and aeration porosity. You may need to add either lime or sulphur to change the ph. You should add superphosphate (unless your analysis indicates otherwise) to the amendment mix because this mineral is the least available to plants. You may wish to add a general fertilizer such as a 10-10-10 so that the plants will have a good start.

After the beds have been planted, you should mulch with one or two inches of shredded bark mulch that has been aged. If you use fresh mulch, it will leach nitrogen from the soil. The mulch will help keep moisture in the soil and will deter weeds. Be sure to keep the mulch away from the crown of the plant to avoid rot.

It is important to know that soil high in organic matter must be replenished on a periodic basis (every year or two) because organics decompose. The best way to do this is to add one to two inches of a humus-type material alternating with one to two inches of shredded bark as a mulch each year. It is usually easier to do this in the fall when a large percentage of your planting has been cut down after a frost. It you add this mulch in the early spring, you will delay warming of the soil.

The success of a garden starts with a proper foundation. Investing in quality soil preparation will pay dividends for you and your clients in the long run.

Ten Tips for Combining Perennials

The creation of a perennial garden is an effort in building relationships to achieve a satisfying marriage of plants. Plant "personalities" must be considered when combining them in a garden. Characteristics include height, bloom (color, type, size and time), foliage (color, size and texture), fragrance, structure, seasonal interest and cultural requirements. Here are ten tips and examples to help you achieve a harmonious relationship in your garden.

1. Use the foliage of a nearby plant to echo the blossom color of a neighbor.
   Example: *Miscanthus sinensis* 'Strictus' (green- and yellow-striped foliage) near or next to *Coreopsis verticillata* 'Moonbeam' (lemon yellow blooms).

2. Use varying foliage textures to give interest to a grouping of plants.
   Example: *Hosta* 'Frances Williams' (large and quilted), *Alchemilla mollis* (medium, pleated and scalloped), and *Corydalis lutea* (small, biternate – meaning twice divided into three leaflets – and slightly scalloped).

3. Vary the colors of foliage: shades of green from light to dark, types of green from matte to shiny, blue-green, yellow-green, yellow, purple and variegated.
   Example: *Asarum canadense* (matte), *Alchemilla mollis* (grooved and pleated), *Asarum europaeum* (shiny).

4. Always keep in mind what the foliage of each perennial looks like when it is not in bloom (which is usually most of the time). Try to vary the foliage textures and sizes (as in #2) and colors (as in #3).
   Example: *Acanthus mollis* (large, lustrous deeply lobed) with *Stachys byzantina* 'Big Ears' (furry and silver) and *Sedum* 'Autumn Joy' (medium and succulent).

5. Use varying heights but do not be rigid in their placement, which means not always placing short in front, medium in the middle, tall in the back. Vary their placement and do not be afraid to use tall plants in the front of the bed, particularly if they are wispy or give a veiled effect.
Example: *Crambe cordifolia*, a tall, airy, white perennial, which has short but large foliage, or *Verbena bonariensis*, which is a tall, narrow, purple reseeding annual.

6. If the colors you like seem to clash or to be too strong, use silver-foliaged perennials as mediators, not white-flowering plants as you might have thought. White is the strongest color of all and will compete, not mediate.
Example: *Rudbeckia fulgida* 'Goldsturm' and *Lychnis chalcedonica* separated by *Artemesia ludoviciana* 'Silver King'.

7. If your garden will be viewed primarily in the evening, or is in shade, combine perennials that have white or pale blossoms with others whose foliage is silver or has a lot of white variegation.
Example: *Liriope spicata* 'Silver Dragon', *Hosta* 'Patriot' and *Phalaris arundinacea* 'Picta'.

8. Don't be afraid to use the element of mystery. Plant something tall and dense in the middle of a curve so as to block sight of the rest of the bed or landscape, thus beckoning the viewer onward.
Example: *Aster novae-angliae* 'Hella Lacy' or one of the *Miscanthus*.

9. Remember that there are four main types of blossoms (daisy, rose, flat and spike) and try to use as many as possible. A garden of only one type will be boring.
Example: '*Rudbeckia fulgida* 'Goldsturm', *Trollius* 'Lemon Queen', *Achillea* x 'Paprika' and *Veronica* x 'Icicle'.

10. Try to use some plants that will give you winter interest.
Example: *Iris siberica*, which has orangey-brown foliage and stiff-stemmed seed pods (assuming that you didn't cut them down when the blooms were finished), *Allium tuberosum*, which has

grayish bronze seed heads, *Sedum 'Autumn Joy'*, which has bronzy flat heads, and *Pennisetum alopecuroides*, an ornamental grass that turns beige in the fall and maintains that color throughout winter.

These are some solid guidelines to use as a foundation. Above all, don't limit yourself to a few of the same repetitive patterns. Explore the full range of plants available to you and don't hesitate to be creative or experiment with the potential to create truly stunning gardens.

Design Tools

Color:
The Great Enhancer

Color enhances all facets of our lives: from the clothes we wear, to the paint on our houses, to the interior and exterior furnishings of these houses. The exterior furnishings include the plants in our landscapes as well as all the aspects of hardscaping: paths, water features, ornaments and furniture. Let's spend some time looking at how color influences the way we design and even live. I'd particularly like to consider color in relation to the design and building of water features, whether they are swimming pools or ornamental water shapes. Their design will win more ready acceptance if they are fashioned with color in mind. Many aspects of water features present color choices: tile, plaster, exposed aggregate and stone. Then, of course, there are the plants and furniture that will surround these features, which should echo those color choices in order to create a unified design.

Let's begin by discussing the nature of color with the color wheel. The color wheel displays the spectrum of color by alternating the primary (red, blue and yellow) and secondary (purple, orange and green) colors known as hues. The secondary colors are created by combining any two primary colors. So where are pink, white and black? Pink is actually a tint of red (combined with white), white is the sum of all colors and black is the absence of color.

Each hue has many values. Technically, lighter values are called tints, achieved by adding degrees of white, while darker values are shades, achieved by adding degrees of black. For ease of discussion, however, I will use the term "shades" to encompass both of these values since it is more commonly employed. It is relatively easy to use several shades of one color, thus creating a monochromatic but very interesting color scheme. The difficulty arises when the shades have differing undertones.

If you look at paint chip strips, found at hardware stores, you usually see five shades, from light to dark, of a particular color. It is the darker ones that are most telling, alerting you to the undertones. The best example I can give you is this: I picked what I thought was a clear, medium-toned yellow for my dining and living rooms, which were to be painted while I was on vacation. When I returned, I found walls of vomit-greenish-yellow. It was so bad that the walls had to be completely redone. If I had looked at one of these strips, I would have saved myself and the painter dismay, time and money.

Once you understand how color is created, you should develop an insight into how color works and ways it affects us. Color impacts upon the human body, both physiologically and psychologically. Knowledge of this relationship is crucial to fulfilling your clients' needs and aspirations. What is the purpose of the water feature that your client wants you to design and build? Soothing? Inspiring? Stimulating? A swimming pool, for instance, can and should be much more than just a place to swim. Yes, it provides a place for exercise, fun and entertaining. The pool has to be functional but it should also be beautiful in order to enhance both property value and enjoyment.

A client who leads a frenetic life will probably want to come home to a pool that uses pink, green, or blue tones because these colors are calming and relaxing.

Pink will contribute to friendly conversation while entertaining and would be particularly appropriate in a warm climate where stucco walls are often colored in these shades. Green helps your eyes recover from strain and imparts an air of richness and luxury. (Just think of emeralds and malachite.)

Blue, besides being relaxing, is also stimulating. This seems to be a contradiction but research has shown it to be true. Particularly in hot climates, blue gives the illusion of coolness; that is why swimming pools have traditionally been painted blue or blue-green. A pool painted red would seem hot. I can't decide, however, whether I would want a "hot" pool even in a cold climate.

A client who leads a more sedate life might want stimulation. This situation calls for hot colors. Yellow and red are the first colors that the eye registers, so this is a great way to call attention to key areas. You can pull attention away from something that you would prefer to disregard by using these colors opposite that feature. Red and orange trigger adrenaline and stimulate the appetite, so use these colors to excite people. Experiments have shown that food eaten in red surroundings tastes better and stimulates conversation – important attributes for clients who like to entertain.

White should be used for clients who need precision because it conveys a sense of neatness and orderliness. Keep in mind, however, that great masses of white can be hard on the eyes. Gray is said to be another creative color but I think the shade of gray is very important. Dark or medium gray conveys a feeling of imprisonment to me while light gray or silver convey a sense of richness and magic.

Next, I want to discuss the relationship of color to distance. This knowledge can be used in a couple of ways. Bright red, yellow and orange can be perceived from long distances; therefore, you can entice and lead people to a somewhat distant feature by using these colors. You can also make a long, narrow plot of land seem more shallow by using bright colors at the end because they visually pull that end in closer. Conversely, a small plot can be made to seem deeper and wider by using cool colors on the edges because these colors recede, particularly blues, purples and pale pinks.

There also exists a relationship of color and light. Color can and will change according to the time of day, the angle of the light, the type of surface and the color of neighboring features. At dawn and dusk, the light is hazy. Strong colors are softened while pale ones become almost ethereal. Yellow *Helianthus* (Sunflower) and *Rudbeckia* (Black-eyed Susan) become soft while blue *Delphinium* almost fade away. An hour or two after dawn and before dusk, the light is warm and low. Blues are very effective in low light but reds become darker and disappear. Summer light during the day is strong and harsh, thus washing out color, both literally and figuratively. A pink, purple and silver perennial border loses all of its bright color during the middle of the day.

Most Daylily catalogs will advise situating red cultivars in afternoon shade so that the petal color does not fade. Such light also casts sharp shadows on the ground and a good designer will capitalize on this by positioning plants, sculpture or raised hardscaping to create shadow patterns where they will be seen to the best advantage. Shadows thrown by tree branches create patterns against a fence, bench or patio and add depth to a landscape.

Autumn and winter light, low and weak, is similar to early morning and late afternoon summer light in the northern United States. In the southern states, closer to the equator, the autumn and winter light will be more like summer light but still not as strong or as high. Evaluate the site to determine what light Mother Nature is providing and incorporate it to your advantage.

There are several ways to design with lighting. Position plants that display seedheads in autumn and winter for backlighting. Backlighting will tend to create a halo around these shapes, giving them a totally different aspect than at other times of the day. Just as importantly, it can be used to outline unusual shapes. Backlighting will also illuminate colored foliage. *Miscanthus sinensis 'Purpurascens'* (Flame Grass), when backlit, looks like it is on fire. Backlighting can also be used to create light patterns. Morning light coming through fence slits casts dappled light on *Miscanthus sinensis 'Variegatus'* (Striped Maiden Grass) and creates patterns of light on the lawn.

Many articles on natural lighting talk about the beauty of backlighting but few mention the beauty of front-lighting. The lovely white inflorescences of *Luzula nivea* (Snowy Woodrush) are highlighted by the early morning sun as they nestle among enveloping green foliage. I have a grouping of *Miscanthus sinensis 'Adagio'* (Adagio Maiden Grass) on the west side of my front yard that looks as though it is lit from within during early morning as the eastern sun strikes it. For the rest of the day, during fall, winter and early spring, this ornamental grass is beige.

There are two colors that can be put to great use in achieving certain moods in the landscape – silver and white. Silver or pale gray plants enhance and cool vivid hues as well as help blend them. For example, *Stachys byzantina* (Lamb's Ears) weaving through magenta *Callirhoe involucrata* (Purple Poppy Mallow) is a complementary pairing that provides textural contrast as well. Silver and white surfaces also gather and reflect light. Thus this part of the spectrum is very useful for evening entertaining as is white because it is the last color to fade from sight. An example of this would be a grouping of yellow *Helianthus* and *Rudbeckia*, with blue *Delphinium*, and, in the foreground, white Shasta Daisy, which actually stands out in the dim light. If you use white, pick the shade carefully. White is the strongest hue and stark white is overpowering, but creamy white and pinkish white are warming. As dark descends, paths edged with white plants are easier to see and navigate, even without supplemental lighting.

Water features that have an aggregate or pearlized surface will sparkle and shimmer as the light strikes them while those with matte finishes will look flat. Which effect will your client want? Glazed surfaces, like tile, will reflect light while surfaces like concrete and stone will absorb light and thus be hotter to walk on.

Delphinium

Balance is usually achieved in design by arrangement of lines but it can also be obtained through the use of color. A small, dark shape will balance a larger but light shape. This is just as true for pool decking or edging design as it is for plant design, where we frequently use one large foliaged plant to balance several finely textured ones. If you were designing a small ornamental pool for a large, dark, shaded lawn area, incorporating a pale gray stone edging would provide balance. Large foliage gives the illusion of weight and thus darkness while fine foliage gives the illusion of buoyancy and light. Create the illusion of shadows with dark surfaces to provide relief from very bright surfaces, which can be overwhelming.

Repetition of color is one of the most effective ways to unify a landscape, but dibs and dabs of color merely make one think of a bouncing ball. Massed repetition is infinitely more potent whether it is with hardscape patterns, a particular plant, or a flower or foliage color. Try to limit the number of hues used in any given setting in order to prevent a feeling of discomfort, but feel free to use innumerable shades of a few, varying the intensity. The interaction between shades will deepen some while making others more subtle. Use varying shades to dramatize designed shapes and their interplay. Remember that varied shapes generate a visually stimulating landscape but too many will give headaches. Be sure that you have some peaceful focal points or areas.

When designing with more than one shade of a particular hue, be aware that you must see the shades side by side before using them. Descriptions in catalogs frequently do not give you enough information. Additionally, shades look different to the eye when used side by side instead of singly. If you plant the annual *Gaillardia 'Yellow Sun'* next to *Rudbeckia nitida 'Herbstsonne'*, you will have clashing yellows because the undertone of the former is green while the undertone of the latter is orange. If either were planted by itself, it would just be yellow. Only in the context of contiguous planting do you realize how different the two shades are. Similarly, if you plant red Petunias, which have a blue undertone, next to the red annual *Salvia splendens,* that has an orange undertone, neither you nor your client will be happy. This is just as true of elements like stone and plaster as it is of plants. And you will certainly want to use materials in hues and concomitant shades that are compatible with the buildings nearby, so pick shades very carefully.

Repetition of color can also be used to reinforce unity with existing or new structures. One such example is that of a pool built near an old stone wall that was topped with brick and repeats the use and color of that brick in the pool deck. Another example of color repetition, also known as color echo, is the use of furniture that repeats the color of pool tile at the inner edge of the pool. Don't forget that repetition of color can also be used in design of accompanying landscape beds. Everyone remembers to do this with flower color, but few do it with foliage color. While white flowering perennials in an island bed within a pool can reflect the color of surrounding stone decking, the green and white variegated leaves of *Euphorbia marginata* can echo the variegated color of stone fountains.

Cultivating color in our designs at many depths is a worthy goal – a higher level, if you will. These examples of the use of color to enhance design will, hopefully, heighten your artistry. Just think how much more exciting your designs can be. It is incumbent upon us as knowledgeable designers to create more than just the adequate – we should be creating the best!

Bulbs:
Hidden Treasures

Every avid gardener, particularly a perennial gardener, lusts for as much long lasting color as possible in the garden. Several strategies can be used to extend and intensify the season of bloom. Incorporating bulbs is a very effective design tool for addressing color and length of season.

To begin with, consider using several different types of bulbs. We often neglect many of the so-called "small bulbs" in favor of *Narcissus* and tulips that give us bright blasts of color. With little effort, you will find many other bulb types that, used in masses, are just as attractive. For example, *Eranthis* (Winter Aconite) and *Galanthus* (Snowdrops) are the first harbingers of spring, blooming before most perennials have even begun to push their green tips out of the soil. Most of us use the large Dutch Crocus, but I love the Snow Crocus that are bi- or tri-colored, such as 'Advance', which is bright yellow on the inside and bluish violet and white on the outside. 'Gipsy Girl' is bright yellow with feathers of deep bronzy purple; 'Ladykiller' has purple violet petals with white edges; and 'Saturnus' is dark yellow with dark purple stripes. The Snow Crocus offer a greater range of color and they also better withstand the vagaries of winter weather than the larger Dutch Crocus. Take care to use greater masses of them since they are smaller.

I also like to use the species tulips because they frequently perennialize, unlike their larger brethren, which should be treated as annuals. For years, I've used *Tulipa bakeri* 'Lilac Wonder', which is pale pink-lilac with a yellow center, because my garden is based on a pink/purple/blue/white color scheme. Another pink species is *Tulipa pulchella* 'Persian Pearl', a real eye-catching magenta pink! It did not come back the following year, but that may have been my fault. They were planted near a sprinkler head and thus may have rotted.

Another lovely and very old (since 1596) little treasure is *Tulipa humilis*, which is a bright rose-pink. Many other species Tulips are in shades of red or yellow. Most species tulips are found in the wild in dry habitats; therefore, to grow them successfully, we need to duplicate that habitat as closely as possible.

For those like me who love blue, there is also *Chionodoxa* (Glory-of-the-Snow), of which there are three species of varying shades: *Puschkinia libanotica*, which is pale blue and white, and *Muscari* (Grape Hyacinth). The best-known species is *M.armeniacum*, which is deep violet-blue. There is also a lesser-known species called *A.latifolium*, which is blue on top and violet on the bottom instead of completely blue.

Planting these little bulbs in tandem with larger ones (*Narcissus*, tulips and hyacinths) that bloom at approximately the same time provides wonderful displays. I must emphasize the importance of carefully selecting the cultivar for timing in order for this to work. When digging the holes, dig large ones to accommodate several bulbs at a time rather than individual ones. Plant the larger bulbs first, approximately six to eight inches deep. Cover them with a few inches of soil and plant the small bulbs right on top of them; then finish filling the hole. At bloom time, you will have a carpet of tiny blossoms through which emerge the larger ones to provide sometimes analogous color and sometimes, complementary color. Whichever type of color scheme you choose, spring glory will brighten your spirits.

Mentioning hyacinths leads me to share with you a special hyacinth that I am using. First, you have to understand that one of my personal prejudices is a dislike of hyacinths. To me, they are large blobs with a scent that is overwhelming. After reading about the blue cultivar *Hyacinthus multiflora* 'Borah', I decided to give it a try and discovered that I love its more informal look of loosely arranged florets on multiple stems. This hyacinth is an heirloom bulb that is still quite fragrant, but I don't find the scent as offensive. I am waiting to see if it will naturalize.

I first saw *Leucojum aestivum* (Summer Snowflake) in a woodland setting with late *Narcissus* and didn't know what they were, but I was determined to find out. Then I saw them again in a Charleston cemetery and discovered their identity. Not long ago, I planted them in my own garden in a partially shaded, slightly moist spot, conditions that most bulbs will not tolerate. Their pendulous white bells on twelve- to eighteen-inch stems bloom from early May well into June, and their foliage remains green until the end of summer. I had planted them among a shade-loving ornamental grass called *Luzula nivea* (Snowy Woodrush), but I have found it necessary to move the *Luzula* in front of them because the *Leucojum* foliage overwhelmed them. Last year, I planted *Tricyrtis* 'Tojen' (Tojen Toad Lily) among them. Their height (three feet as opposed to the eighteen inches of *Luzula*) and large leaves allows them to compete and flourish with the *Leucojum*.

Most of us focus on spring blooming bulbs, but some of the summer blooming bulbs are worth our attention, especially *Allium*. My favorite is the late June/early July blooming *Allium sphaerocephalum* (Drumstick Allium). Its unusual shape and maroon color add excitement to my pastel border. I've planted it behind *Ruellia humilis*, the pale violet Wild Petunia, and one of my favorite annuals, *Zinnia angustifolia* 'Classic White', which blooms nonstop until frost. Another *Allium* I can't live without is *Allium giganteum* for its shock value. Everyone, regardless of age, is amazed at its height and size — four- to five-inch spheres on four-foot stalks! I've planted them next to the late blooming (June) Dwarf Lilac, *Syringa meyeri*, which is a paler purple and only a little bit taller than the *Allium*. I've also planted them in a client's garden for the contrast value — the tall purple balls behind a bright yellow *Potentilla fruticosa*.

There are several design and planting practices that will enable you to use color to its best effect. I have found that the technique of color echoing is one means of achieving this result. For instance, I always cringe when I see a front yard with a pink flowering Dogwood but red and yellow tulips. For better color coordination, I would have added pink and purple tulips, or perhaps pink and rosy red tulips. In a client's front yard, I planted a Crabapple with red buds against the white house. Then, in beds going down the driveway, I planted red and white tulips, creating an echoing vignette. Sometimes an effort to coordinate house and floral colors fails for lack of another color. An example of this is white tulips planted against a white house. What is needed is something as simple as a green hedge to provide a dark background for the white bulbs so that they don't fade into the house and thus become almost unseen. One of the most effective color echoes I've seen is a gray house with a yellow door echoed by yellow Narcissus and yellow tulips.

Maximizing space is another issue that needs to be addressed. I have three techniques that I find particularly useful in this regard. The first is planting bulbs with perennials that bloom at the same time. A mass of the soft blue bells of *Scilla sibirica* (Squill) next to one of *Arabis caucasica* (Rock-cress), whether it is a white or rosy-pink cultivar, intensifies the color of each. Another eye-catching combination is red tulips such as 'Red Shine', a lily-flowering type, planted among *Iberis sempervirens* (Candytuft). Thus the *Iberis* serves as a base from which the tulips emerge. One could also use *Muscari* (Grape Hyacinth) and *Myosotis alpestris* (Forget-Me-Not) in a weaving pattern, thus creating a flow of shades of blue.

The second technique involves planting bulbs between perennials with leaves that enlarge later to hide the dying bulb foliage, which is always unattractive. A good example is planting *Narcissus* between *Brunnera macrophylla* (Heartleaf Forget-Me-Not). First the *Narcissus* bloom; then quickly the *Brunnera* emerges. At first, the leaves are relatively small, the better to see the tiny flowers, but they enlarge to three times their initial size, ably hiding the dying foliage of the *Narcissus*. The same is true for a combination of *Muscari and Heuchera* 'Palace Purple'. The lavender blue of the *Muscari* enhances the reddish purple of the *Heuchera* foliage and then the *Heuchera* foliage enlarges and hides the limp *Muscari* foliage as it goes dormant.

The largest foliage for hiding bulb foliage is that of *Hosta*, which makes it invaluable for hiding tulip leaves, which are larger and stiffer than that of other bulbs. In addition, *Hosta* foliates late and many tulips are among the latest blooming bulbs.

The third technique, which is alluded to with the *Hosta*/tulip combination, is planting bulbs among perennials that foliate late and thus allow full enjoyment of the bulb bloom before hiding the dying foliage. Examples of such combinations are *Narcissus* among *Aster frikartii*, *Narcissus* between *Iris siberica*, *Narcissus* and *Scilla sibirica* between ornamental grasses such as *Pennisetum* (Fountain Grass) and *Scilla sibirica* at the base of *Perovskia* (Russian Sage), *Buddleia* (Butterfly Bush) and *Caryopteris* (Blue Mist).

My garden is an unending delight to me twelve months of the year. Creative use of a variety of bulbs and smart planting strategies guarantee a long, gorgeous display. The effort involved in accomplishing this will be well worth it. Let bulbs put on a show in your garden too!

Nature:
Butterfly Gardening

In the past few years, gardens that attract wildlife have become very popular. As designers and landscapers, we must educate our clients and discuss the reality in relation to their expectations. How many of us have "surprised" clients by telling them that foliage in a butterfly garden will have holes in it and that edges will be ragged because the caterpillars that will become butterflies are using them as a food source? We can, however, reassure the clients that natural predators keep caterpillar populations under control and that most butterfly larvae (caterpillars) will eat only specific plants.

Some of the books I've read on butterfly gardening say that it is necessary to leave some weedy patches and long grass for egg laying, but my garden is full of butterflies without the weeds and tall grass. I will admit that I have one small patch in the back that I would call brushy rather than weedy, so perhaps it's only a matter of semantics. Assuming that the client accepts these "problems," one can then concentrate on how to attract these beautiful creatures.

Several components are needed to put together a butterfly garden. Chief among them is the absolute need for sunlight and a dependable food source. One can attract butterflies by providing color, nectar and ease of feeding. Finally, length of bloom must be taken into consideration so that the garden provides blossoms from early spring to frost.

The number one requirement for a butterfly garden is sunlight. Butterflies avoid shade and windy areas. Try to create a windscreen with shrubs that will provide nectar as well. Pesticide use must be either non-existent or very limited. Mud puddles for the males are another essential requirement. The puddles provide additional nutrients, particularly the salts that plants lack. Plants that will provide this element are:
- *Philadelphus* (MockOrange)
- *Syringa* (Lilac)
- *Buddleia* (Butterfly Bush)
- *Viburnum*

Providing a food source can be tricky. If your client has a spot that can be somewhat weedy, the butterflies in their caterpillar munching stage can do their damage where it will be little noticed. There they can feast on goodies that appeal to them. Butterflies are very finicky but generally they prefer weeds to vegetables. They love umbelliferous plants such as carrots, parsley, fennel and anise, but if you have Queen Anne's Lace, they'll gladly dine there. Plants that will provide this element are:
- *Asclepias syriacus* (Common Milkweed)
  (Be advised that this plant is impossible to pull)
- Clover
- Nettles
- Thistle
- Queen Anne's Lace

You should then look to provide color, nectar and ease of feeding. Purple will catch a butterfly's attention first; other favorite colors are yellow, pink and white. A comfortable perch will make feeding easier. Blossoms with flat surfaces or ball types work well. Try to provide large clumps of each type of flower rather than just one or two plants of each type and choose plants for diversity of height, bloom time and color. Plants that will be attractive and provide easy feeding are:
- *Hieracium species* (Hawkweed)
- *Chyrsanthemum leucanthemum* (Ox-Eye Daisy)
- *Anaphalis margaritacea* (Pearly Everlasting)

Late summer and early fall nectar sources are:
- *Sedum spectabile* (Upright Stonecrop)
- *Phlox paniculata* (Garden Phlox)
- *Rudbeckia* species (Black-Eyed Susan)
- *Aster divaricatus* (White Wood Aster)
- *Aster novae-angliae* (New England Aster)
- *Chelone* species (Turtlehead)

The *Sedum* and *Phlox* require full sun and excellent drainage but the others will tolerate partial shade and some moisture.

To meet the needs of the migrators and hibernators, nectar must be available until frost. To provide this element use:
- *Buddleia* (Butterfly Bush)
- *Eupatorium fistulosum* (Joe-Pye Weed), the tallest of the fall bloomers at 5-8', is a magnet for Monarchs during fall migration.

Of course, some plants offer multiple benefits. You can use these plants to incorporate several elements:
- The clustered petals found on *Eupatorium fistulosum* (Joe-Pye Weed) provide easy perching and late season nectar.
- Large-lipped petals found on *Nepeta sibirica* (Siberian Catmint) provide an easy feeding perch and butterfly-attracting color.

A butterfly garden needs to be in bloom from early spring to late fall in order to provide food for the many species of butterflies that, hopefully, will appear. The earliest spring butterflies are hibernators. As they come out of dormancy, an immediate food source is essential. There are several plants that provide this element:
- *Salix caprea* (Goat Willow) is one of the first woody plants to flower. It is a small tree suitable for damp, sunny areas.

Other early-flowering plants can be found among these April blooming perennials:
- *Arabis* (Rock Cress)
- *Primula* (Primrose)

These varieties, which flower in May, require full sun and good drainage:
- *Aubrieta deltoides* (Purple Rock Cress)
- *Lavandula angustifolia* (Lavender)
- *Dianthus barbatus* (Sweet William)
- The old -fashioned favorite, *Syringa vulgaris* (Lilac) is also a butterfly favorite. Although people tend to plant it in partial shade, *Syringa* really does not bloom well unless it is in full sun.

To encourage these visitors throughout the early and mid summer, you may use any of these plants to provide a source of food and color. These perennials need full sun and average to dry soil.
- Any of the *Verbena*, whether perennial or annual
- Any daisy-type flower (particularly those with yellow centers or petals) such as *Leucanthemum superbum* (Shasta Daisy)
- *Coreopsis lanceolata* or *C.verticillata* (Tickseed)
- *Echinacea purpurea* (Purple Cone Flower)
- *Gaillardia x grandiflora* (Blanket Flower)
- *Centranthus ruber* (Red Valerian)
- *Monarda* (Beebalm)
- *Liatris spicata* (Spike Gayfeather)

There are two plants in particular that are virtually synonymous with butterfly gardens: *Asclepias* and *Buddleia*, as evidenced by their common names, Butterfly Weed and Butterfly Bush. *Asclepias tuberosa* is the most common species used in the perennial garden and it is, of course, bright orange. There is a cultivar called 'Gay Butterflies', which is a mix of orange, yellow and red. All of these plants are generally two to three feet tall and are native to prairies. They do very well in sandy, well-drained soil but also in clay soils. *Asclepias incarnata* (Swamp Milkweed) is pale to rosy pink, grows three to four feet tall and prefers moist sites but not standing water although it will perform nicely in well-drained soils. It also has a mild vanilla scent that attracts butterflies. *Asclepias* blooms from June until the middle of July. Full sun is a necessity.

There are two species of *Buddleia* but *davidii* is the one most frequently found in gardens. Colors range from purples to shades of pink to white. A mature plant will be eight to ten feet tall and wide, but finding space in the landscape for this plant is a necessity for me. To my eye, there is little that can compare with the sight of a Monarch feeding on a purple truss of *Buddleia*. There is a Petite Series which is useful for the gardener limited to smaller sites. The Petites grow only four feet tall and have smaller leaves with a bluish cast. *Buddleia* blooms from the middle of July until frost and requires full sun and average soil. *Buddleia* is woody and usually dies back to the ground in winter in zones 6 and above. Because it foliates quite late, often not until early May, do not prune it back until at least a week after the new foliation emerges.

I have only touched on the diversity of butterfly-attracting plants that can be integrated into any type of garden or landscape. There are numerous books and magazine articles that can be used as resources for additional material. By including these basic techniques, you can create a garden that will be filled with these beautiful winged creatures without necessarily designing it exclusively for them. As their natural habitats disappear, they'll be happy to show up in yours.

Culinary Plants:
Herbs in the Perennial Garden

I wish, as does almost every gardener, for more space. Then I could have an herb garden, a woodland garden and a fall border as wall as my perennial garden. This is not to be, however. Thus I incorporate them all into the general landscape with perennials and ornamental grasses leading the way. There are, of course, woody ornamentals, which provide the bones of the landscape, as well as bulbs, annuals, vines, and herbs. Many of the herbs are useful in the commercial landscape because they are extremely durable and require very little maintenance.

Herbs lend fragrance, colorful foliage and flowers. The first that comes immediately to mind is Thyme. Its tiny leaves impart a texture different from that of most other plants in the perennial garden. Thymus minus, also known as *Thymus praecox 'Minor'*, and *Thymus praecox ssp. arcticus* are two very low and tight creepers that I use on slopes and between stepping stones. I frequently use *Thymus vulgaris 'Argenteus'* (Silver Thyme) wherever I want small but white- and green-variegated foliage. However, I have been frustrated by its inability to survive Cleveland winters. It is possible that it succumbs because of poor drainage in my garden rather than lack of hardiness since it, like most thyme, is rated hardy from zones 5 to 8.

Thyme is one plant whose flowers I cut off because I think they detract from the beauty of the foliage. It looks lovely in front of *Sedum 'Autumn Joy'*, particularly when the *Sedum* is still in its broccoli head stage. I tried to pair it with *Arabis caucasica 'Variegata'* but its variegation is cream and green, not white and green. The variegation of *Arabis ferdinandi-coburgi* is the same as that of the thyme but its foliage is too small to provide enough size contrast. It does pair well with any green foliaged plant, such as the common *Arabis caucasica 'Snowcap'*. Those who like yellow-variegated plants could use some of the cultivars of Lemon Thyme.

Oregano is a valuable addition to the perennial garden. I became acquainted with *Origanum laevigatum* 'Herrenhausen' in the early 1990s. It came to us from the German estate called Herrenhausen which was the home of some of their 18th and 19th century nobility. Planted on eighteen-inch centers, it fills in fairly quickly and seeds a bit but not so much as to be troublesome. Hardy to at least zone 6, this Oregano has reddish-purply-green foliage. The flower spikes, which do not appear until mid-July, are pale lilac to purple and hold themselves above the foliage so that the ultimate height of the plant is approximately eighteen to twenty-four inches. For the first few years, the spikes stay erect, even in the winter, but after that, they become lax unless divided. Supposedly the cultivar 'Hopley's Purple' remains more erect but I have not grown it long enough to verify that. Otherwise, I see no difference between the two cultivars. One other Oregano that looks particularly fetching at the edge of a rock wall or between rocks is *Origanum vulgare* 'Wellsweep'. It has tiny green- and white-variegated foliage and ten-inch spikes of pink flowers in July and August.

Salvias are an incredibly large genus that includes species which are annual, half-hardy perennial and hardy perennial. Many of these, such as *Salvia x superba*, are mainstays of the perennial garden but are not really considered as herbs even though their common name is Sage. *Salvia officianalis* (zones 4-7) has been used as a food flavoring for centuries, but it is only in the past hundred years that it has also been recognized as a colorful addition to the perennial garden. The passion for purple-leaved plants has brought *Salvia o.* 'Purpurea' to prominence. The grainy texture and ovate shape of the foliage make this plant an excellent foil for delicately foliaged plants such as those mentioned immediately below. It is twelve to twenty inches when in bloom and, of course, much lower when not in bloom. This makes it an excellent plant for the foreground, where it can sit in front of purple- or pink-flowered *Linaria purpurea* (Toadflax) or one of the purple-flowered hardy geraniums such as *Geranium x magnificum* (Showy Geranium).

Salvia o. 'Tricolor' is another useful cultivar, especially when sited near a purple-foliaged plant such as *Penstemon digitalis* 'Husker Red' or *Sedum x* 'Mohrchen', an improved hybrid of *Sedum x* 'Atropurpureum'. It would probably work well with one of the purple-leaved hybrids of *Heuchera* as well, but I hesitate to recommend this because I find that these hybrids tend to bleach out or burn in the sun.

For me, one of the old standbys (which does not lessen its value) of the perennial garden is *Nepeta* (Catmint). I most often use *Nepeta 'Dropmore Hybrid'* at the edge of a walk or a wall so that I can enjoy its sprawling nature and its floriferousness. In an average year, I usually coax three flushes of bloom by pruning it back after each flush. During the past few years, in my travels to gardens in other cities, I have fallen in love with *Nepeta sibirica 'Souvenir d'André Chaudron'*, which grows three feet tall and wide, sporting rich blue flowers that last all summer. Although it is not as fragrant as the low spreaders, its beauty more than compensates. It is also a zone hardier, to zone 3 rather than 4.

Monarda

I can attest to the fact that Beebalms have been planted in herb gardens for centuries, having seen it in a 12th century monastery garden in France. But as beautiful as the flowers are, the foliage usually becomes disfigured with powdery mildew. You can, of course, cut down the plants when this happens and they will regenerate, but a better solution is planting some of the new cultivars that are at least mildew resistant and, in some cases, seem to be mildew proof. *Monarda 'Jacob Cline'* appears to be the best of the red flowering cultivars, highly superior to *Monarda 'Gardenview Scarlet'*. An excellent pink cultivar is M. *'Marshall's Delight'*. There is also a series coming out of Germany with Indian names, such as *'Cherokee'* and *'Comanche'*, which has been bred for mildew resistance. These mildew-resistant cultivars are generally taller (four to five feet) than *Monarda didyma* cultivars because they have been crossed with *Monarda fistulosa*, which is four feet but mildew resistant. A few dwarf cultivars are beginning to appear on the market such as M. *'Petite Delight'* and *'Petite Wonder'* but my sources tell me these are not as vigorous as the taller varieties. This could be an asset, however, since *Monarda* would probably cover the earth if left unimpeded.

The last herb I want to mention is Hyssop, not *Hysoppus officianalis* but *Agastache foeniculum* (Anise Hyssop). A new cultivar called *'Blue Fortune'* was introduced a few years ago. It is hardy in zones 6 to 9 and has the typical lavender-blue spikes that bloom for months, particularly if pruned to lateral branches after the first flowers fade, which effectively reduces its height from three feet to two feet. I have used it quite effectively in front of a late blooming New England Aster, *Aster novae-angliae 'Hella Lacy'*, to hide its leggy stems. *Agastache* attracts bees by the hundreds and I never have to worry about pollination or lack thereof in my garden. One of the greatest attributes of A. *'Blue Fortune'* is its sterility, thus no seedlings to pull each year.

It may be heresy to say so, but who needs an herb garden when you can integrate the best of them into your perennial garden or commercial landscapes?

Pot It!:
Containers in the Garden

Container gardening is a term that covers a lot of territory and refers to a type of gardening characterized by great versatility. Container gardening is suitable for virtually every site you may encounter; in some cases, it can provide green space where it would have been impossible to garden. With its versatility and unique design considerations, container gardens provide a wonderful opportunity to let our imagination and creative spirit run a little wild. Since this is a broad topic, I will first discuss some of the concepts and elements that make up container gardening. Specific examples to illustrate these ideas can be found at the conclusion.

Why use containers? First, containers can be used in all kinds of settings: very formal with citrus boxes as seen at Villandry; semiformal with *Argyranthemum frutescens* (Marguerite Daisy) and Rose or Fuchsia standards as seen at Giverny; and informal with a simple but beautiful terracotta pot filled with one large *Hosta* at the edge of a shade garden. Secondly, containers give the gardener/designer a head start of a month or more. Perennials can be put out as soon as they're available from nurseries. Add annuals after the last frost free date has passed.

In early April, I planted *Scabiosa columbaria* 'Butterfly Blue' and *Sedum spurium* 'Tricolor' in concrete containers on my front porch wall. I had immediate color from the *Sedum* foliage. Then in early May, I added *Verbena tapiens* purple and two weeks later, the container was full and blooming. The one mistake I made was in not choosing a *Verbena* that would have more color distinction from that of the *Scabiosa*. A true pink would have supplied that. Finally, containers provide fresh dimensions to established gardens: depth, height, bursts of color and the ability to re-locate easily. All in all, containers have much to recommend themselves to any site.

Understanding the nuances of a perennial garden that evolves, as well as an annuals garden that is static, is helpful in combining both in a container. Many of the same design principles that apply to working with them on full-scale gardens still apply; however, they need to be scaled down to much smaller proportions – a daunting task! So often we limit ourselves to annuals, overlooking many effective perennials and ornamental grasses.

The choice of plant material is crucial when it comes to planting containers, so expanding our options makes sense. Perennials, like annuals, can be used for quick color changes in prominent spots. A pot of *Lilium 'Casa Blanca'* is just as effective as a pot of tall Snapdragons, perhaps more so because it is unexpected. Perennials grown for this purpose can later be planted in the garden or taken into the greenhouse to be held for the following year. If perennials are grown in non-ornamental pots, be sure to disguise their presence in an ornamental pot by either mulching or planting something else around the edges.

I think one of the best attributes of perennials in containers is their winter presence. Containers of annuals are either empty during the winter or look terrible. Containers that are filled with overflowing grasses and/or some evergreen perennials make winter more bearable. Grasses have large masses of foliage, sway in the wind and, if *Chasmanthium* is used, also rattle in the wind. Most grasses are beige during the winter but some, like *Festuca ovina 'Elijah Blue'*, retain their color. Evergreen perennials such as *Fragaria, Heuchera* or *Lamiastrum galeobdolon 'Variegatum'* also give color and presence where there would otherwise be none.

Using perennials and ornamental grasses in containers can also lessen our chores in the spring when we wonder how we'll ever get everything done. If they winter over, we need only add a few annuals once the frost free date passes. Wintering over is usually successful in unprotected containers if they are large because the soil mass insulates the roots from the cold. I can offer no definitive record for window boxes. Because of their shallow nature, I suspect that even plants that would be hardy to zone 3 in the ground may not survive in window boxes but I'm going to test that proposition this coming winter.

Since containers can be placed virtually anywhere, the next step should be determining where to place them. This is influenced by your overall goals – are you looking to add additional color, draw attention to or away from a certain feature, or create a green space in a barren area? Containers should be placed in prominent locations so that they can enhance their surroundings. Put them on either side of a doorway, on a patio or deck, or on stairs, being careful to coordinate the colors of the pots and the plants in them with the color of the hardscaping. For instance, white stucco walls cry out for Mediterranean or desert plants with gray foliage or herbs with blue-green or very green foliage. Nurseries or garden centers can place unusual containers (such as large wooden carts) near their entrances or on the roadside of the business. Containers are also very effective when integrated into the garden. Be aware that directional location is also crucial. Placement of a container facing south or west will necessitate much more frequent watering than one on a north or east wall. Some other considerations for container placement are:

- Awareness of the viewing angle or angles.
- Placement of cascading plants on a pedestal or overturned pots or on a hook that is high enough that they are viewable but not in the way.
- Recognition of lack of rain under eaves of a building.
- Recognition of windy areas where plant material will dry out faster and plants with brittle stems may break.
- Accessibility for watering – will you or your client open and lean out windows to water window boxes? Grouping containers eases the chore of watering while the proximity of several pots adds humidity to the group.
- Artful grouping hides many of the pots and emphasizes the foliage and flowers.

When selecting a container you will want to consider its location and coordinate the container to complement the surrounding area (home, garden, patio, etc.). Determine whether the container is going to be distinct from the plants or blend into the overall display. Try to coordinate the type and color of the container with its background or the material on which it is placed. If the building is white concrete, then white concrete or fiberglass pots are a natural. If pots are being placed on a green stone patio, choose ones that will blend, such as gray stone or fiberglass rather than terracotta, which will focus the eye on the pots rather than the plants. Use of gray-foliaged plants would also integrate a grouping here. Terracotta pots on brick patios look wonderful while wooden tubs or barrels on a deck or against a wood background make excellent choices.

Another consideration is the shape of the hardscaping. A round stone or concrete "pad" in the middle of a brick patio, for instance, cries out for a round container. Watering needs can also influence the size and type of container. If it is possible that a client may not water with the frequency that is necessarily needed, select a larger container since the greater soil mass will hold more water.

There are innumerable choices for selecting pots, limited only by your imagination. Terracotta is available in a wide range of sizes and styles, from very simple to very ornate. One of the more unusual configurations is the strawberry jar, a series of openings on the sides as well as a large planting opening in the center of the top. Although originally designed for strawberries, it is much more interesting when planted with a variety of herbs or *Sempervivum* (Hen-and-Chicks). The one drawback of terracotta is that it cannot be left outside during the winter. For small containers, this is not a problem but trying to carry large ones inside for the winter and then back out each spring is both time consuming and back breaking.

An excellent alternative is a concrete or fiberglass container. Such containers are now becoming readily available in beautiful patterns that have been cast from molds of old European containers. Plastic is another possibility. Its primary virtue is its lack of weight as opposed to the concrete and fiberglass containers, which are quite heavy. If you haunt antique shows, flea markets or salvage yards, you may find any number of items that could be used as containers, such as lead urns, copper boilers or whatever else your creativity can convert to use. Troughs are especially appropriate for alpine plants since it is easier to create the particular soil mix necessary for them in a small confined area than to amend the soil in a garden. Troughs also work well for *Sempervivum* and small plants that might get lost in a large garden.

Then there are Mother Nature's containers. A very creative lady from Cleveland turned the root system of a dead tree into a huge planter for *Sedum, Sempervivum* and Cacti. A hollowed out tree stump in the

Woodland Garden of the Cleveland Botanical Garden is a natural planter for *Aquilegia canadensis*, *Viola*, *Oenothera* and *Geranium maculatum*. In a Denver garden, I saw *Phlox subulata* planted in a rock depression with a container beside it that was filled with *Sempervivum*.

Window boxes enhance a building in a way that no other feature can. An ordinary garage can become a cottage. Most window boxes, permanently affixed to a structure, are very shallow so keeping them watered is particularly difficult. Search for the deepest ones you can find. The larger the soil mass, the less frequently water will be needed and the greater the chance that the perennials will survive the winter. Be prepared, however, to plant anew the following spring. Because of their size, the plants chosen for them need to be ones that will not become too big and out of scale.

Hanging baskets can be wonderful but, to my mind, the typical white plastic variety detracts from the overall display. Since the plants rarely entirely cover the plastic basket, put it in a natural basket or lift the plant out of the plastic and insert it into a wire basket that has been lined with coconut fiber or sphagnum moss. Or create your own combinations in wire baskets. Baskets for sun are easy to create. An unusual combination at Kingwood Gardens in Mansfield, Ohio, was composed of *Chlorophytum* (Spider Plant), *Houttynia cordata* 'Chameleon', *Plectranthus* (Swedish Ivy) and *Echeveria leucotricha* (Chenille Plant). Here is a place where *Houttynia* can run wild without concern that it will invade the whole property. Baskets for shade could use *Lamiastrum galeobdolon* 'Variegatum' as a trailer with one of the annual tuberous Begonia.

Containers that can accommodate water gardens open up a whole new realm of possibilities. Without discussing it at any length here, you will find a few suggestions for suitable plant combinations with the other examples at the end of this essay.

Now I want to talk about designing what goes into these containers. The same principles that we apply to our gardens apply here: unity and balance. Unity can be easily achieved by repetition of either container material or plant material or both. Sometimes, containers are used as we would a specimen plant but more often we group them. When a series of pots is used, they will be more effective if they are similar in form but different in size. In addition, there should be some unifying plant element such as a particular genus and species or a particular color of foliage or flower. I find repetition of foliage color, such as the silver of Artemesia, to be especially effective. In frost-free areas, a series of pots filled with Agapanthus would again repeat the plant material in both color and form.

Balance is the other crucial ingredient in creating eye-catching container compositions. To achieve this balance, it is necessary to carefully select plants for their height and width relative to the size of the container. Some plants, usually the ones in the back or center, depending on the angle from which the container is viewed, should be at least as high as the container. Then they should be combined with plants that will mound and trail. Or as seen at Sissinghurst, a container could be planted with something like Euphorbia characias 'Wulfenii', which is almost the exact shape and size as its container.

The use of containers also enables us to add dimensions of height, depth and width to our design. Where extra height is desired, we can choose vining plants by putting tall, narrow trellises in the pots. On decks or in window boxes, we can choose plants that trail down, such as Akebia quinata or Clematis. In the garden itself, where most of the plants may be relatively short, we can insert a pot, which when filled, will be taller than the surrounding plants. Containers allow us to go down as well as up. Where raised beds border a patio, put containers on the patio using plants that echo the textures and forms in the garden or add to them. Just as important as the height of the plants is their width. The height needs to be balanced by the width of the same or additional plants. An excellent perennial for this purpose might be *Gaura lindheimeri*, which although two feet tall has lax stems which lean outward.

Pay attention to the habit of the plants being chosen. Cascading plants can direct the eye toward new areas and provide transition. When considering which trailing plants to incorporate, don't hesitate to take "houseplants" out of the house. Such plants as *Plectranthus* (Swedish Ivy) and *Chlorophytum* (Spider Plant) have been mentioned earlier, but there is a vast array from which to choose. We need not limit ourselves to one type of trailer in a pot; a combination of two or three can be stunning. But keep in mind that, as exemplified by the Sissinghurst container, it is not necessary to use multiple varieties of plants in a container. We could use one large *Artemesia* in an urn or we could use three or four of one type of plant, such as the interesting *Carex ornithopoda* 'Variegata', in a low round bowl. Or we could use several different herbs in a window box or a basket. Choose some plants for their architectural interest. One of the most stunning pots I ever saw was planted with *Foeniculum vulgare*, which was in bloom, *Salvia coccinea* 'Lady in Red', and *Rex Begonia*. The tall airy foliage of the Fennel against a stucco wall combined with the color of the *Salvia* and the *Begonia* was breathtaking.

Attention to the size, color, form and texture of both bloom and foliage is essential to a winning composition. Since bloom is more often the focus, I want to concentrate on foliage. Foliage can take a leading role to create very unique looks. One effective design would be a combination of several gray foliages of different sizes and textures with one long blooming perennial and one short blooming perennial that has outstanding foliage. In the examples addressing foliage color and form, you will see a combination that includes *Lactuca sativa* (Red Lettuce). Including vegetables in containers is an excellent way of incorporating the element of surprise (the "oh-wow" factor), since most people do not expect to see them used in this way. Grasses are another plant not usually associated with containers. A beautiful grass for containers is the unusual yellow-and-green-striped *Hakonechloa macra* 'Aureola', which could be used with one of the scented geraniums and a plant with purple foliage. If you want your container gardens to be noticed, take a common plant like *Hedera helix* and use it in an uncommon manner. Train it in loops around and halfway down a large container and then fill the center with annuals.

Combining the elements of foliage and flower leads us to the concept of color echo. This describes the way plants appear in relation to their surroundings, based on the color play between one or more plants, the container and/or surrounding elements. To illustrate by example, the flowers of *Coreopsis verticillata* pick up the yellow stripe in *Miscanthus sinensis 'Strictus'* and the yellow streaks in *Aquilegia 'Variegata'*. *Crocosmia 'Lucifer'* would echo the color of a terracotta pot while a purple-leaved cultivar of *Heuchera* would provide a stunning contrast. Again, refer to the example section for more ideas that utilize color echo.

Of special note: If you are ever designing containers for public spaces, such as downtown sidewalks, choose containers that do not have an edge wide enough to sit on. Unfortunately, many people disregard the fact that sitting on the containers will damage the plants. Pick plants that have a long season of interest that will continue into the winter, particularly in locales where most perennials go dormant. Add perennials that have evergreen foliage and grasses to lend a winter presence.

Now we come to the nitty-gritty of installing the container of choice. The first essential is good drainage. Without space between soil particles for air, plant roots will sit in water and rot (suffocate). Contrary to common belief, putting a different medium in the bottom of the container does exactly the opposite of the installer's intention. It does not improve drainage; instead it impedes the dispersal of water. If the container is quite large, pebbles could be added to the soil mix to help fill some of the space.

The second essential is the soil mix. The problem with premixed potting soils is that they need to be thoroughly moistened before being placed in the container. If they are allowed to dry out after planting, they are almost impossible to completely remoisten. I have used 100% leaf humus with great success. At the end of the season, annuals planted in it are very difficult to remove because their root systems are so large. For commercial installations, try 1/3 humus, 1/3 topsoil and 1/3 very sharp sand well mixed with super-phosphate and slow-release fertilizer.

For ease of planting, the containers should initially be filled only two-thirds full. Once the plants are in, additional soil can be added as needed, remembering to leave one-half to one inch between the top of the soil and the top of the container in order to facilitate watering and to prevent unnecessary water runoff or washing out of soil. When you water initially, water slowly, then tamp down the soil to press out air pockets that will cause roots to dry out.

How many plants you need and how far apart you plant them depends on the habit of the plant and the dimensions of the container as well as the growth pattern of the plant. Since most containers will automatically impose constraints on root size, keep in mind that plants will probably not grow as large as they would in the ground. Most clients will need a great deal of education if you are planting on the spot. The container will not look full immediately unless you are using mature plants, a situation that rarely occurs unless you have a greenhouse at your disposal.

Now a few reminders are in order to help you keep these beautiful containers looking their best. During the first week, water every other day unless the containers are in full sun. In that case, you may need to water twice daily using a watering can or a water wand on the end of a hose. Regular morning watering is the key to success and the best way to prevent plants from becoming heat and wind stressed. If the soil dries out, it may never completely remoisten. A well-balanced slow-release fertilizer mixed into the soil before planting or liquid fertilizer applied once every three to four weeks will keep your plants growing and blooming. Many annuals, which tend to become lanky, should be pinched upon planting. Many perennials that tend to bloom in flushes should be deadheaded just as they would in the garden. Grooming is crucial to keeping containers looking their best. Yellowing or dead foliage as well as deadheads should be removed as often as possible. Weeds can grow anywhere; be alert for their presence and remove them as they appear.

If the containers being used are not weatherproof, they should be emptied after the first hard frost in order to keep them from cracking. Containers that can stay outside for the winter will, of course, have some perennials and grasses that you have installed but some of the plants will probably be dormant. In this instance, cut the stems and foliage back to the base. Then you could add cuttings of conifers or berried branches for extra interest and fullness.

The examples below are starting points on the way to designing your own creations. Remember that once the location is selected, you must determine the cultural variables that are present: amount of light/shade, wind, natural water and potential stresses. Select plants suitable to the intended location. Additionally, you should ensure that all selected plants have the same cultural requirements. Mediterranean, desert, and alpine perennials, which require very little water, will be excellent choices for hot and sunny spots. Woodland plants, which like moisture and humidity, will thrive in shady spots.

EXAMPLES OF CONTAINER GARDEN COMBINATIONS:

For Early Color (and good foliage combination)

This combination was planted at the same time in window boxes: *Arrhenatherum elatius* 'Bulbosum', *Fragaria vesca* 'Variegata' and *Centranthus ruber*. I had immediate foliage color although the *Fragaria* and *Centranthus* wouldn't bloom for at least a month or two. Then, in early May, add *Ipomoea batatas* 'Tricolor' (Tricolor Sweet Potato Vine) for even more foliage color and trailing habit as well as *Evolvulus* 'Blue Daze'.

To Blend Annuals and Perennials

Fill a hanging basket with *Veronica* 'Goodness Grows', *Verbena tapiens* pink and *Ipomoea batatas* 'Tricolor'. The annuals give color until the Veronica begins its bloom period. However, this combination illustrates a design error: Never use a dark blue flower against a dark background; it just can't be seen from a distance even though it is part of a beautiful combination when viewed up close. A better choice would have been *Veronica* 'Icicle' or 'Red Fox'.

A container of *Sedum* 'Vera Jameson' and *Sedum* 'Autumn Joy' would have no flower color until August if it did not also include *Salvia farinacea* 'Victoria'. Large plastic pots of *Caryopteris nepalensis* would just be tall green foliage until August if *Torenia 'Blue Wave'* and *Dahlia 'Dandy'* weren't planted in the foreground.

To Blend Annuals and Perennials for a Shady Location

A composition for partial shade that doesn't rely as heavily on annuals is one containing *Chasmanthium latifolium, Campanula poscharkyana, Ceratostigma plumbaginoides* and *Verbena tapiens* pink. The *Campanula* blooms from May until early July, the *Chasmanthium* infloresces in July and the *Ceratostigma* blooms in August and September while the *Verbena* blooms from the time it is planted in May.

For a Hot/Sunny Location

An excellent combination for a hot, sunny location would be *Sedum 'Vera Jameson'* and *Artemesia 'Silver King'*, both of which have lovely foliage, while *Oxypetalum caeruleum* adds sky blue flowers.

Another combination I have used is *Sempervivum 'Sanford' Hybrid, Sempervivum arachnoideum, Sedum spurium 'Red Carpet', Lavandula angustifolia 'Hidcote'* and a tender perennial, *Anagallis monelli linifolia.*

In a companion pot, I used all of the above but I substituted *Salvia nemerosa 'Plumosa'*. This was a huge mistake because the *Salvia* requires more water than all the other component plants.

Herbs, most of which are of Mediterranean origin, can be placed in a trough, which is then placed in an herb garden. *Sempervivum* are usually chosen for their foliage, but their blooms are also quite interesting.

For a Shady Location

Most shade combinations need to place the emphasis on foliage color and texture because the majority of shade-loving perennials do not bloom for a long period of time. Try combining one of the *Carex* with *Hosta, Epimedium, Arisaema* and *Astilbe simplicifolia 'Sprite'*, which will have a succession of bloom from spring through late summer depending on the choice of *Hosta*. A spring combination would be *Houstonia caerulea, Hosta, Aquilegia* and *Viola*.

Water Container Garden

Water gardens present us with a whole new realm of possibilities. Half barrels or molded plastic make excellent containers for these kinds of gardens. When planting them, it is just as important as in a garden to remember to mix heights and textures. Try combining *Carex 'Ogon'*, *Houttynia cordata 'Chameleon'*, *Caltha palustris* and *Juncus effusa 'Spiralis'*.

Flowerbox Container Garden

An excellent combination that emphasizes foliage color but still has some flower color would be *Salvia officianalis 'Tricolor'*, *Heuchera 'Palace Purple'*, *Fragaria frei 'Pink Panda'* or *'Lipstick'* and *Ajania (Chrysanthemum) pacifica*.

Another is *Imperata cylindrica 'Red Baron'*, *Lonicera nitida 'Baggesen's Gold*, *Dianthus gratianopolitanus 'Firewitch'* and *Ceratostigma plumbaginoides*. This combination has excellent foliage color and all seasons of bloom except midsummer, which could be achieved by replacing the *Lonicera* with *Gaillardia 'Golden Goblin'*.

Clematis are wonderful plants for window boxes; they can be used instead of *Vinca major* or in addition for a trailing plant that blooms.

Hanging Basket for Sun

An interesting combination is *Achillea millefolium 'Summerwine'*, *Artemesia stelleriana 'Silver Brocade'* and *Ipomoea batatas 'Blackie'*.

Hanging Basket for Shade

For partial shade situations, try *Lamiastrum galeobdolon 'Variegatum'* and trailing varieties of tuberous *Begonias*.

Color Repetition for Unity

A stunning and eye catching combination is orange Nasturtiums, bronze and yellow *Coleus*, *Phygelius*, *Plectranthus*, *Cyperus*, *Phormium*, *Ipomoea batatas 'Marguerita'* and *Agave*.

Planting for Balance

A lovely combination that can be used as annuals in the north or as half and half in frost-free areas is *Ipomoea batatas* 'Marguerita' and the popular burgundy grass, *Pennisetum setaceum* 'Rubrum'. This is a grass that is worth bringing inside for the winter, or if that is not feasible, replacing each year.

Adding Height in Shade

In a shade garden filled, for instance, with *Lamium maculatum* 'Beedham's White', *Euphorbia amygdaloides* 'Purpurea', *Arachnoides simplicior* 'Variegata' and *Hosta*, fill a container with a yellow *Carex* and place it on a pedestal in the garden to add height and echo the colors on the ground as well.

Trailer Combinations

Combine two or three trailers such as *Ipomoea batatas* 'Blackie' for its dark and large foliage, one of the *Hedera helix* (Ivy) for its medium-sized and green or variegated foliage and *Bacopa*, which has hundreds of tiny white flowers and tiny foliage. Use them to surround an ornamental grass that is upright yet bushy.

Architectural Interest

Achieve high drama by using a wide but somewhat shallow pedestal urn with a tall *Dracena* complimented by bushy *Heliotropium* and *Pelargonium* and trailing *Lobelia erinus* and *Diascia*.

Bloom Form

Complementary bloom form can be achieved by using *Coreopsis verticillata* 'Moonbeam', *Pennisetum setaceum* 'Rubrum' and *Galtonia candicans*.

Foliage Form

A combination of *Geranium cantabrigiense* 'Biokovo', *Fragaria frei* 'Pink Panda', *Hedera helix*, *Lonicera nitida* 'Baggesen's Gold' and *Imperata cylindrica* 'Red Baron' satisfies all the requirements of designing with foliage.

Another combination would be *Nasturtium 'Alaska'*, *Petroselinum* (Curly Parsley) and *Lactuca sativa* (Red Letttuce), which also lends an element of surprise because people are not accustomed to seeing vegetables in container compositions.

A third combination might be *Coreopsis verticillata 'Moonbeam'*, a fern, *Artemesia 'Powis Castle'*, *Salvia argentea*, *Artemesia 'Valerie Finnis'*, *Iris pallida 'Variegata*, *Thymus x citriodorus* and *Thymus x c. 'Argentea'*.

Color Echo

The foliage of *Echeveria* and *Helictotrichon sempervirens* would pick up the veining in a *Rex Begonia*, while the blooms of the *Echeveria* would pick up another color in the foliage of the *Begonia*. Two other examples of color echo combinations are *Liatris spicata 'Kobold'* with pink Petunias and purple Flowering Kale and a grouping of two pots, one with *Fragaria frei 'Pink Panda'* and the other with a pink *Dianthus* and *Thymus lanuginosus*.

Installing container gardens can add excitement and dimension to any setting. Designing and working on a smaller scale allows us to easily manipulate our design and experiment in new and creative ways Hopefully, the examples above have stimulated your imagination and you will greet spring with a myriad of containers and ideas for planting them.

Stone Impressions

When we refer to someone as "stone-faced," we're implying that the person shows no emotion. But, in truth, stone is a highly expressive material that imparts a sense of antiquity while giving impressions of permanence, security and serenity. And when you factor in its durability and flexibility, it's easy to see why stone has been the material of choice for countless generations of designers and builders.

Stone has been used in construction for centuries. The ancient Celts of Britain transported huge slabs of stone over long distances to create religious circles like the ones at Stonehenge and Avebury. The Romans used stone to build their aqueducts. From the pyramids of Egypt to the Acropolis in Athens, from the Great Wall of China to the magnificent castles of Europe, stone has been the raw material of choice for our greatest and most enduring structures.

Many qualities make stone a desirable material. Nothing is absolutely permanent, but stone withstands the ravages of weather better than brick or concrete. Not only is stone durable, it is readily available. It's hard to find a town in Europe without walls made of local stone. New England is full of walls constructed with the stones farmers dug from their fields. Here in Cleveland, I have a good friend and fellow gardener who swears that every time she wants to plant something new, she just has to swing her pickax in the soil to excavate a rock for a ready-made planting hole.

How, then, can we create exciting landscapes with this versatile material? Even a quick survey of what has been done with stone through the ages gives us a treasure trove of ideas and design touches. In addition to walls and structures, stone can be used in the artful imitation of nature. For centuries, the Chinese and Japanese have used it to replicate the mountainous terrain of their countries. These gardens and their borrowed landscapes also integrate stone into the landscape as paths and altars, and as ornamentation, such as lanterns.

We can transmute these approaches by our placement of stone in landscapes, watershapes and garden structures to help create the illusion that the viewer is looking at the work of nature. And from the beginning, designers and installers have understood that stone in a natural setting must be *believable*.

Too often, however, boulders look as though a giant dropped them into the landscape with no sense of unity or design. That's the wrong approach. Multiple boulders should instead be thoughtfully placed, with at least the bottom third buried in the soil. The color and grain should be similar so that several pieces appear to be merely part of an outcropping. In addition, the angle of the rocks should be similar. This requires thought and planning, especially when large stones are involved.

Stone connotes power, partly due to its size and feeling of permanence but also because many cultures believe that spirits abide in it. This is probably why stone has frequently been used to create prayer niches or altars by the roadside or in the woods.

Stone also conveys a sense of age, particularly when it is somewhat eroded and covered with lichens or moss. Such stones are almost always used in Oriental gardens, but you don't need to go to the Orient to see examples. I suspect that similar stones can be found almost anywhere in the world. In Northeast Ohio, where I live, a section of the Cuyahoga Valley National Park called The Ledges has huge, glacially striated and pockmarked rock outcrops that are covered with lichens. Few designers would ever try to duplicate the grandeur of The Ledges, but it should be possible to create, on a smaller scale, similar effects through a study of the shapes, striations and manner in which plant material (particularly ferns) grows here. Such an outcrop could, under the right circumstances, be the basis for a spectacular waterfall.

And of course, stone doesn't have to be in a near-natural state to play its role in a landscape or watershape. Old European gardens usually contain aged pieces of stone that have been carved. Some are statues or monuments; others serve as pedestals for statuary or urns. The front gates of Herrenhausen, a German garden that dates from the early 18th century, are attached to carved stone pillars. Many English gardens of the late 17th and 18th centuries copied architectural elements of Italian Renaissance gardens, appropriating their stone arches, staircases and balustrades as well as their stone piers and columns used as ornaments or as supports for pergolas.

When you look at these traditional applications of stone – regardless of the period or culture – the richness, subtlety and beauty of stone that has been in place for a long time is instantly apparent. No matter where it's found or how it is used, stone ages gracefully, and its presence lends an immediate sense of antiquity and tradition to any setting.

If you look carefully (and even not so carefully) at pieces of old stone next to pieces of new stone, you will notice that no piece of old stone is exactly like another and that each has blunt edges. New stone tends to have an Industrial Age accuracy to it, with its very even, sawn edges. Therefore, Step One in making a new installation take on what I consider to be a desirable air of antiquity might be to blunt all those new edges with a chisel or other tool.

Another noticeable difference in old stone is color. The steps and pond edging at the Hohenpark Killesberg, a public garden in Stuttgart, Germany, are very dark and look very old, but the park opened only in 1939. Weathering, dirty shoe soles and pollution all contribute to that darkening. New stone is much brighter. This is an instance where dirt is truly useful. As Step Two, rub it into new stone to start the darkening process.

Under favorable conditions, old stone is also a magnet for plant growth. Given the opportunity and a bit of moisture, plants will root anywhere space is provided by crumbling mortar. If you are using new stone to build a wall, Step Three in the aging process calls for leaving gaps to sustain plant growth and, in shady settings, encouraging the growth of lichen and moss by either transferring existing growth or administering a buttermilk mixture to the stone.

In areas with little rainfall, succulents such as *Sempervivum* could be planted into the wall. Over time, rain falling on the foliage will create stains that color the wall. Naturally, you will need good drainage behind the wall to ensure the stability of the wall as well as survival of the plants.

We should seize any opportunity to open our eyes to the vast heritage of the stonework of the ages and exploit it to create lasting stone impressions.

Lasting Impressions

Walls, paving, path edging and steps are probably the uses that first come to mind when thinking about stone, but there are myriad other ways of using stone to beautify the landscape.

Ornamental pools, which can be created in every size and shape imaginable, are a perfect example. Like other stone structures and features, pools should engender a feeling of age. One way to do this is to design the pool as part of a niche in a wall that has been built using an old pattern. Or a very simple water garden can be added to an existing foundation wall. The use of an antiqued wall plaque above it would contribute to the feeling of age, as would the veined stone used to outline the water garden.

When a landscape is renovated, it is a challenge to blend the old and the new, especially when the old stone is darkened. In a Boston garden, an innovative designer devised a channel water garden that runs between an old stone wall and new stone paving. It was edged first with stone cobbles but then curbed with sawn stone, which was, alas, glaringly new. (Chisel, chisel, chisel!) A timeless look can be given to a path by placing dark stone (at a comfortable stepping pace) in gravel. If a boulder is then added and chiseled out to create room for a recirculating pump, one combines a contemporary yet timeless fountain with a seemingly aged path.

Bridges are among the most striking of all the stone structures I've seen. While movement through rock gardens provides something of a sculptural dance, bridges slow down the impressions to a more deliberate and contemplative pace. They do not have to be large or grandiose to be effective. Even small bridges can make a huge impression, as is certainly the case with the beautiful arching stone bridges at Stourhead, a former English estate that is now a National Trust garden. Such bridges would be difficult to duplicate today because of the cost; however, they suggest ways of organizing and connecting settings in both space and time that can be applied in different ways today.

Our budgets frequently limit us to small or modestly scaled installations. The minimalist approach seen at Iford House would be simple and inexpensive to copy or use as a basis for design. Following a stone path, the visitor crosses a rill by walking over a long, monolithic stone bridge. What makes this bridge unique is its placement. Instead of being a direct extension of the path, the bridge stone is offset, forcing the walker to contemplate the scene rather than forging straight ahead. In this way, the designer at Iford House used a small and subtle bridge to create a distinctive focal point. On yet another terrace, crossing the same body of water is a different experience. This time, the stone path is more direct, but the walker still has to slow down because the stones across the water are uneven.

A contemporary version of this type of bridge can be seen at a private garden in Toronto, where the use of cantilevered stone slabs over a koi pond has the effect of virtually immersing the adventurer within an aqueous environment. This is a relatively new garden where the stone still looks new, but the combination of shade and moisture should quickly age it.

A pair of projects designed by Oehme/van Sweden in the Baltimore area demonstrate an even simpler concept. One uses concrete rounds to traverse a pool. The other uses a series of polished stones (which appear as a long slab) as a water garden deck as well as a shortcut across it. Both of these looks are sculptural and architectural. They would seem more natural if submerged rocks with flat tops were used as a substitute.

Another effective and intriguing use of stone is in the form of cascades – something that is probably nearer and dearer to watershape designers than any of the other stonework forms we've encountered so far except pools.

We're all more or less familiar with concepts of stream-building and waterfall design and are aware of the use of stone to create naturalistic water effects both large and small. What interests me, however, is a different approach – more sculptural and architectural – to the use of cascading water in built spaces.

Stone cascades have been with us since antiquity, probably contemporaneous with early irrigation systems. Certainly they were in wide use by the time aqueducts served as a means of water distribution. But artistic usage of moving water really hit its stride in Europe during the Italian Renaissance, when places such as the Villa d'Este took the decorative potential of water to totally new levels of grandeur and inspiration.

From that creative source have come cascades such as the curvilinear water chain in the Children's Garden at the Royal Botanical Garden, which entices youngsters and adults alike. A more formal architectural impression is made at the RBG Visitor Center, where water from arching fountains falls into a pool before overflowing as two cascades into a lower pool. The plantings on either side of the cascades cleverly echo the form of the fountains.

Ingenious minds, however, have created cascades with much more commanding presence, the distinctive quality that causes viewers to take second and third looks. One of these is the polished stone cascades that are part of the Franklin Delano Roosevelt Memorial in Washington, D.C. These cascades are an integral part of the memorial, which has many water features as well as stone monoliths engraved with FDR's most powerful words. All of these facets of the memorial evoke powerful emotions.

The Parc André-Citroën, a public garden in Paris that opened in 1992, has a very distinctive cascade. It is tiered on a slant facing another cascade that is a simple sheet of water. Both of these cascades invite the eye and the ear to move across the enclosing berm to the river Seine.

Thus far, all of the discussion of stone has been centered on its use in structures or paving. We must not forget, however, that one of its oldest uses is for the construction of rock gardens. The biggest problem with most rock gardens is that they look like a pile of rocks among which plants have been placed. Seeing the rock garden at the Edinburgh Botanical Garden was a real eye-opener. Putting aside the fact that it is the largest rock garden I've ever seen (with large plants to match its scale), what entranced me was that it seemed to be a landscape that just happened to have rocks in it. This is a concept worth copying.

Rock gardens are most appealing when they appear to be old. This is possible only when the stone itself looks old. Paul Zammit and Uli Havermann have designed a new residential garden in Toronto that looks old because they have used old rock to retain the soil and to create paths and steps through the garden. The stone, from the nearby cottage country to the north, was hand selected, piece-by-piece, for shape and color. Uli specifically looked for exposed rock with mosses, lichens and bits of twigs and then laid the rocks so that they would mirror one another, always keeping the stress lines consistent. The marvel of this garden is that it looks as though the stone has been there for eons, well before the house was built. The plant material, particularly in the front half of the garden, was selected for its ability to survive with only natural rainfall. This rock garden happens to be in the front yard, but it could just as well be adjacent to a swimming pool.

Why, particularly in areas with very little rainfall, do designers rarely take advantage of an opportunity to do something different by creating rock gardens or xeriscapic gardens next to swimming pools? A pool area should be an extension of the house, considered as though it were an outdoor room. Just as a homeowner decorates the indoors, we need to decorate the outdoors. The nature of rock lends itself to inventive design.

A very different twist on a rock garden is the two-level raised bed at Upton Grey in England. It serves as a focal point in the middle of the lawn, which is then surrounded by raised flowerbeds. The designer's use of stone similar to that in these surrounding walls creates a feeling of unity.

In a sense, the Upton Grey rock garden also serves as a planting container. Containers made from stone are, however, more likely to look like one I saw in a Boston garden. A large rectangular piece of stone had been hollowed out so that it could serve as an ornamental pool with a fountain in it. Because the fountain was a classical type of statue, the whole thing took on an air of antiquity.

Stone can and should be used as an accent in the landscape, not just as a construction material. It can be used in an infinite number of ways. An unusual rock can be a focal point in the landscape. So can a beautifully carved pedestal that is then placed upon a stone base. A single column carved in one of the ancient Greek styles evokes a sense of the past, even in a suburban Boston setting.

The oldest seating in the world, other than the earth itself, is probably a large piece of stone set upon two other pieces. Such a bench would be quite suitable in a rustic setting. A more refined version is not difficult to make or find in a good catalog.

Stone is an incredibly versatile material. Plants and even water may come and go, but stone is eternal. Hopefully, some of these descriptions of old and new uses will give inspiration to those of you who constantly seek it.

Vintage Impressions:
Patterns of the Past

Studying the works of past masters, many of whom are unknown, is a way to explore the world's rich resources for ideas about walls, pathways and stairways that can be used to work magic in a variety of settings.

It's the little things that often make the biggest difference in creating beautiful spaces within gardens or near watershapes. A well-articulated retaining wall here, a clever treatment of a stone footpath there or the perfect placement of a stone stairway can, at various points, lend variety, balance and even a sense of antiquity to the work. By exploring these classic and often subtle stone treatments, we stand to gain inspiration along with very specific design ideas – a powerful brew that will help us enliven and enrich our garden spaces now and in the future.

Walls are used mainly to define the external boundaries of landscape spaces. But walls also find use *within* those larger confines, either to define or divide smaller spaces or to manage transitions in elevation.

When I look at most contemporary work, I can't help noticing many missed opportunities. Particularly bothersome are the glaringly "new" retaining walls that make it seem as though the designer installed a purely functional structure without much, if any, thought about turning the necessary presence of the wall to the client's visual advantage.

In classic gardens, you don't find this pale, flat attitude. Indeed, the master gardeners were adept at taking advantage of every opportunity offered by walls, and they used a variety of approaches aimed at making both retaining and freestanding walls enhance, complement or reflect their surroundings.

At Vann, for instance, the designer of this private English garden set large slabs of stone against a straight cut as a retaining wall and then put smaller slabs into the wall as seating. Set against a cut-stone patio, the wall extends and harmonizes with the patio as a serene, sheltered refuge.

Or consider the use of stacked-stone walls with beautiful ornamental caps, as we find at Iford House in England. The property's steep terrain is governed by a series of stone walls, terraces and staircases designed by Harold Peto, who owned Iford House from 1899 until 1933. It's a beautiful combination of sound engineering with a real visual treat – and not a missed opportunity in sight. Peto was a landscape architect who firmly believed that the most beautiful gardens are those that combine plants and architecture, a sentiment he picked up from his architectural predecessors who designed the gardens of the Italian Renaissance. This influence can be seen in his axial design and use of ornamentation. He also employed walls as "room" dividers, always using larger stone as a cap.

There's no limit to the patterns and aesthetic touches that can be picked up in the study of classic designs. The best thing about such study is that it leaves plenty of room for creative interpretation – and for transmuting a general construction idea into an almost magical creation.

At Hadspen House in England, for example, you'll find a spectacular garden that contains an unusual watershape. There's a tall (approximately twelve-foot) brick wall on the far side of a rectangular lily pond that was once a water tank. Above the wall you'll see more gardens and a path between them. The whole composition is set up to manage views and make the pond a pleasant surprise when you approach it from above.

If I were building this sort of space now, I'd think about using stone instead of brick and then adding to the potential delights of the space by accenting the wall with small water spouts – something along the lines of the Hundred Fountains wall and walkway at the Renaissance garden of the Villa d'Este outside of Rome, although a hundred spouts would be somewhat overwhelming in this space!

The fact is, in drawing inspiration from the classics, designers are never beholden to them, never required to imitate them slavishly. Inspiration means literally filling one's mind with the spirit of a thing rather than directly borrowing form or function. I would use the classics as touchstones to create new, innovative, site-specific projects that evoke the same feelings and emotional responses I find in the originals.

Observation of the past also shows us that walls need not be solid, monolithic masses to get the job done An unusual stone wall at Spadina House in Toronto is used as a "room" divider. It has several arches that serve as display niches for flowers in containers, and the wall itself is also the base for a vine-covered pergola.

Mundane, practical structures can be made into distinctly ornamental and visual elements within the overall garden composition. Why don't do we do this more often?

What is a pillar but a wall in a very constricted space? History books about ancient Greece and Rome are full of drawings or photographs of carved classical columns, but we need not rely solely on these models for our inspiration. Sir Edwin Luytens, a famous landscape artist with a very fertile mind, constructed pillars out of stacked stone in both round and square designs as well as a combination of the two. Some were used as focal points and some, in alternating sequence, as supports for pergolas. Just think what a visual difference it would make if we designed garden pergolas with supports made of a material other than wood.

Extending that thought, we frequently need to design small buildings as shelters or as pool houses. The ones I have seen are usually constructed of wood, but why couldn't we incorporate stone? Perhaps we could use a stacked pattern like the one found in the Luytens pillars as did a couple who borrowed Luytens' idea to build a small shelter on their property.

Other than wall construction, stone is most often used as a paving material for walks or as edging for walks or driveways made of another material. Gravel is frequently used for walkways or driveways in Europe but is often frowned upon in the United States as being "messy." One can handle this objection by using an aggregate, which looks like gravel but has the solidity and permanence of concrete. The aggregate could then be edged with narrow stone pieces as I saw at St. Goarshausen, a small town along the Rhine.

As for paving itself, there are many old patterns that can inspire us. One is the use of wide stone slabs laid horizontally to create a sidewalk as seen in a centuries-old German cemetery. At Iford House, Harold Peto laid a very similar walk but edged it with stone squares of a corresponding color. This approach has been applied elsewhere, sometimes with the edging elevated to create a channel, other times with the edging at the same grade as the walkway. Is it heresy to suggest creating this aged look by laying new stone and then deliberately cracking it?

Another pattern, from the ancient Italian city of Siena, is the use of different sizes of rectangular stone set horizontally and perpendicularly to create a pattern that seems consistent yet somewhat irregular.

A beautiful but highly unusual pattern was designed for the entrance to Cranborne Manor in England in the mid-1800s. This pattern consists of squares and rectangles of cut stone intermingled with squares and rectangles of brick.

Sir Edwin Luytens was a master of pattern. At Hestercombe, he created a decidedly unusual pattern using large pieces of stone laid in a long rectangle, edged on both sides with narrow stone laid perpendicularly. The large pieces are very uneven in shape. Copying this quality, as well as the pattern, would contribute greatly to a feeling of age in new construction.

The patterns I have just mentioned are all fairly regular, but "cracked glass" patterns can also be employed. In Siena, I saw a very simple rooftop garden set into a terrace of irregular stone. In the Toronto Music Garden, a similar pattern is used, though with larger pieces and pieces of more than one color, which are coordinated with boulders of like colors. The feeling of age can be enhanced by encouraging the growth of crevice creepers or perennials that seed between the stones. There are any number of plants that can be used, the choice being determined primarily by the zone hardiness of the site.

Of course, the range of opportunities available with stone paving is virtually limitless. The few examples given here are just a sampling of what's been done by our predecessors to combine the durability of stone with an aesthetic approach that makes structures as common as walkways a source of visual interest in their gardens as well as the perfect potential complement to well-designed watershapes.

We've already addressed garden walls as one way of managing elevations, and now we come to a second: stairways, and the role they have in guiding visitors from place to place within a landscape. Steps should be more than a pragmatic means for conveying the stroller from place to place; they should beckon us to discover a new world and give us visual pleasure as we traverse them.

Steps can take on any number of "looks," from the rustic to the formal. Among the former is the rough-hewn stairway of the Rock Garden at the Royal Botanical Garden in Hamilton, Ontario, which seems as though it were carved out of an old quarry. In fact, all of the stone was brought in and placed in the 1930s, a reminder that one of the characteristics of stones is that the larger their size, the older and more permanent they seem.

Designers and pool builders, of course, have the opportunity to use stone stairways, whether rustic or formal, as a source of access and egress from their pools, as was the case in a project I saw in suburban Boston. There, a set of irregular (but basically triangular) steps leads up, alongside and over a small, meandering stream to an irregularly shaped swimming pool with a stone deck. The steps then continue right into the pool itself.

A more formal approach is found in the pattern of arcing steps popularized by Sir Edwin Luytens in his English landscapes. When he renovated the gardens at Great Dixter for the father of Christopher Lloyd, one of the 20th century's most eminent garden designers, he used the arcing pattern over and over again. The sweeping stairway at the Morris Arboretum in Philadelphia is a close duplication of the steps at Great Dixter, but the vegetation between the steps has been carefully cultivated and pruned for a formal look instead of being left to grow naturally to soften the hard edges of the stone. To my mind, this pattern lends grace to what is frequently pedestrian.

As with the other patterns I've mentioned, the arcing pattern need not be copied exactly. It could be implemented with brick for the riser and stone for the tread, or it could be combined with linear lines into an arc-and-tangent pattern for use in pool decking and elegant steps for entering a pool. A California designer used this pattern as his inspiration while incorporating the Islamic tradition of canals for a walled garden in the Petaluma area.

Of course, cost is a factor when using stone for design projects. On one hand, it's probably easier than it's ever been to get your hands on good-quality stone in a huge variety of types, textures and colors; on the other hand, it's true that stonework can run through a heavy portion of any given budget.

But sometimes, all it takes is a creative approach rather than a monster budget. At Iford House, for example, steps were made with dirt or gravel, and stone was used only as the riser and as edging for the stairs. The riser-only principle can be seen in the ancient amphitheaters of Greece and Rome. Julie Moir Messervy used it at the Toronto Music Garden in the amphitheater, but with grass instead of dirt or gravel. Her steps look new rather than old only because they are sawn, not chiseled, stone. There are, of course, other compromises that don't work as well, such as mixing good-quality stone risers with pre-cast concrete pavers as treads. This mixture of media would work better with treads made of well-packed gravel fines, grass or even dirt.

One of the key concepts underlying all of the examples discussed so far is the designers' use of patterns. Repetition of a certain shape or line is a wonderful way to create continuity within any physical space, and patterns of stone, in particular, serve as wonderful visual foundations for the ever-changing whimsy of plant life or moving water. The point is, whether you're working to mimic the masters or striving to create something innovative and new, the past can be used as a template or source for ideas that fit into a variety of visual contexts.

Steps at Great Dixter

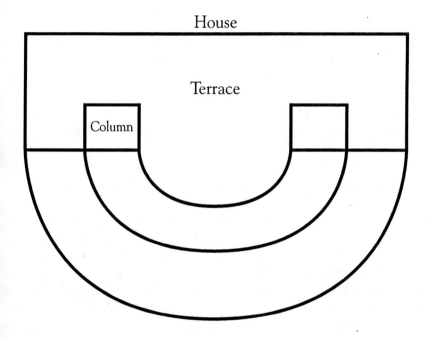

Steps at Morris Arboretum

Similar to above, but six steps, wider and vegetation between each step

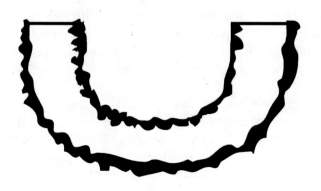

New World Impressions:
Stone in Mesoamerica

During the last four thousand years, civilizations the world over have used stone to create structures of durability, beauty and timelessness. While the stone aqueducts of ancient Rome are well known, unfamiliar or forgotten are the stone constructions of Maya cities in Mesoamerica (Mexico, Guatemala, Honduras and Belize) as well as those of their descendants who live in the rural areas near these lost or rediscovered cities.

The Maya had a very sophisticated civilization that was based on knowledge of astronomy, mathematics, hydraulics and engineering. They were able to quarry stone and move it hundreds of miles on rollers, as did the ancient Celts. Maya civilization flourished from approximately 600 B.C. to 1200 A.D. and was not really rediscovered until the 1800s, although the Spanish were aware of some of the ruins after they invaded Mexico in the 1400s. The Maya pyramids are as amazing as the Egyptian pyramids, but they are not nearly as well known. Nevertheless, it behooves us to study the stonework of the Maya for inspiration in our designs.

Most of the Maya patterns used for wall construction in Mexico are quite different from those in the Old World (Europe) and lend themselves to a more informal and rustic plus xeriscapic style of landscape design. For starters, the stone is rough rather than clean-sawn, although one side does have a smoother finish than the others. This can be seen at Uxmal, one of the Maya ruins in the western Yucatan, where a partially reconstructed wall has loose stones, not yet reintegrated, sitting atop the wall.

The Maya heritage of wall building is evident throughout the Yucatan. While driving from Cancun to Merida, I saw a simple, dry-laid stone wall used to delineate ownership of an agave field. Demonstrating both the beauty and simplicity of uneven, rough stone, it was a tangible reminder of that heritage. At Hacienda Chichen, a hotel near Chichen Itza, a low wall of irregular, rough stone is similar but capped with square blocks of stone. Either would be appropriate in a xeriscapic setting today. At a restaurant in Izamal, I could see that the art of wall building has been passed down from one generation to another. The differentiation in color where the wall had been repaired recently was the only clue to where the new part began.

At the ruins of Kinich Kokmo, on the outskirts of Izamal, there is an interesting juxtaposition of an old Maya wall and a more recent one. The older one, although only partially reconstructed, shows much more care in the selection of the stone faces. This may not be so amazing when one realizes that the Maya were a rich society and probably employed thousands of slaves who were directed to build carefully and well.

At the Temple of the Warriors in Chichen Itza, alternating layers of carved and plain stones are separated by a row of stones that jut out. (Figure 1) The idea of a protruding layer of stone is also found in some of the walls at Tulum but in a much simpler design. Relatively flat stones are built into varying height layers, which are then separated by the protruding row. (Figure 2) This pattern makes a strong impression, even from a distance.

Figure 1

Figure 2

Some patterns, created by plain stones, demonstrate great attention to detail. On the walls of the Nun's Quadrangle at Uxmal, the stones are the same height and laid either all vertically or horizontally in rows. (Figure 3) A partially reconstructed wall at Uxmal suggests another pattern that we might use – alternating large patches of smooth, fairly regular stones with patches of very rough but similarly sized stones. (Figure 4)

Figure 3

Figure 4

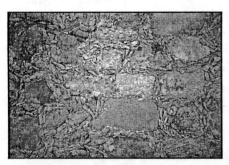

Figure 5

A very different wall pattern can be found at the partially reconstructed city of Dzibilchaltun, where small pieces of stone were set on end into the mortar between large and medium, somewhat rectangular pieces of stone. (Figure 5) Thirty miles south of Dzibilchaltun, in the vibrant city of Merida, the walls of a church school are very similar. Much larger rectangular pieces of stone were used to form the lintels of the windows and doors. In Izamal, a modern interpretation of the pattern at Dzibilchaltun was used on the façade of a shopping mall around one of the squares, but the small stones were aligned on the diagonal before being set into the mortar. At the Hacienda Chichen, a cruder version of this pattern can be found in a low wall that encloses a small courtyard. The stones seem more randomly placed, but the alternation of flat side and end side remains. (Figure 6)

Figure 6

As mentioned earlier, many of the Maya walls are composed of a series of layers; some are embellished with carvings, others with columns. In Kabah, the walls of the first level of the Great Palace are inset with round, simply carved columns at regular intervals. Eight miles southeast of Kabah, this pattern is repeated almost exactly on the Palace of the North at Sayil, except that the columns either form a section of wall or stand alone to provide openings to the interior of the palace. (Figure 7) By contrast, the columns of the courtyard wall at Uxmal are made of stacked round stones and are not set into the wall but provide openings in the walls. (Figure 8) I wonder whether Sir Edwin Luytens read about Uxmal since the design of his columns at Hestercombe in England is very similar.

Figure 7

Figure 8

When the Spanish colonized Mexico, they used the natives to construct their walls, homes and churches. Thus the methods and patterns reflect the heritage of the builders but incorporate Spanish methods as well. At Hacienda Chichen, the architect combined the rounded arches of Spanish architecture with the round, stacked stone columns of the Maya as supports for the creation of a large veranda. Using the same concept, a modern pergola in Merida is supported by similar stacked stone columns, though they are square rather than round.

In Maya architecture, stone was used dramatically or decoratively, even for such commonplace elements as foundations. Whereas in modern architecture the base of a building rarely shows, at the Great Palace of Kabah, cylindrical stones are placed side by side as the base of the wall. (Figure 9) More striking was the use of projecting panels called talus, which echo the angle of the staircases. (Figure 10) Kukulcan, the great pyramid at Chichen Itza, is basically a series of taluses built atop each other with a grand staircase on each side. The same concept has been used in the construction of the Governor's Pyramid at Uxmal. While none of us will be building pyramids, might we use the talus concept to make our walls more interesting?

Figure 9

Figure 10

Figure 11

Entrances in Maya buildings are carefully framed with plain stones on the sides and as the lintel above. In Merida, where the Spanish probably used the natives to construct their buildings, many of the windows have large pieces of stone above the windows, carved on the bottom in an arching shape to accommodate the arch of the window. (Figure 11)

One of the architectural elements continually repeated in Maya construction, regardless of period, was the vaulted arch. This is basically an upside-down "V" set into a wall as an opening or as an inset. The stones are placed in rows, each one projecting farther into the center of the "V," until the intervening space between the two walls can be bridged by a single capstone. In this way, the force of gravity supports the stones and forms an opening. The Maya used the vaulted arch in each city but in different forms. At Government House in Uxmal, some vaults are set into the wall as a decorative feature and appear to be supported by extra horizontal walls at the back of the vault. (Figure 12) Elsewhere in the city, the vault is used as an entrance. In one instance, after walking through a vault that is perfectly centered on an entrance behind it, one proceeds up a staircase to that rectangular building entrance. (Figure 13) At Kabah, there is a freeform vault that is both a hypothetical reconstruction and

Figure 12

Figure 13

a symbolic marker for the beginning of the causeway that connected Kabah to Uxmal and other smaller communities. At Tulum, there is a very primitive vault that functions as one of the few entrances to this old walled city on the Atlantic.

If one should be fortunate enough to have or be able to construct a wide, gentle slope, the opportunity to create a staircase arises. The long entrance staircase to the reconstructed buildings at Uxmal is composed of huge slabs of stone with a riser of two inches and a tread of approximately two feet, edged with long narrow stones. Its gradual rise eases the ascent for everyone but especially for those who are older and may be short of

Figure 14

Figure 15

breath. While the staircase looks old, it is relatively new. By contrast, the Convento de San Antonio de Padua in Izamal was built by the Spanish on the site of a Maya temple that was razed, leaving only the stairs, which are constructed in a simplified Dzibilchaltun wall pattern. (Figure 14)

An interesting and unusual pattern of tread and riser can be seen at Uxmal. The treads consist of large stone slabs, but the risers are rectangular pieces of stone set on the vertical, side by side. (Figure 15) I can easily imagine creating stairs using this pattern in brick or clay tile, or even in concrete that would be carved before it set completely.

In our efforts to find patterns in the past that we can use to make our newer construction look old, one of the simplest and easiest is to imitate the Maya example of path edging by using stone to line cement paths that have been divided into squares or rectangles. Rough cutting the seams of the concrete and edging the path with rough-cut, narrow rectangular stones will impart a feeling of age.

The Maya placed great importance on symbols, many of which had religious connotations, since religion was inseparable from other aspects of their civilization. The artisans of the Maya created sculptures from stone -- witness the two-headed jaguar in front of the Governor's Palace at Uxmal. Some sculptures were used as ornaments on buildings. A series of turtles waddle around one of the upper layers of the House of the Turtles at Uxmal. At Chichen Itza, carved serpent heads (the symbol for the god Kukulcan) protrude from the walls of the Platform of Eagles and Jaguars as well as the base of the Great Pyramid. Carved and sculpted serpent heads are also seen on the corners of the Nun's Quadrangle buildings at Uxmal, where carvings tended to be quite elaborate. The walls of Government House at Uxmal display carvings of Chaac, the rain god, and of spirals, which represent the source of life and the shape of the galaxy, while eagles and jaguars are carved at the base. Skull carvings are found on the base of the Platform of Skulls, where skulls were displayed before final disposal. Wouldn't it be interesting to see a client's reaction when told that his or her symbol could be incorporated into a project? Finding a symbol to use would personalize a project in a very unique way

Sometimes the carvings seem to appear randomly, but frequently they are utilized to create beautiful wall patterns like those found at the Governor's House in Uxmal. (Figure 16) There, spirals and X's alternate in an elaborate pattern on the top of the two layers that compose the wall. Similarly, two carved alternating themes of X's and small triangles decorate the walls of the Kodz Poop in Kabah. (Figure 17) For our purposes, we could adapt this type of pattern by inserting squares for the X's, thus reducing the labor and concomitantly, the cost.

Figure 16

Figure 17

After visiting several partially reconstructed Maya ruins, I began to see a pattern of carved repetition. For example, one of the walls of the Kodz Poop shows a series of arcs on repeating stones, a series of verticals on repeating stones, a series of spirals on repeating stones and a series of zigzags on repeating stones, but the pattern always started as

Figure 18

repetition of one design within one stone. (Figure 18) Lacking time and money to hire craftsmen to carve such walls for us, why couldn't these patterns be used as a template for one of the polymers or resins? Stretching our imagination even further, the patterns could be painted onto walls or fences, especially since archeologists have found traces of paint indicating that these carvings were brightly painted in shades of red, blue and yellow.

Stand-alone columns are both sculptural and sculptured at Chichen Itza. At the Temple of the Warriors, the square, stacked columns told tales through the carvings. Adjacent to the Temple of the Warriors is the Plaza of the Thousand Columns. These round columns are composed of stones that are gradated from large to small as the column

Figure 19

rises from bottom to top, with small stones embedded in the mortar between them, similar to the wall pattern described earlier. (Figure 19)

At Tulum, the round columns vary in size without any apparent logic. Archeologists theorize that these columns supported thatch roofs. I can imagine using such columns instead of wood to support a pergola in a rainy climate where the wood might rot after a period of time. A variation can be seen at Uxmal, where round columns are composed of rectangular stones exactly like those in the walls, but they are mortared (around an unknown core material) as a façade of the columns. (Figure 20) Today, many people use vertical artifacts in their landscapes. While I am not suggesting that we duplicate these columns, I am suggesting that a column of some kind could be used as a focal point.

Water features are a very popular element in today's landscapes. Unfortunately, they rarely seem to be an integral part of a landscape but more often appear to be an afterthought. The pools, or cenotes, at Maya sites were natural wells supplied by underground streams that were usually surrounded by

Figure 20

layered stone. It is difficult to determine whether the stone was added to aid access or was already there. The stone around the cenote at Dzibilchaltun looks so natural that one can only guess. If only all pool surrounds looked so natural! The study of such sites is invaluable to anyone designing water features.

As any gardener, designer or contractor knows, regular maintenance is essential to the survival of any landscape. This is just as true for the hardscaping elements as it is for the natural elements. How many concrete driveways or stone patios and paths gradually disintegrate because weeds germinate in the cracks and are not pulled? Many of the Maya sites are in the desert; others are in the jungle or other humid locations where plants can grow at an accelerated rate. Weed seeds, however, can survive anywhere, as seen in the ruins of Tulum, where little flowering plants bloom between fallen stones. Even at a well-tended hotel like the Hacienda Chichen, seeds germinate everywhere, including walls. A few look charming, but too many will lend an air of decay – a lesson for all of us.

In a world of constant change and new construction, stone imparts a sense of antiquity and timelessness. We tend to look for examples from Europe and Asia, forgetting that an incredible civilization existed just south of us. We can use many of the Maya concepts as the genesis for new concepts of our own.

Ornament:
What It Is and Why We Use It

Everyone knows the old conundrum "Which came first, the chicken or the egg?" A similar quandary is "Which comes first, the landscape and its design or the ornament?" Naturally, there is no correct answer. Sometimes the design is done first, and the designer will specify the location of appropriate garden accents, which become the finishing touches. But other times, the owner of a garden or landscape chances upon an object that calls out to be purchased and then a niche must be found for it.

Garden ornamentation has a long history. The Chinese and Japanese have long used decorative containers as well as unusually shaped plants as accents. Clay pots have been found in Egypt, and urns and statues were abundant in ancient Roman and Greek gardens. Renaissance and Islamic gardens were filled with fountains and urns as well as parterres, canals, steps and terraces, which are ornamental in a grander sense. Victorian English gardens frequently highlighted balustrades of stone or wrought iron as well as cast iron urns.

In the 20th century, the definition of ornament became wide enough to encompass almost any kind of art form, from serious to whimsical. Containers of every kind and size, statues, sculpture in an incredible array of sizes and materials, pedestals and plinths (either to stand alone or to raise another object to a better viewing height), seating that is beautiful or funky as well as functional, water features, birdhouses and mirrors – these are just some of the possibilities. What we use in the garden is limited only by our creativity, but we should also try to think on a large scale as our predecessors did. Structural elements can be ornamental. Just imagine how much beauty we can add to our landscapes by utilizing unusual walls, fences, arches, arbors and pergolas.

To make the most of garden accents, we must first understand why we use them. A well-designed landscape is an effort to create nature with form. What is lacking is the human element. Happily, the answer lies in something that is man-made, whether a chainsaw sculpture created from a dead tree or a bentwood arbor. Letting the client choose the ornament nurtures a strong feeling of participation and ownership. In our mobile society, it is also important for people to be able to take important pieces of their landscapes with them when they move.

Garden accents frequently make a statement. An animal sculpture set in a large swath of lawn will attract small children. It might as well be saying, "Please walk on the grass." A bench placed midway on a long path is an invitation to rest and enjoy the view. A topiary rabbit mowing the grass or a metal robot set in a grouping of *Miscanthus* evokes laughter and the element of childhood delight in the unexpected.

Accents also reflect our personalities and interests. Found art, such as an old iron gate used as a partial screen when hung from a pergola, tells us that the owner is probably someone who is interested in the past. Romantics may be drawn to elegant arches and gates. A statue of Pan set in a woodland garden lets us know that the owner is well acquainted with the symbolism of the ancient Greeks. Sports fans can make their interests known through their ornaments.

Ornaments received as gifts can sometimes require us to redesign part of a garden. I am the recipient of a Cleveland Indians birdhouse and an Ohio State Buckeyes birdhouse. (Having lost another decorative birdhouse to the elements, I recommend spraying them with polyurethane, which does not discourage birds from building nests in them.) Since the birdhouses are primarily red, but my garden is primarily pink and blue, I deliberately added red-flowering perennials, making sure that the reds had tones of blue in them but not orange so that they would blend in.

Accents can link a garden to the past, present or future. Decorative structures made from bentwood by a Celtic artist in Canada evoke ancient Ireland. On Algonquin Island in Ontario, a modern painted totem created from a dead tree trunk summons both an image of the artist and of the Indians who once lived there. Tools from the 18th and 19th centuries displayed on a shed door remind us of our agricultural heritage. Those wishing to create an English garden reminiscent of the 19th century might incorporate a Luytens bench and echoing hedge shape behind it. A futuristic metal sculpture could be the centerpiece of a garden bed with lines that imitate those of the sculpture.

Most people bring home wonderful memories from their travels. What better way to capture those experiences than to buy something special to place in the landscape? The aforementioned Luytens bench would remind anyone of a trip to English gardens. A Charleston bench would elicit images of camellias and the South. A Parisian street sign affixed to a fence or a wall would bring smiles to anyone who has been to Paris. Someone with plenty of space might try to duplicate the mood of Monet's garden at Giverny by installing a series of black arches and then planting perennials and annuals on either side. (I've seen this done in Belgium and in Youngstown, Ohio.)

The right ornament can also accentuate the style of the garden. A country garden calls for rustic seating, while a formal garden calls for a more stylized arrangement. A naturalist's garden, if divided into areas for specific types of wildlife, would benefit from signs designating those areas – for example, Frog Garden, Bird Garden or Butterfly Garden – so that visitors know what to expect. Fence styles can reflect both mood and history. A white picket fence would be perfect for a saltbox home but not for a Tudor, which would cry out for an iron fence. Fanciful fences create anticipation of the unexpected. Fences and low or see-through gates constructed on the lot line can create the illusion of a larger garden or landscape by making it appear that one may continue through the gate. Another way to make the garden seem more spacious, if one has a tall hedge, is to cut a "window" into the hedge so that it is possible to peek through to another interesting landscape.

Large structures such as fences and pergolas impart a sense of stability and permanence that is emphasized when covered with plant material. This enduring quality also can be achieved by using large pieces of stone, particularly stones of staggered heights.

Blank walls are boring, but it seems as though almost every landscape has at least one, usually a garage wall. The traditional design would place an interesting assortment of plant material against this wall, but what about doing something different? One could use a large piece of wrought iron art or an interesting fountain on the wall. If the designer or the client is very talented, the wall could be used for a mural or as the backdrop for a three-dimensional vignette.

Many people hate winter, not only because of the cold and snow, but because most landscapes appear dead. This illusion can be partially negated by evergreens and ornamental grasses, but garden ornaments are also helpful, particularly colorful ornaments such as sculptures that can be seen from indoors. Walkways covered by arbors that focus the eye on an unusual plant structure would also be helpful.

There are an infinite variety of accents that can be used to satisfy innumerable considerations. What is yours?

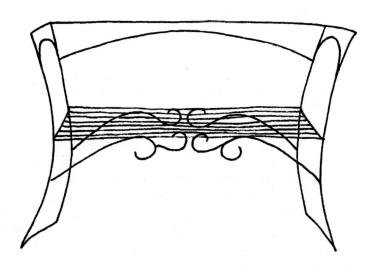

Ornament:
The Importance of Placement

When a garden accent is well placed, the viewer not only stops in his tracks, he also notices the setting, the light and the plants surrounding it. I once saw what had been a narrow driveway (which directly abutted the house) transformed into a magical container garden by covering the former garage door with lattice and erecting a lattice wall on the other, open side. Numerous containers, filled with an array of vines, shrubs and perennials, were placed on the concrete "floor" along these "walls." One might not think of lattice as an ornament, but any item, small or large, that isn't living and that changes the mood of a landscape can be an accent.

How one places an accent depends on both the site and the personality of its owner. Placement can be so subtle that the eye of the viewer almost has to search for the accent; for example, a small fountain can be nestled under the branches of a shrub with other plantings in front of it. The sound of water will lure the viewer to find it. In contrast, a brightly colored sculpture planted within a mass of equally bright flowers will draw the viewer's attention in the garden and from within the house all year long, but especially during the bleakness of winter.

Whichever kind of ornament is chosen, it must be in keeping with the scale and style of the site, particularly when it is close to the house. In England, hedges adjacent to large buildings sometimes become ornaments because they are sheared in a style that reflects the nearby architecture. Placing large pieces of sculpture can be difficult. In a sculpture garden, large pieces are quite appropriate, but great care must be taken when placing them in a residential landscape. All too frequently, the bed is not large enough or the surrounding plant material is too puny.

Ornaments such as lanterns are usually found in Japanese gardens. The style and size depend on the site itself. Where tall trees surround the garden, a tall lantern on a large base would be perfectly in scale with the site. Where the garden is of shorter stature, smaller and shorter lanterns would be more appropriate. Sometimes, sculptures are placed on a base in order to make them more prominent, but the site must be viewed from the building as well as the ground to assure that the height is correct. A very large sculpture probably would not need a base, but would require an appropriate background, perhaps a huge tree or a combination of large container plantings.

Kitchen gardens are utilitarian, but there is no reason why they cannot be both functional and beautiful. Take another look at watering cans, standpipes and terracotta or glass cloches used to cover tender plants when frost threatens. All of these can have lovely shapes as well as very real functions. Entrances to kitchen gardens, which are normally surrounded by some kind of fencing to keep out marauding animals, can be enhanced by a beautiful arbor and gate. Forget treated lumber; create an arbor from young branches in keeping with a rustic setting and then grow cherry tomatoes on it. Don't use ugly tomato cages; substitute twig tepees or shiny, spiraled metal supports that are sculptural.

One of the most difficult placement problems concerns multiple accents. Sometimes the result is laughable. I'm sure that everyone has seen a front yard crammed with "stuff." It is easy to get carried away. But there are some things that can help assure cohesion and comfort. One is using ornaments of the same color, though they may be made of several different materials, for example, wood furniture and window boxes that will age to gray, a stone table and a fiberglass fountain with a gray finish.

Large accents are often part of the landscape design itself. For instance, a backyard that needs screening from a neighbor could incorporate a Japanese-style pavilion situated along the lot line while a bamboo fence screens the other side. Then add a waterfall and pond to provide sound and movement, and a statue and/or a lantern amid the plantings, and you have a setting in which all of the ornaments have a common theme.

Effective accent placement means keeping in mind the design principle of the focal point. When the eye has too many places to look, the area can feel disjointed. The object is to lead the eye and draw the body, to command attention to a particular space. A beautiful urn placed at the beginning of a path, whether used as a planted container or, unplanted, as an ornament, calls out to the viewer. So does an arbor over the path with a planting that frames the walk and leads the eye to the end of the path where a bench awaits under another arbor.

Use accents to affect the stroller's pace and direction through the garden. A well-placed ornament, like a statue of a child amid a perennial planting, will make the stroller pause or stop. Whimsical sculpture, such as a large, brightly colored dragon, can be very effective and fun when placed amid large plants. Where the stroller has a choice of paths, accents will influence that choice. Containers on steps encourage one to climb up. A statue or a sculpture at the end of a path entices the viewer to come that far and then decide which way to continue.

Seating accents that act as focal points also provide visual rest and physical relief. How restful it is, on a hot summer day, to see a pool with a bubbler surrounded by lovely flowerbeds, and know that as soon as you walk down that path, there is a bench waiting for you. Well-placed seating may also provide a view to another focal point that will draw the viewer even farther.

Use walls of stone or brick or living walls (hedges) with openings that offer views of another garden room. Obviously, there will be a path from one to the other. At the end of the path, place an accent, such as an urn, as the focal point. A landscape with an axial design will naturally provide such opportunities.

Accents used as focal points help move people through a landscape, but they also create a sense of discovery that enhances the experience. A moon gate set in a fence beckons the viewer to discover what is beyond. Huge twig balls that seem suspended in mid-air draw the puzzled viewer to come closer only to discover that the balls are sitting on tall posts that are initially hidden from sight by the plantings.

Some accents are meant to be seen at particular times of the year. A stone ball placed at the foot of an ornamental grass provides interest in early spring when the grass has been cut to the ground. As the seasons progress, the ball becomes partially hidden by the foliage of the grass, only to be rediscovered in spring again.

Do keep in mind the natural light of the site. An ornament placed in a dark spot may not be seen; this could be a good place for something white or shiny. Alternatively, elevating the accent on a pedestal may bring it into enough light.

I hope it is now apparent that placement of ornaments is just as important, if not more important, than the ornament itself. Poorly placed, your beloved object may not be seen by anyone other than you.

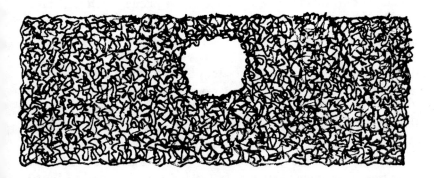

Ornament:
Complementary Plants

Now that we've decided why we want to use an accent in the landscape, what it will be, where we want to place it and how best to place it, we are ready to enhance the placement with plant material. Question: What effect do we want the plants to create? Do we want them to echo and emphasize the character of the ornament? Provide a foil for it? Frame it? Soften it? Stage it? Ground it? Cause it to come forward or recede? Plants can do all of these things.

If the objective is to emphasize the character of the ornament, first examine its form and then find a plant that will echo it. A narrow, vertical sculpture could be placed next to or in front of an upright hardy cactus, a fastigiate *Ilex crenata* such as '*Skypencil*' or '*Schworbel's Upright*', or a fastigiate conifer such as *Juniperus scopulorum* '*Skyrocket*'. If the ornament is round, such as an urn, it could be placed on a round base that sits atop a circular pattern of stone. The urn could be planted with a globular Boxwood or a simple annual combination of *Pelargonium* (Annual Geranium) and *Verbena*, which together provide a rounded contour.

Another way of echoing the character of an ornament is to repeat the material or the color. A Philadelphia designer's garden has a bamboo grove into which she has placed a bench made of bamboo. A steel sculpture could be complemented by using the similarly colored *Juniperus scopulorum* '*Grey Owl*'. An Ontario designer, instead of lamenting the distraction of a yellow fire hydrant at the back of her garden, integrated it by using the yellow grass *Carex* '*Bowles Golden*' as well as perennials with yellow flowers.

To accent an ornament, provide a foil for it. Metallic wire ornaments, in particular, need dark, dense backgrounds in order to be seen. Many coniferous evergreens would serve this purpose, as would a dark fence. The cogent factor here is supplying sufficient contrast so that the ornament is easily seen. Placing a series of wooden human figures in front of a dark green hedge, perhaps Boxwood or Yew, would provide such contrast. Mature trees behind the hedge could then emphasize the upright form of the figures. The foil could also be one of form rather than color. Take an abstract, linear sculpture and place it amidst a sea of mounding ornamental grasses such as *Pennisetum alopecuroides* or *Miscanthus sinensis*.

I love to frame garden accents in order to call attention to them. Sometimes, the frame already exists in the form of tree and shrub branches. If it doesn't, we can create it by careful selection of woodies with an open branching character such as *Betula nigra* (River Birch) or one of the more open *Acer palmatum* (Japanese Maple). Beautiful steps and paths can be framed with containers and interesting plants such as ornamental grasses to call our attention, not only to the steps and paths themselves, but also to the specific area to which they lead.

Ornaments with a very linear character may be enhanced by softening them. For instance, a wooden obelisk, mainly used as a support for climbing roses, would benefit from having its feet hidden by a stand of *Iris siberica* foliage. While the *Iris* foliage is also linear, its overall form is fan-like, the obverse of an obelisk. A swooping metal bird attached by a thin arm to a metal stake loses much of its effectiveness if the stake is not hidden by plant material. Not only are most pedestals more effective if they rise out of plant material, there may be other reasons – birdbaths, frequently set on pedestals, provide more shelter and safety for birds if they are surrounded by a sea of *Hosta* or set into a border of perennials and grasses.

Water features enhance any landscape, but we can augment their character by staging a compatible sculpture, such as a heron, in the midst of bog-loving ornamental grasses like

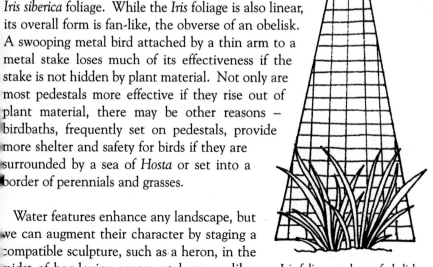

Iris foliage at base of obelisk

Scirpus tabernaemontani 'Zebrinus' (Zebra Bullrush) or *Butomus umbellatus* (Flowering Rush). In a Baltimore garden, I saw a pelican sculpture that had been nestled into a bed of *Sarcococca* (Sweetbox). The upright but short, linear growth of the *Sarcococca* was an excellent contrast to the heavy, rounded form of the pelican.

It is important to consider carefully the color of the plant material as it relates to the ornament. Black ornaments recede and are particularly difficult to see in the shade. This is a time to use variegated plants such as *Kerria japonica* 'Picta', *Brunnera macrophylla* 'Variegata' or one of the variegated *Hosta*. If a black urn containing a plant with red foliage, such as *Imperata cylindrica* 'Red Baron', is placed against the background of a dark hedge, the urn will not be seen, even in the sun. A bright yellow sculpture will be seen from any vantage point, but it will appear closer if yellow foliaged plants such as *Carex* 'Bowles Golden' or *Spiraea x bumalda* 'Goldcharm' are planted in front of it.

There are an infinite number of ways to complement ornament with plant material, and so many factors to consider. What is most important, however, is that the end result is pleasing.

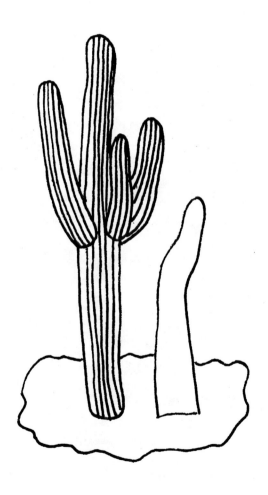

Creating the Design:
Plant Material

Old Favorites:
New Cultivars
Part 1

We are all familiar with the old standbys that are reliably hardy and relatively maintenance free. These perennials are invaluable to the landscaper and the homeowner. But for the sake of variety and interest, try incorporating some of the newer cultivars of these old standbys.

Achillea millefolium (Common Yarrow) has two noteworthy cultivars. One is 'Credo', a Karl Foerster introduction, which is actually a hybrid between *A.millefolium* and *A.taygetea*. It is three to four feet tall with strong stems, green foliage and light yellow flowers that fade to cream. In fact, during the summer of 2000, when the temperatures were relatively cool, the flowers were white. This cultivar is a clumper, unlike A.'Summerwine', which is a true millefolium and thus a spreader. What distinguishes this latter cultivar is its color. Spill any deep red wine such as cabernet or zinfandel and you will produce 'Summerwine'. Unlike most *Achillea* blossoms, the faded ones are still attractive. Be sure to plant them in full sun.

Asters are native plants and thus in vogue but be aware that most of the wild species have tiny flowers. The cultivars of *A.novae-angliae* have more imposing flowers on relatively tall plants (four to six feet). The beauty of A.'Purple Dome', besides its deep purple color, is that it only grows to a very manageable height of eighteen inches, never needing to be pinched as its taller cousins do. Two other new cultivars are A. 'Woods Purple' and A. 'Woods Pink', which are even shorter – only twelve to eighteen inches. They too need no pinching and all three are disease and mildew resistant. Again, plant in full sun.

There are so many *Astilbe* that it's hard to keep track of all the cultivars. But a new one appeared a few years ago. Its color, a deep raspberry pink, is its claim to fame. A member of the *chinensis* species, its spikes are thicker and more plume-like than those of the *Astilbe* we most often see. Called *'Visions'*, it only grows eighteen inches high. Because of its membership in the *chinensis* family, this *Astilbe* will spread. It does best (and spreads most quickly) in moist soil and partial shade.

Coreopsis (Tickseed) is used effectively to brighten many a garden and landscape with its bright yellow flowers. Most *Coreopsis* grow anywhere from twelve to eighteen inches, but *'Flying Saucer'* will reach up to twenty-four inches with flowers that are larger than those of any other cultivar. Naturally, full sun is required to keep it blooming from June until frost.

Astilbe

Dianthus (Pinks) make wonderful groundcovers for hot, dry sites with their lovely linear foliage but until recently, extra moisture would cause rot. Now we have two cultivars from the Deep South where humidity weighs heavily on people and plants. *D.'Bath's Pink'* and *'Itsaul White'* seem to tolerate average soil moisture instead of demanding very dry soil. Like most *Dianthus*, they bloom heavily in late May and June. *'Bath's Pink'* is a soft pink that grows four to six inches high, while *'Itsaul White'* is eight to twelve inches high; both have lovely silvery-blue foliage.

Gaura is not known nearly as well as other genera I have mentioned but it has quickly become a favorite of mine for its durability, its length of bloom (from June to frost) and its ability to look good without maintenance. The species seeds prolifically but its cultivars are sterile. *'Whirling Butterflies'* is the white cultivar that has been around for several years. Then came G.*'Siskiyou Pink'*, which is a striking bright pink, and G.*'Corrie's Gold'*, which has white flowers fluttering above yellow- and green-variegated foliage. Now we also have several new cultivars, some with dark foliage and one with variegated foliage. Most *Gauras* grow approximately thirty inches high in full sun and somewhat dry to average soil but some of the newer cultivars are only twelve inches high.

Heuchera sanguinea (Coral Bells) has almost been forgotten in the rush to canonize the purple-leafed varieties. The green-leaved cultivars have much more colorful flowers and one of the best of the newer ones is 'Raspberry Regal', which has panicles of bright raspberry-red tiny bells that are eighteen to twenty-four inches high. This particular cultivar usually stays in bloom four to eight weeks.

Shasta Daisies are a staple of the perennial garden, but most of them bloom for about a month and then flop over. *Leucanthemum maximum* 'Becky' has very strong stems, which are usually four feet tall when 'Becky' first blooms. If you deadhead religiously, 'Becky' will keep blooming until frost. By that time, she is only two and a half feet tall. This Shasta is also a very quick spreader. Grow in full sun for best results.

Although I've never grown *Lobelia cardinalis* because I don't have a site that is moist enough, I have seen it growing elsewhere and thought that it was stunning. Now with *L.* 'Ruby Slippers', I too can grow *Lobelia* for this hybrid doesn't need as much water. The color is a stunning ruby red and when the plant blooms in August and September, it sends up spikes that reach three to four feet high. This *Lobelia* will grow in full sun or partial shade but leans in partial shade and stretches an extra foot. Rabbits seem to love the new foliage, so a chicken wire cage around the base and lower extremities is advised.

Some of the cultivars I've discussed are not readily available but requesting them from your suppliers will increase interest and availability. Expanding our plant palette will give us the opportunity to provide fresh and original landscapes – something new from something old!

Old Favorites:
New Cultivars
Part 2

Continuing with the venture of adding new cultivars from old favorites to bring a fresh note into the landscape, let's look at some of the noteworthy newcomers. There are so many that it would be nearly impossible to include them all so I will just touch on just a few.

Lysimachia punctata (Yellow Loosestrife) provides lots of color in moist shady spots, where it is very aggressive, but it also thrives in full sun and drier soil, where it is less invasive. The new cultivar 'Alexander' has caught many people's eye because the foliage is green and white and variegation seems to be the current rage. This perennial will grow from one to three feet tall and bloom from late spring through most of the summer. It is hardy to zone 4.

There are two new cultivars of *Nepeta* (Catmint) that I particularly like. One is *Nepeta fassenii* 'Walker's Low', which will be useful where a plant more compact (only ten inches wide as opposed to fifteen to twenty) than *Nepeta* 'Dropmore Hybrid' is desired. I love 'Dropmore Hybrid' but it does sprawl. In some situations, like softening the hard edge of a wall or sidewalk, this characteristic is desirable. Where one wishes to create a low compact edging, however, this new cultivar will be more desirable. Both of these cultivars are hardy to zone 4.

The other *Nepeta* I want to call to your attention to is *Nepeta grandiflora* 'Dawn to Dusk', which is hardy to zone 5. This species is not well known but the flowers are similar although much more upright and will bloom throughout the summer. This particular cultivar is pink rather than lavender and will grow to three feet. Be aware, however, that this *Nepeta* is a rampant seeder. All *Nepeta* have wonderful gray-green foliage and thrive in full sun with dry to average soil but will also do well in partial shade, although there they will sprawl even more.

One of my favorite native woodland plants is *Polemonium caeruleum* (Jacob's Ladder). I love the delicate, fern-like foliage. A new cultivar, *'Brise d'Anjou'*, has leaves that are edged with creamy white. This cultivar will provide color long after the traditional lavender flowers are gone. Plant in full sun or partial shade but beware of slugs in partial shade. The species is hardy to zone 2 and I have no reason to think that the cultivar will be less hardy.

Tiarella cordifolia (Foamflower) is another staple of the woodland garden. Just as the purple-leaved *Heuchera* are being hybridized, so too are the *Tiarella*, but they are being hybridized for dark and prominent veining in the foliage. One of the best is *'Tiger Stripe'*, which has light green foliage with dark red veins. It also has beautiful pyramidal flower spikes that are purplish-pink near the top and white throughout the rest of the spike. The flowers generally appear in May for three weeks. Be aware that these *Tiarella* are stoloniferous and form large colonies if given organic soils, which are moisture retentive but well-draining; wet feet in winter, however, will kill them. Under the right conditions, they are hardy to zone 3.

When *Saponaria* (Soapwort) is mentioned, most people think of *S.ocymoides* (Rock Soapwort), which is a groundcover-type perennial that blooms in early summer, or *S.officianalis* (Bouncing Bet), a summer blooming wildflower. Almost no one knows about *S.lempergii 'Max Frei'*, an excellent plant for the front of the sunny border. Its pink flowers rise twelve to fifteen inches above the small green foliage for most of the summer. Then, after the petals fall off, unusual radiating bud-like pods remain for the rest of the growing year. I have yet to encounter any pests or diseases on this plant and it never grows out of bounds. Unfortunately, not all of you will be able to use this cultivar because it is supposedly hardy only to zone 6, but it might be worth a try for some of you in zone 5. Just put it where it will be in a warm microclimate and/or against a wall that will be bathed in winter sun and thus retain some of its heat.

I want to remind you of two cultivars of *Sedum spectabile* that are easily overlooked in favor of the more famous cultivar, *S.'Autumn Joy'*. One is *Sedum 'Matrona'*, which has paler pink flowers than *'Autumn Joy'* and has leaves that are edged with rose as well as stems that are rosy pink. Now that it's grown in my garden for a few years, I can tell you that its stems are also much stronger than those of 'Autumn Joy' and thus they better withstand the vagaries of winter. The other cultivar is 'Frosty Morn', most distinguished for its green- and white- variegated foliage. Its pale pink flowers become almost white with age. It is not as strong a grower as 'Matrona' but the variegated foliage is worth having. These perennials are hardy to zone 3 and, of course, you know that they need full sun and excellent drainage. Over-watering is the kiss of death!

Ever since I saw the pods of *Trollius* (Globeflower) planted en masse in a public garden in The Hague, I have been a fan of this perennial. Most cultivars of *Trollius* are golden yellow or orange. What I love about the new cultivar 'Cheddar' is its pale yellow flowers (they look good enough to eat — where are the crackers?) that blend so well with the lavender/blue/pink color scheme that is so popular. It blooms in May for two to three weeks but the succeeding pods last for at least another month. Hardy to zone 4, this perennial needs lots of moisture, particularly in full sun, or grow it in partial shade. When the foliage starts to look ratty, cut it back to the ground.

You may have noticed that there seems to be a recurrent theme in several of the new cultivars — that is, the creation of perennials with variegated foliage. Who knows if this trend will continue? What will be next year's theme? What new cultivars will arrive on the scene? I'll let you know.

Old Favorites:
New Cultivars
Part 3

One of the things I love about the green industry is its constantly changing nature which reflects the essence of the plant world. How boring our landscapes and gardens would be if we were restricted to an unvarying plant palette. Aren't we fortunate that we are blessed with people who are constantly searching for new and better plants?

The rage for variegated plants continues unabated, so I want to warn you against of these trendy perennials, i.e. *Veronica chamaedrys* 'Miffy Brute' (zones 5-8). The species is an excellent groundcover for full sun and this green- and white-foliaged cultivar with its sky blue flowers is lovely, but it has a tendency to revert to all green.

A much better variegated perennial, but one for the shade, is *Brunnera macrophylla* 'Variegata' (zones 3-7). This cultivar has the same large, heart-shaped leaves of the species as well as the sky blue flowers that lend charm to the spring garden. Its most winning feature, however, is its foliage, which has wide white margins as well as white streaking throughout. Thus a plant that formerly had one season of interest now has three. You would be amazed at how much only one plant can lighten up a shady spot. There is also another relatively new cultivar named 'Langtrees', which has white teardrop markings near the edge of the leaf but it is not as colorful.

Another new perennial for shade is *Geranium phaeum* 'Samobor' (zones 4-8). This hardy geranium from Bosnia has delicate pink flowers on fifteen- to eighteen-inch stems in late May and early June above a compact mound of foliage that is distinguished by the dark purple blotches centered in the maple-like foliage. Here again, we have a plant that prolongs its attraction in the garden with its interesting foliage.

Although *Geranium phaeum* tends to be a shade-loving geranium, this one will tolerate full sun and the blotches will be brighter in the sun. A site with full morning sun would probably be ideal.

Geranium 'Dilys' (zones 5-8), a cross between *G.procurrens* and *G.sanguineum*, is one for the sunny border. I have been happily growing this one for two years in the sunny border and delight in its long time of bloom – from July to October – as well as its dimunitive stature of two inches, which allows it to weave around and through other perennials without overwhelming them. Mine weaves through *Veronica spicata 'Icicle'* and the dwarf Balloonflower, *Platycodon 'Sentimental Blue'*. The brightness of its magenta blooms is somewhat mitigated by its dark eye and venation.

The next two perennials are suitable for full sun or partial shade sites. *Lobelia 'Grape Knee-Hi'* (zones 4-9) is a backcross between *Lobelia cardinalis* and a compact form of *Lobelia siphilitica*. Because of its parentage, it will do well in moist sites as well as average moisture sites. The lush purple florets stay in bloom from August to October on twenty-two-inch stems and do not fall over like the taller relatives. This purple perennial will make the late summer and autumn garden glisten. Rabbits seem to enjoy the young foliage but you can foil them with chicken wire.

Echinacea purpurea 'Kim's Knee High' (zones 3-9) is a smaller version of the common Purple Coneflower. Although it actually grows a bit taller than Kim's

Echinacea

knee (she's only five foot, two inches), it is definitely shorter than normal, approximately twenty-four to thirty inches, but has all of the wonderful characteristics of the species: long bloom (July to October), excellent seedheads, good foliage and no disease problems. I have sited mine next to *Pennisetum orientale*. The slightly taller and mounding habit of the *Pennisetum* as well as the slight pink tinge of the inflorescence provide an excellent foil for the *Echinacea*.

Speaking of *Pennisetum orientale*, which is showier than *Pennisetum alopecuroides*, I want to bring the cultivar *'Karley Rose'* to your attention. Both the species and the cultivar are hardy in zones 5-9 and start blooming in late June. *P.o.'Karley Rose'* has inflorescences that are much pinker than those of the species and seem to hold up better through the winter than those of *P. alopecuroides*. The species and the cultivar are both the same size with the mound of green foliage about twenty-four inches high and wide and the inflorescences adding another twelve inches. I grow both in my sunny dry border.

I have been using the tall cultivars of *Molinia caerulea* (Purple Moor Grass) for quite a while. Although I have seen *Molinia c.'Variegata'* (zones 5-8) in gardens in Europe and Canada, I had never seen it for sale until recently. This is a grass for full sun to partial shade. Moist soil is optimal; although it will grow well in drier sites, it will not flower well there. This cultivar has green foliage striped with either cream or light yellow. While the inflorescences are very nice and even better if backlit, I will be growing *M.c.'Variegata'* for its beautiful eighteen-inch foliage, particularly since flowering is undependable in hot weather. I would recommend siting it beside a perennial with yellow flowers such as *Chrysanthemum* rubellum *'Mary Stoker'* or a yellow-foliaged shrub, perhaps *Berberis thunbergii* *'Bonanza Gold'* or one of the golden Spireas.

As you can see, there are a multitude of new choices. Isn't that what makes life so interesting?

Designing with Ornamental Grasses:
Uses

Grasses have covered the earth from time immemorial but they have not been used as ornamentals in landscapes until relatively recently. To give you some idea of the history of these versatile plants, it can be said that they were first mentioned in the 18th century in an English gardening catalog and used extensively during the 19th century in Victorian gardens. An 1890 Philadelphia seed catalog listed fifteen grasses and some were listed in an Ohio catalog in the early 1900s. As popular taste and fashion changed, grasses fell into disfavor around the 1930s. Not until the 1960s were grasses re-introduced by the firm of Oehme and van Sweden, which used the grasses in large, sweeping masses in very visible landscapes in downtown Washington, D.C.

Exploring ornamental grasses in some depth is a worthwhile endeavor. As I speak of grasses, I will also include grass-like plants such as sedges, woodrushes and Lily-Turf. Once you are acquainted with the inimitable attributes of these wonderful plants, you will be inspired to use them in new ways. At botanical gardens around the world, grass gardens demonstrate these attributes. Ornamental grasses, planted side by side, create pictures of great beauty and incredible variety in height, form, color, texture and type of inflorescence. All of these differences can and should be utilized to create well-designed landscapes that distinguish themselves from the mundane.

There are approximately six hundred genera and nine thousand species of grasses, sedges, rushes and bamboos, all of which I include in the general classification of grasses and grass-like plants. Obviously, not all of these are appropriate for use in Ohio, but at least sixty-two genera and a great number of species may be used. Grasses range in height from a few inches to twelve feet and in diameter from six inches to six feet. Several *Carex* species and cultivars as well as *Ophiopogon plansicapus* 'Nigrescens' (Black Mondo Grass) come to mind for the tiny grasses, while *Saccharum ravennae* (Ravenna Grass), formerly known as *Erianthus ravennae*, and *Arundo donax* (Giant Reed) evoke the image of towering grasses.

Grasses also vary in form. When more than one genera is being used, it is incumbent upon the designer to choose the best genera for contrast of form and texture. The common name of *Pennisetum alopecuroides*, Fountain Grass, immediately tells us its shape. A strong contrast would be *Calamagrostis acutiflora* 'Karl Foerster' or 'Stricta', which have inflorescences that are very stiff and upright. The foliage of *Calamagrostis* is somewhat mounding but the eye focuses on the inflorescences, which appear in late May/early June. Another upright grass is *Sorghastrum nutans* 'Sioux Blue' (Blue Indian Grass). This grass is nearly six feet tall and has blue foliage.

Some grasses have stiff but fan-like foliage rather than upright foliage. The two best known are *Festuca ovina var. glauca* (Blue Fescue), which grows approximately twelve inches high, and *Helictotrichon sempervirens* (Blue Oat Grass), which is similar in appearance but twice as large. Both require excellent drainage, particularly during the winter in order to extend their life.

Other graceful grasses besides *Pennisetum* are *Miscanthus*, *Molinia* and *Hakonechloa*. Several *Miscanthus* cultivars are available and give the designer a choice of height from three feet for 'Adagio' and 'Yaku Jima' to five or six feet for most other cultivars. Some cultivars such as 'Morning Light' have very narrow foliage with a fine white edge conveying a feeling of delicacy while 'Cabaret' is the exact opposite, having wide foliage with a wide white stripe down the center of the leaf, conveying a feeling of majesty. *Molinia caerulea subsp. arundinacea* has mounding foliage that is only two to three feet high. The outstanding characteristic of this grass, however, is its arching inflorescences which reach six to eight feet high.

Hakonechloa macra 'Aureola' and 'Albostriata' are cascading grasses, ideal for partial shade and moisture situations, that look like waterfalls when well grown. They look their best on slopes or falling over rocks.

In addition to using grasses to contrast with each other in form, a designer can take advantage of these forms to contrast or echo the architecture of the site. Many storefront buildings and office buildings are quite stark. They present the perfect opportunity to use some of the graceful grasses to mitigate that starkness. On the other hand, when I was presented with a site where the pool paving and an adjoining pool pergola were very linear, I echoed those lines with a grouping of *Calamagrostis a.'Karl Foerster'*.

I have alluded to the attribute of texture, but I would like to develop this theme a bit more. Texture of ornamental grasses derives, not only from width and length of foliage, but also from density of foliage and of the inflorescences. I mentioned earlier the varying widths of some of the *Miscanthus* cultivars, but even the narrow foliage of *'Morning Light'* is not as narrow as that of *Helictotrichon sempervirens* or *Festuca ovina var. glauca*.

Because the foliage of many *Miscanthus* is quite dense, one cannot see through it; thus, it is an excellent eye-stopper. By contrast the foliage of M.*'Morning Light'* is delicate and is somewhat more see-through. Although its foliage is fairly dense, its inflorescences are very airy. *Molinia* is even more see-through. *Arundo donax*, looking like a giant corn stalk, is dense in and of itself and, if planted closely, would look like a cornfield.

Ornamental grasses are very useful to a designer who is attempting to devise compositions that accentuate contrasts of texture. A very simple but effective composition is the coarse foliage and bold-colored flowers of *Rudbeckia fulgida 'Goldsturm'* with the delicate foliage and inflorescences of *Deschampsia caespitosa* (Hair Grass). Another example is the mounding foliage and bottlebrush inflorescences of *Pennisetum alopecuroides* with the succulent foliage and broccoli-like heads of *Sedum 'Matrona'*. A third example could be the thread-like foliage of *Chamaecyparis pisifera filifera 'Aurea'* (Threadlead Golden False Cypress) in front of an upright *Calamagrostis a.'Karl Foerster'*. The possibilities are really infinite.

Ornamental grasses have so many wonderful attributes that I can't even enumerate them all in one article. Guess I'll have to continue next time.

Designing with Ornamental Grasses: Foliage Color, Inflorescence and Winter Interest

Adding winter interest is often one of the main reasons ornamental grasses are included in landscapes. Now we all know that, in life, there are good things that get even better. Here are a few reasons to include these good things in the landscape.

I'll admit that color is not usually the first attribute that comes to mind when considering ornamental grasses. How many of us commonly think of the grass palette as having a range of colors: blue, yellow and red as well as green, green with white and green with yellow or cream? The primary blue grasses are *Festuca*, *Helictotrichon*, *Panicum virgatum* cultivars and *Sorghastrum*. The primary yellow grasses are *Carex* 'Bowles Golden', *Hakonechloa macra* 'Aureola' and *Milium effusum* 'Aureum'. *Imperata cylindrica* 'Red Baron' is the best known of the red grasses but some of the *Panicum virgatum* cultivars such as 'Shenandoah' and 'Rotstrahlbusch' are also red and become more so with the advent of fall and cooler temperatures.

There are several variegated grasses. *Miscanthus* cultivars abound, with varying degrees of variegation but let me mention the ones with yellow variegation. Variegation is usually along the length of the leaf but the yellow variegation in *Miscanthus* is across the leaf. The older cultivar 'Zebrinus' has been mostly replaced with 'Strictus', which remains fairly upright, and with 'Puenktchen', which is a dwarf and stiffer version of 'Strictus'. The other clumping variegated grass I frequently use is *Carex*, particularly the cultivar 'Ice Dance' because its thrives in partial shade and tolerates less than ideal conditions. It does spread, but slowly. Most other variegated grasses are runners rather than clumpers, such as *Glyceria* and *Phalaris*.

Many grasses provide ongoing interest as their foliage color changes when cooler fall temperatures arrive. *Miscanthus sinensis 'Purpurascens'* and *Schizachyrium scoparium* (Little Bluestem) turn bright orange in the fall and keep this coloration through the winter. The red cultivars of Panicum become even redder. As fall advances and brings frosts with it, most other grasses turn beige although the blue grasses, *Festuca* and *Helictotrichon*, keep their blue coloration. When winter descends, the grasses provide us with beauty and spectacle as they sway in the wind and the snow.

The striking appearance of grasses is most apparent in the winter, but grasses can be used to add drama at other times of the year. Drawing on European influence, you may use grasses in new ways to capitalize on various site conditions. Gardens in European front yards are typically quite small and one that I saw in Antwerp was no exception. I suspect that the garden was no larger than ten feet deep and eight feet wide. Most of the space was occupied by a huge *Miscanthus* which flanked the front door. This concept could certainly be used in small condominium gardens, which are becoming quite common. Drama can also be supplied by the element of surprise. Imagine placing an eight-foot *Molinia* with its veil of inflorescences at the front of a border. The observer's view of the landscape would barely be impeded.

Pennisetum

I have mentioned inflorescences, which are the flower spikes of ornamental grasses, but now I want to elaborate on the differences of which a designer will want to take advantage. The first form is that of the bottlebrush, most commonly found on *Pennisetum*. The species bottlebrush is purply-beige but that of the cultivar '*Cassian*' is light brown, that of '*Hameln*' is creamy-white and that of '*Moudry*' is dark purple, almost black. Then there are the large feathers of *Miscanthus*, which vary in color from creamy white (on most of the early-blooming cultivars) to purply-pink on several of the newer cultivars and the smaller feathers on *Molinia*. The third type is the airy panicle found on *Panicum*. They vary in color from cream on the blue cultivars to pale rose on the red cultivars. Whatever color the inflorescence may be, the color is always muted and thus a designer's dream. Muted colors can be thought of as nearly neutral and will, therefore, work well with any color scheme.

Another very good reason to include ornamental grasses is that they require very little maintenance, basically an annual scything and that's it. Too much water and fertilizer tend to make grasses lanky so the keyword is LESS! for most of them. In addition, grasses mature relatively quickly so a new landscape looks well established within a few years.

Best of all, the four-season interest of ornamental grasses reminds us that nature is not static but ever changing and dramatic. The act of cutting down the grasses is the epitome of the renewal of the life cycle: from "death" comes life.

Because the areas where grasses are planted will look somewhat bereft after they have been scythed, interplant them with spring-blooming bulbs. The advent of the bloom of the bulbs will also help remind you to scythe the grasses. If you don't do it early enough, you will miss the blooms of the bulbs. Then in late spring, as the grass foliage emerges, it will hide the dying foliage of the bulbs.

In late spring and early summer, the cool season grasses like *Calamagrostis* bloom, in midsummer *Pennisetum* blooms, and in late summer and early fall, the rest of the grasses grace us with their blooms. Some grasses such as *Molinia* are too floppy to maintain their form during the winter, but many of the grasses stand erect and remind us that they are merely dormant, ready to recommence their cycle soon after the robins return.

Designing with Ornamental Grasses:
Color Echo, Variety and Lighting

Now that you are aware of the many attributes of ornamental grasses, I want to discuss actually designing with them. Ornamental grasses have a timeless quality that makes them usable with any type of building, whether traditional or contemporary. They were, in fact, quite the rage during the Victorian Era. One of the greatest assets of grasses is their texture and nowhere is it more needed than in old landscapes of stiff evergreens.

Where does one place grasses in the landscape? Those with large foliage and inflorescences, like *Miscanthus* (Maiden Grass), can be used almost anywhere but the grasses with wispier inflorescences, such as *Pennisetum alopecuroides* (Fountain Grass) and *Molinia* (Moor Grass), need a dark background to be seen effectively. In fact, these can be planted at the front of a border because the viewer can see through the inflorescences to the plants behind them. Those grasses with light green foliage such as *Pennisetum* will be more effective if placed between plants with dark green foliage.

Scale is always a consideration. Some of the grasses like *Miscanthus floridulus* (Giant Maiden Grass), *Erianthus ravennae* (Ravenna Grass) and *Arundo donax* (Giant Reed) are extremely tall (ten to twelve feet). Unless their backgrounds and accompanying plants are also quite tall, these grasses will seem out of scale. They would be very effective if used with a background of fastigiate trees or if accompanied by perennials such as *Eupatorium fistulosum* (Joe-Pye Weed), *Helianthus salicifolius* (Willowleaf Sunflower) or *Vernonia noveboracensis* (Ironweed), which are all five to six feet tall.

Spacing of ornamental grasses will depend on the look you hope to achieve. Normally, one spaces grasses as far apart as they are tall. This spacing enhances their massed effect and gives the appearance of an ocean of grass. But wider spacing will emphasize their mounding character. Some grasses, such as *Calamagrostis acutiflora* (Feather Reed Grass), which have extremely vertical inflorescences, will make a stronger statement with closer spacing to accentuate their verticality.

Increase the effect of grasses by using the concept of color echo. Try planting *Imperata cylindrica* 'Red Baron' (Japanese Blood Grass) near a red cultivar of *Acer palmatum dissectum* (Japanese Maple) or a variegated grass such as *Miscanthus sinensis* 'Variegata' (Variegated Maiden Grass) with perennials that have white flowers such as *Clematis recta* 'Purpurea' (Ground Clematis), *Anemone hybrida* 'Honorine Jobert' (Japanese Anemone) or *Tricytis hirta* 'Albo-marginata' (Japanese Toad Lily). You could also plant a variegated grass with woody ornamentals that have either white flowers, such as one of the *Viburnum*, or that also have variegated foliage, such as *Kerria japonica* 'Picta'.

When designing, I tend to use more than one type of ornamental grass in order to repeat that texture while varying the height and/or color. Sometimes, I will repeat the color with two or three different genera. *Helictotrichon sempervirens* (Blue Oat Grass) and *Festuca ovina var. glauca* (Blue Fescue) are very similar in color but Helictotrichon is twice as large. For a taller, more upright blue grass, use one of the blue cultivars of *Panicum virgatum* (Switch Grass). There are several variegated grasses, from the very short *Arrhenatherum elatius bulbosum* (Tuber Oat Grass), to the short *Phalaris arundinacea* 'Feesey' (Ribbon Grass) to the middle-sized *Calamagrostis acutiflora* 'Overdam' (Overdam Feather Reed Grass) and ultimately, to the taller, variegated *Miscanthus* and *Arundo donax* (Giant Reed).

A common landscape color scheme is blue and yellow. It is tricky to get the ratio correct so that the yellows do not overwhelm the blues. Keep in mind that this can be done with foliage as well as flowers and that the blue grasses are an excellent color modulator.

Think of natural lighting as another way of emphasizing color. Inflorescences that are backlit become translucent rather than opaque. Foliage that is backlit can become translucent too, turning from red to flame. In Autumn, after their foliage has turned red or orange, just look during early morning or late afternoon at *Imperata* or one of the red cultivars of *Panicum virgatum* or *Miscanthus s. 'Purpurascens'* (Flame Grass) for a glimpse of a fiery spectacle There is so much emphasis on backlighting that it is easy to forget that front lighting can also be used to create an appealing display. *Miscanthus sinensis*, in late fall, winter or early spring before being cut down, is beige. However, early morning sun on *Miscanthus* turns it to burnished gold.

Ornamental grasses can be used as companion plants to any other type of plant. I have seen them used very effectively with trees, conifers, perennials and groundcovers. The principle to keep in mind is textural contrast. Use a variegated *Miscanthus* with *Taxus* or *Chasmanthium latifolium* (Northern Sea Oats) under a tree. Try a groundcover or low spreading Rose next to an ocean of *Pennisetum* or in back of a foreground grass such as *Festuca*.

Use bold-foliaged perennials such as *Acanthus spinosus* (Bear's Breeches) with a fine-foliaged grass such as *Molinia caerulea* (Moor Grass). Use a delicate fern with *Liriope* (Lily-Turf) or *Ophiopogon planiscapus* *'Nigrescens'* (Black Mondo Grass) in a shade situation. Try *Spodiopogon sibiricus* (Frost Grass), a bamboo-like grass, with *Perovskia atriplicifolia* (Russian Sage), a finely textured perennial.

Because ornamental grasses change in character with the seasons, they add interest to an otherwise static landscape. They are a diverse group of plants, able to fill many needs while providing beauty and drama year round. Hopefully, these characteristics will motivate you to use them extensively in your landscapes.

Designing with Ornamental Grasses:
Placement

Now it is time to consider where and how to incorporate grasses into our landscapes. Grasses are the backbone of meadow, prairie and wetlands restorations. Their root systems are extensive and adaptive to drought as well as boggy conditions. They help to restore wildlife habitats by providing food (seeds) and shelter for birds and small animals. The natural (or wild) landscape, in direct contrast to the manicured landscape, is usually a mix of forbs (non-grassy herbaceous plants) and grasses that bloom in succession with the latest blooming plants being the tallest. Most of us do not work with design areas large enough to support a natural meadow or prairie. But we can design stylized meadows and prairies, using cultivars of the wild grasses along with cultivars of the perennials (forbs) that would likely be found in association with the grasses as well as adding some that give the illusion of a meadow.

Grasses can be used in many other ways in the landscape. Ornamental grasses can help make the transition from lawn to woodland and from the woodland to the horizon by providing an intermediate layer to bring the eye up from the ground to the trees and then to the sky. They can be integrated as small masses or used as weavers in mixed or perennial borders. They can be repeated throughout the landscape to unify it. For instance, groupings of one type of grass could be used by the driveway, in the front of the house, and again in the back of the house. If different sizes were needed, one could use grasses that are the same color but similar in texture such as *Festuca 'Elijah Blue'* (Blue Fescue), *Helictotrichon sempervirens* (Blue Oat Grass) and *Panicum virgatum 'Heavy Metal'* (Heavy Metal Switch Grass).

Certain grasses lend themselves to use as a specimen or focal point. These grasses usually have a distinguishing characteristic whether it be large size, as is found with one of the *Miscanthus* (Reed Grass); unusual texture, as on the foliage of *Spodiopogon sibiricus* (Siberian Frost Grass), which looks like Bamboo; or unusual color, with *Andropogon gerardii* (Big Bluestem), which turns a rich orange and copper-red in the fall.

Grasses can also be used as screens or hedges. Those that are used as screens will usually need to be tall. Try *Arundo donax* (Giant Reed), which looks like corn on steroids, or one of the *Miscanthus* or *Panicum virgatum* 'Cloud Nine', which will grow six feet tall. A hedge can be any height you wish but the usual height is three to six feet tall. A three-foot-high hedge could be composed of *Pennisetum alopecuroides* (Fountain Grass). *Panicum virgatum* 'Rotstralbusch' (Red Switch Grass) would make a nice four-foot-high hedge. For a four- to five-foot-high hedge, try *Miscanthus sinensis* 'Adagio'. The beauty of this one is its capacity to absorb being beaten down by heavy rain or snow and then to become upright again.

Try using grasses as edgers. Excellent candidates would be *Liriope muscari* (Lily-Turf), although technically not a grass but a perennial, or *Festuca* (Blue Fescue). Both stay low and contained and need minimal maintenance. On the other hand, if a groundcover is needed, *Liriope spicata* will grow in the shade and under trees with extensive, shallow root systems where nothing else will grow.

Phalaris arundinacea 'Picta' (Reed Canary Grass) and *Leymus (Elymus) arenarius* (Lyme Grass) are aggressive spreaders for sunny sites. These running grasses are also a natural for covering slopes. Why mow a slope if you don't have to? Twenty-three thousand pots of *Phalaris* were used on a steep slope by the entrance to the Pittsburgh airport so that no mowing would be necessary. Although *Miscanthus* is a clumping grass, rather than a running grass, it too can be used on slopes. Oehme and van Sweden used several different cultivars of *Miscanthus*, interspersed with large masses of perennials, on slopes surrounding a large shopping center on Long Island to great effect.

Ornamental grasses are a wonderful group of plants to use in or near water. Even if a pool is situated in a backyard, the grasses convey a feeling of the seashore. And if the pool is situated not too far from a natural body of water, the grasses provide a very natural transition from that body of water to this one. Grasses make beautiful reflections in water, whether lake, pond, swimming pool or ornamental pool.

Some grasses, such as *Glyceria maxima 'Variegata'* (Variegated Manna Grass) and *Spartina pectinata 'Aureo-marginata'* (Cord Grass), are very happy in boggy situations and can thus be used along waterways, both in and out of the water. They are, however, very aggressive and this factor should be taken into account. Others such as *Arundo donax, Calamagrostis acutiflora* (Reed Grass), *Carex* (Sedge) species, *Chasmanthium latifolium* (Northern Sea Oats), *Deschampsia caespitosa* (Hair Grass), *Hakonechloa macra 'Aureola'* (Golden Hakonechloa), *Luzula* (Woodrush) species, *Miscanthus* and *Panicum virgatum* either tolerate or like moist conditions but do not like to be in water.

The grasses can be used very effectively near hardscapes. Mounding grasses at the edge of a walk can counter the hardness of the surface material and also soften the edge by hiding part of it. If the walk happens to be curvilinear, the habit of the grass can also echo the grace of the walk. If grasses flank both sides of an entrance, they will call attention to and emphasize the entrance. If grasses are planted behind a sitting area, they will add movement and sound to the experience of the garden visitor.

Grasses have so many desirable features and characteristics that it is difficult to consider a landscape as being complete without them. The investment in educating ourselves (and our clients) as to their variety, beauty and benefits is very worthwhile.

Miscanthus

Perennials and Ornamental Grasses
for Form and Function:
Groundcovers

Homeowners and landscapers face many problems, not the least of which are areas that are difficult to mow but need to look good. This includes short but steep slopes, larger, gentler embankments and large swaths of flat or rolling ground. Such areas cry out for an evergreen groundcover that will form a thick mat to prevent the germination of weeds and slow erosion.

Forget the traditional three – *Hedera helix* (Ivy), *Pachysandra* and *Vinca minor* (Myrtle) – and try one of the following suggestions:

Arabis caucasica (Rockcress) has felty, gray-green foliage that is scalloped and spreads over the ground in no time at all. It has lavender-pink or white flowers, depending on the cultivar, from April to the middle of May and is only two inches high. Grow it in full sun to partial shade in well-drained soil.

Geranium cantabrigiense 'Biokovo' or 'Biokovo Karmina' has small-lobed leaves that form a tight mat which becomes tinged with red in the fall and remains that way all winter. In May and June, its six-inch-high flowers are pale pink or bright pink, depending on the cultivar. Even after the long blooming flowers (four to six weeks depending on the temperature) lose their petals, the red calyces remain for another month. Grow in full sun to partial shade in average to moist soil. Another hardy geranium that is particularly useful is *Geranium macrorrhizum* (Big Root Geranium) because it will thrive in heavily shaded, dry areas. Its foliage is twice as large as that of the previous Geranium and is more deeply lobed. The pink flowers bloom at the same time as those of *G.cantabrigiense*.

Campanula poscharkyana (Serbian Bellflower) has heart-shaped leaves that grow on long runners and bear star-shaped lavender flowers from the beginning of May through the first week of July. Grow this one in full sun or partial shade in average to dry soil. It will do very well among the roots of trees. Mine cavorts happily under an old Dogwood.

Although most ornamental grasses do not remain evergreen, the few that do would serve well in these situations. Both *Festuca ovina var. glauca* (Blue Fescue) and *Helictotrichon sempervirens* (Blue Oat Grass) have steely blue foliage that keeps its color twelve months of the year, and both have wheat-colored inflorescences in early to mid-summer that are attractive but showy. Use one of the cultivars of Fescue such as *'Elijah Blue'*, which is better than the species. All of the Fescue grow twelve inches high while the Blue Oat Grass grows twice that size.

Another blue-evergreen is *Leymus arenarius* (Blue Lyme Grass) but care must be taken with its use. While the two grasses mentioned above are clumpers, this one is a rampant runner. Placed on the right site, this can be an advantage. All three of them require full sun and average to dry soil.

For shady sites, *Liriope* (Lily-Turf) makes an excellent substitute for grass. *Liriope muscari* has many cultivars. *'Big Blue'* has especially large flower spikes held well above the foliage, while *'Monroe's White'* is the only white-flowered one. There are also some with variegated foliage, always a plus in the shade. While *L.muscari* is a clumper, its cousin *L.spicata* is a runner and copes easily with shallow tree roots. Both grow only twelve inches high. If the foliage becomes tattered during the winter, a quick pass with the weed whip or a mower will take care of that.

The *Carex* family also has members that can be used as evergreen groundcovers, some for sun and some for shade. *Carex morrowii* *'Aureovariegata'* (Goldband Japanese Sedge) will grow in either sun or partial shade at twelve inches as a dense mound of foliage as will *C.'Ice Dance'*, which has a wide white edge. Mine is growing under the worst of circumstances – very little light and only as much moisture as Mother Nature contributes. An excellent *Carex* for sunny, wet places is *C.muskingumensis* (Palm Sedge), which will grow eighteen to thirty inches and slowly creeps along the ground. This one looks more like a miniature palm than grass, as do the other *Carex*.

So give the old threesome a rest and try something different!

Perennials for Form and Function:
Hedgers and Edgers

When the need for privacy, wind barriers or division in the landscape is needed, we most often think first of hedges. Frequently we turn to the tried and true (same old, same old) shrubs, particularly conifers. Let's expand our horizons and consider other options. Which grasses and perennials can be used for these purposes? The most obvious option is the ornamental grasses that can provide a hedge from three to twelve feet high depending on selection. The only drawback is that the hedge must be cut to the ground in early spring each year. However, that chore reminds us, and everyone who sees it, of the cycle of life.

The grasses that first come to mind are probably *Miscanthus* and *Panicum*. *Miscanthus* have beautiful and long-lasting inflorescences in the fall and winter when there is frequently little else to attract our eye in the wind and snow. Cultivars range in height from three to eight feet as a rule and all have beige winter color with the exception of *M.s.'Purpurascens'*, which is orange. *Panicum* will range in height from four to six feet. The airy panicles appear in mid-summer, either rose or cream depending on the cultivar, and the foliage will be reddish green or blue, again depending on the cultivar. Another grass, which bears a striking resemblance to corn, is *Arundo donax*. The cultivar *'Variegata'* is quite striking. This very tall grass (twelve- to fifteen-foot) has strong stems and would create a very unusual hedge. All of these grasses do best in full sun and average to dry soil.

Some perennials could also be used as hedges. A few years ago, I saw a mass planting of *Boltonia asteroides 'Snowbank'* at the top of a long wall. Its blue-green foliage on strong, narrow, three-foot stems was very striking and I'm sure that when it came into bloom in September with thousands of white daisy type blooms, it was breathtaking. The same thing could be done with *Eupatorium rugosum 'Chocolate'*, which would provide a purplish-green hedge instead of a blue-green one. This *Eupatorium* has white flowers that start blooming in August on four-foot stems. Both of these perennials can be grown in full sun or partial shade, average to dry soil. I have read recently that the *Eupatorium* may lose some/all of its purplish coloration if planted in full sun instead of partial shade or morning sun only.

Another *Eupatorium* that would be useful in this situation is *E. fistulosum* 'Gateway'. This cultivar of Joe-Pye Weed is only five feet tall instead of the eight feet tall of the species. The foliage and height alone are striking but the huge pinkish-lavender flower heads add incredible impact in August and September. Full sun plus average soil and moisture are required. A fourth perennial, technically a self-sowing annual, is *Verbena bonariensis*. Pale lavender, statice-like blossoms on strong, wiry, four-foot stems bloom from July to frost. Although I generally use this plant as a see-through, it could be planted thickly enough to make a very dense hedge. Sun and almost any soil, including wet, are its only needs.

There are many sites that need edgings. In such instances, a clumping, rather than a spreading plant, is generally called for. Otherwise, too much maintenance time will be spent on cutting back these edgers. The exception to this guideline is a site where the hardscaping is so linear that it needs to be softened. Then it would be desirable to have a perennial such as *Nepeta* 'Dropmore Hybrid', which will sprawl over the edges of the bed. The *Nepeta* will have several flushes of bloom. You can either cut it back after each flush to keep it from going further over the edge than desired or install it two feet from the edge instead of one foot. *Nepeta* will bloom profusely in either sun or partial shade and in average to dry soil.

Another long blooming perennial for use as an edger is *Gaillardia* 'Goblin', which is a dwarf cultivar growing only twelve inches high and wide. This yellow and red bicolor blooms its head off from June to frost. While deadheading makes it look neater,

Gaillardia

this *Gaillardia* will keep blooming regardless. Just give it full sun and average to dry soil.

An excellent edger for partial shade is *Dicentra eximia* or *formosa*. The Everblooming Bleeding Heart has foliage that is fern-like and makes a nice contrast to the *Hosta* that are usually found in shade landscapes. The pink or white flowers, depending on cultivar, bloom from late May to October and are self-cleaning. Provide average to dry soil and watch out for slugs.

A small ornamental grass such as *Festuca ovina* 'Elijah Blue' makes an effective edging that will be colorful twelve months of the year. It is only twelve inches high, needs virtually no care and sports a purplish brown inflorescence that reaches to eighteen inches in June. Plant in full sun and dry soil. In a shady site, substitute one of the *Liriope muscari* cultivars such as 'Monroe's White' or 'Christmas Tree', which has a larger bloom spike than most of the other cultivars. *Liriope* will thrive in partial shade and average to dry soil.

Now that I've stimulated your creativity a bit, I'm sure that you can think of many other perennials and grasses that could be used as hedges or edgers. Let your imagination and sense of discovery take over; you will be amazed at what you can create.

Perennials for Form and Function:
Long Bloomers

If you've been asked to design or install a colorful, low maintenance landscape, you will be looking for long-blooming perennials and perennials or woody ornamentals that have colorful foliage. We are familiar with some "standards" that have come to be known for long-lasting color. I hope to introduce some new ones.

There are three relatively new *Achillea* (Yarrow) that lend themselves to commercial or low-maintenance landscapes because they are clumpers rather than spreaders. These cultivars, developed by Ernst Pagels, are 'Credo', a clear yellow, 'Feuerland' (translated as 'Fireland'), a brick red that fades to beigey-yellow, and 'Terra Cotta', a pinkish brown. All of them grow two to three feet high on sturdy stems and have bright green ferny foliage. They will bloom all summer if you deadhead them periodically. *Achillea* require full sun and average to somewhat dry soil.

Centranthus ruber (Valerian) was commonly found in our grandmothers' gardens and could be considered a pass-along plant because it reseeds prolifically. This trait is quite desirable in a commercial landscape because the mother plants frequently die from overwatering. The abundance of seedlings, however, negates this problem. The deadheads do not diminish the attractiveness of this perennial that blooms prolifically from June until frost. The species is a pinky-red and *C. ruber* 'Albus' is white. *Centranthus* usually grows two feet high in the sun but tends to flop in partial shade and thus should be considered to grow only one foot high. Unlike many perennials, *Centranthus* blooms as well in the shade as it does in the sun. While it prefers average to slightly dry soil, it will also grow well in slightly moist soil. (See reference above to seedlings.)

Coreopsis verticillata is probably well known by now to all of you but I mention it because it is a mainstay of the long-blooming, low-maintenance garden. There are three yellow cultivars to choose from: 'Moonbeam' for its lemon hue and eighteen-inch height, 'Zagreb' for its sulphur hue and twelve-inch height, and *'Golden Showers'* for its sulphur hue and eighteen-to twenty-four-inch height. The latter is becoming quite difficult to find. There is also a pink version, sometimes called *Coreopsis rosea* and sometimes *C.rosea 'American Dream'*. The cultivar is supposedly a clearer pink, which would definitely be an improvement on the muddy pink of the species. Relatively new are *C.'Sweet Dreams'*, which is pale pink with a rose center and *C.'Limerock Ruby'*, a ruby-red. These are totally new colors for these *Coreopsis*. They ask only for full sun and average to somewhat dry soil and will bloom in flushes from late May/early June through September and October, particularly if you shear them back by a third at the end of each flush.

One of my favorite perennials, and now more available than it used to be, is *Corydalis lutea*, the Yellow Bleeding Heart. The scalloped green foliage, which is similar to that of Dwarf Columbine, sets off the bright yellow folded blossoms. This perennial is incredibly versatile. It will bloom well in shade or sun and in wet to dry soil. If it is grown in sun, it must be moist. It will reseed copiously under virtually all circumstances. Only twelve inches high, it provides a lovely foliage texture as well as color from the middle of May until frost.

Dicentra eximia and *formosa*, the Everblooming Bleeding Hearts, have foliage and blossoms very similar in appearance to *Corydalis lutea* but, in this instance, the blossoms are pink or red or white depending on the cultivar. Many of the newer cultivars have bluish-green foliage that is particularly attractive with the white blossoms. Like *Corydalis*, the *Dicentra* only grow twelve inches high and from the middle of May until frost. Be aware that slugs and deer are fond of the foliage. Grow *Dicentra* in partial shade and soil that ranges from slightly dry to slightly moist.

The perennials that I have described are only a small part of the long-blooming perennials palette. Rest assured, I'll keep discovering more to share with you.

Perennials for Form and Function:
Low Maintenance

Commercial landscaping, whether it be in parking lots or office building beds, for churches or hospitals, for restaurants or college campuses, is seen by thousands of people every day but most of it is boring rather than inspiring or exciting. If we avail ourselves of an expanded plant palette, we can constructively influence the public's perception of landscaping. Both perennials and ornamental grasses offer long seasons of interest although not necessarily bloom color. But there are other attributes that are desirable in a landscape: colorful or texturally interesting foliage, movement, fragrance, winter interest and seed heads or pods.

Most commercial properties are large and therefore require great masses of different species in order to have an impact. If these masses are arranged somewhat naturally, as in drifts which feather out on either end, they will not look artificial as do masses in which the plants are lined up like soldiers. There is a huge shopping center on Long Island that utilized sweeping groupings of perennials and grasses in the majority of the beds, including slopes that come right down to major streets and would be very difficult to mow. Because large properties often consist of several beds, they could easily be unified by repetition of a specific plant, a particular form (such as pyramidal or mounding), a specific texture like that of grasses, or a specific color.

Choice of color affects how and what the viewer sees. Do you want to make sure that an entrance is readily apparent? Hot, strong colors like red, orange, yellow and white are seen immediately and from afar and thus have great impact. Pastels like pink, lilac, blue and silver fade away from the viewer and may thus make an area seem larger than it is. Pastels are inviting and will not be overwhelming along a lengthy roadway. If a color scheme such as blue and yellow is used, it is important to use more blue than yellow, or the mass of yellow will be overwhelming. The shade of the color is also important. Sulfur yellow will seem like a larger mass than pale or lemon yellow.

It is important to extend the seasons of interest as long as possible. Since most perennials, grasses and woody ornamentals do not bloom until May, convince the property owner that an investment in bulbs is appropriate. Most bulbs, except tulips, will multiply and bloom for years without needing to be replanted. Tulips, other than some of the species, should be treated as annuals. Small bulbs, such as *Crocus* (March/April), *Scilla sibirica* and *Muscari* (April/May), when planted by the thousands, have incredible impact. *Narcissus*, planted by the hundreds, do too. Because *Narcissus* is poisonous to animals, the bulbs are rarely disturbed. With careful selection of cultivars, a landscape can be abloom with *Narcissus* alone from March through May.

Beds are frequently bare during the winter on commercial properties. When searching for evergreens to fill these beds, don't leave out evergreen perennials, many of which make excellent groundcovers for slopes and don't have to be wrapped with burlap, which defeats the reason for using evergreens. Some perennials look like sculptures in the winter landscape and should not be cut to the ground until spring. Ornamental grasses are highly prized for their winter interest; their dried foliage and inflorescences sway in the wind, hold the snow, and add a more natural and appealing look to the landscape.

Textural variety is important in any size bed. This is just as true when using different woodies as it is when using perennials and grasses. This can be achieved by varying the size of the leaf as well as the division of the leaf – entire, bipinnate, lobed, etc. Adding colored foliage is also an excellent way to vary texture. Use darker colors in the foreground or against pale green or silver foliage. Use them against a light-colored wall if they are placed in the mid-ground or background.

All of the issues discussed above, pertinent to designers of commercial landscapes, are just as applicable to the home gardener who wants low maintenance.

Maintenance is always an issue, no matter how much you love to garden, because time is always at a premium. Many perennials and grasses are relatively low maintenance, particularly the grasses that need only to be cut down once a year in early spring, but some plants need more frequent maintenance. This maintenance helps to sustain the plants' overall health and appearance. Can we convince the public that the beauty and enjoyment derived from these plants in the landscape are worth the extra investment of time and/or money?

Perennial Garden Maintenance:
Low But Not No

Designing a perennial garden, installing it and then watching it mature is very satisfying but if it is not well maintained, all of the effort will have been for naught. Nothing is more discouraging than to see a beautiful garden or landscape become a weed-filled patch.

Many clients these days ask for a perennial garden so they may enjoy the beauty of flowers even if they do not have the time (or desire) to take care of it. Thus they ask for low-maintenance gardens. Perennial gardens, by their nature, are basically not low maintenance but there are ways to lower the maintenance. This can be accomplished with several strategies such as:

- Selecting long-blooming perennials that do not require deadheading.
- Selecting plants with attractive foliage that will catch the eye even though the blooms may be long gone.
- Selecting (or installing) plants that are zone hardier than required to lessen the amount of replacement that may be needed.
- Choosing perennials that are insect and disease resistant.

Another way to lower maintenance is by allowing adequate spacing between plants. If perennials are planted too close together initially, the garden may look mature after the first year but in the second year, it will look overcrowded and then division or removal will be necessary. It is often difficult to explain to the client that a properly planted (spaced) garden will look bare for the first year, will be better the second year and will look fairly mature by the third year. Most people, not just clients, lack patience but patience is an essential attribute of a gardener. This is the ultimate dilemma: short-term pleasure versus long-term problems. One can ameliorate this situation by planting annuals of similar color and height between the young perennials for a year or two.

Lower maintenance can be facilitated by not planting invasive perennials in a garden situation. These plants should be saved for areas where they can run rampant or where erosion is a problem. For such areas, plant "thugs" are ideal. If the perennial is otherwise perfect for a design, the invasive plant can be controlled by annual edging or division or by planting it in a very large container, which is then sunk into the garden. Another control for invasive perennials is poor soil. Roots thrive and ramble in rich, moist soil but poor and/or dry soil limits their growth. Yet another control for these plants is the necessity of competing with tree roots, which suck up most of the available moisture. Thus I have planted *Lysimachia clethroides* (Gooseneck) under an old Crabapple and have not had a problem.

The ornamental grasses are a boon to the low-maintenance garden. Cut them to the ground in early spring and forget about them. If the centers die out (as they did in *Pennisetum* and *Miscanthus* during the winter of 1995) just leave them alone and the grasses will continue to grow out from the edges and fill in. Sub-shrubs like *Buddleia*, *Caryopteris* and *Perovskia*, which have woody bases, are pruned in mid to late spring after the new foliation can be seen. Wait at least a week before pruning because late frosts may cause further dieback. After that, they need no attention.

Many spreading, groundcover-type perennials, particularly those that bloom in the spring like *Arabis*, *Iberis* and *Phlox subulata*, benefit from being pruned back immediately after bloom to keep them under control and to prevent them from developing bare centers, but again, that is once-a-year maintenance.

By designing work paths into the garden, you can accomplish the maintenance work with fewer struggles. One path could be at the very back of the garden where it will be hidden by the perennials. A second path could be an attractive asset to the garden by using decorative materials such as stepping-stones that echo another element in the landscape. Such paths help avoid compacting the soil (inevitable when walking on it) and make it easier to reach the plants that need maintenance. Accidentally breaking other plants is so aggravating, particularly when it could be prevented by utilizing a simple path.

One of the most time-consuming components of maintenance is weeding. If the garden site is weeded thoroughly before being rototilled so that weed seeds are not incorporated into the new soil, the time needed later for weeding should be greatly reduced. After installation, use of a weed-free, aged mulch will help greatly to reduce germination of new weeds. Great care should be taken to keep the mulch away from the crowns of the plants to prevent rot. Any of the pre-emergent herbicides could also be spread on top of the mulch to reduce germination of new weeds, but it may interfere with the growth of the new perennials, particularly if they are being encouraged to fill in.

Inevitably, some perennials will need staking. One of the best products on the market is a round metal grid and supporting legs which have been coated in green plastic. They are called Grow-Through Plant Supports and are available in a variety of sizes. I push them into the ground as far as possible in early spring. When the plant foliates, it pushes through the grid openings. As the season progresses, I pull the grid higher as the height of the plant necessitates. At the end of the season, after the specific perennial is pruned back, I then push the grid back down to ground level and leave it for the winter. That way, when spring comes, I don't have to try to remember which perennials need Grow-Throughs. I have found them quite useful for perennials like New England Asters, Peonies and *Miscanthus*. Another staking product that I find useful is linking stakes. These I use along paths or lawn edges to keep leaning or floppy perennials from interfering with walking or mowing. I love *Gaura* and its loose habit but not where it flops onto the lawn. My *Tricyrtis* grows under a tree and in partial shade along a path over which it would lean to reach the sun if it were not restrained by a series of linking stakes. The stakes can be used for an area of any size or configuration.

For me, a large part of enjoying a perennial garden is working in it. But this is not true for everyone. We can't design no-maintenance gardens but we can create lower-maintenance gardens. Hopefully, the methods suggested above will help to accomplish that goal.

The Foliage Palette:
Shapes and Textures

Have you ever looked at a landscape and not been able to decide why it didn't work? All of the plants as individuals were very nice but still something was wrong. Perhaps the problem was not enough distinction of foliage.

What do I mean? I'll give you several examples. If there are several conifers, how many genera are encompassed? The foliage of *Tsuga canadensis* (Canadian Hemlock) is very loose while that of *Picea* (Spruce) is very tight. The needles of *Taxus* (Yew) are very dense and relatively short while those of *Pinus* are much looser and longer. The foliage of *Thuja* (Arborvitae) is whorled and scaly as is that of some *Chamaecyparis* (False Cypress) but some *Chamaecyparis* have long, thread-like foliage. Members of the genus *Juniperus* usually have very short, prickly needles but there are some that are longer and look softer. These characterizations are, of course, very general because there are many variations within each genus. Good design will play off the foliage characteristics of these conifers to create interesting contrasts.

Clients frequently ask for evergreen landscapes in Ohio since winter is long and gray. That's why we see Rhododendrons and Azaleas on so many properties. But there are other broadleaf evergreens that would add different textures and shapes to the landscape as well as berries in the fall and winter when the Rhododendrons and Azaleas are merely green (if they're not desiccated). *Ilex x meserveae* (Blue Holly) has glossy scalloped leaves with a blue tinge in addition to its bright red berries. You will find small to medium glossy ovate leaves on *Ilex crenata* (Japanese Holly) and *Ilex glabra* (Inkberry) with the Inkberry bearing tiny black berries as well. The foliage of *Pieris japonica* (Japanese Pieris) and *Kalmia latifolia* (Mountain Laurel) is also ovate but larger than that of the hollies, and they both have unusual blossoms in May and June, providing an excellent foil for those of the Rhododendrons and Azaleas, which are similar.

The range of foliar differences on deciduous plants is unbelievably wide. Just about anything is possible. There are simple leaves, meaning one leaf per bud, as found on *Aronia arbutifolia* 'Brilliantissima' (Brilliant Red Chokeberry), compound leaves which can be pinnate (*Koelreuteria paniculata*, Golden Rain Tree), bipinnate (*Athyrium felix-femina*, the Lady Fern), or palmate (*Aesculus*, the Ohio Buckeye).

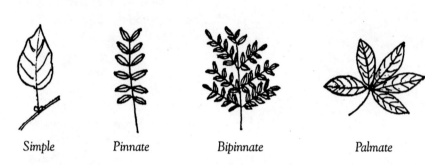

Simple   Pinnate   Bipinnate   Palmate

Consider the many types of leaf margins. First are smooth (entire) ones in many different shapes. *Arum italicum* 'Pictum', a variegated leaf perennial with bright orange, berried spathes in fall, has arrow-shaped leaves. *Pulmonaria longifolia* (Lungwort) has long, narrow leaves. Several varieties of *Hosta* have wavy leaves; and *Iris siberica* (Siberian Iris) has tall, linear leaves. There are also toothed margins, which vary in the size of their indentation. Examples of these are *Mahonia aquifolium* (Oregon Grape-Holly), *Acer* (Maple) and *Crataegus* (Hawthorn). Then there are also lobed or scalloped leaves as found on *Aquilegia* (Columbine) and *Quercus alba* (White Oak).

To take full advantage of the numerous textures available, we must add perennials and ornamental grasses to our landscapes. Keep in mind that the foliage of most trees and shrubs has a matte surface and does not reflect light while shiny foliage does, of course. I've already mentioned that of the hollies, but a groundcover such as *Ajuga* 'Metallica Crispa' has shiny as well as crinkled foliage. *Stachys* (Lambs Ears) will provide furry foliage in the sun while *Luzula nivea* (Snowy Woodrush) will give us hairy foliage in the shade. Heavily veined or pleated foliage can be found on the leaves of *Alchemilla mollis* (Lady's Mantle), which hold dewdrops and rain on their surface long after moisture on most other plants has run off or evaporated. Hellebores have large leathery leaves and display the earliest flowers in most areas.

Succulents add a shape and texture unlike any other. Their thick stems and leaves retain moisture for long periods of time, making them excellent plants for sunny, dry sites. *Sedum* are the best known but don't forget the *Sempervivum* (Hen-and-Chicks), which make an unusual groundcover. These plants come in a variety of colors and look like thick-scaled lily bulbs. Some even look a bit like spider webs, thus the species name *arachnoides*.

Sedum

The ornamental grasses allow for creative use with their wide range of sizes as well as length and width of their foliage. One lesser known, but very hardy, grass is *Spodiopogon sibiricus* (Silver Frost Grass), which looks a lot like bamboo because its foliage is held horizontally.

Unless you are designing for a huge property, it will not be feasible to incorporate every type of foliage, but using as many as possible will guarantee an interesting and inviting landscape.

The Foliage Palette:
Green, Yellow, Silver and Blue

An in-depth discussion of foliage would be incomplete without considering the use of colored foliage to enhance a landscape. When discussing color in the landscape, the first thing that pops into one's mind is bloom. It is important to remember that flowers are fleeting while foliage lasts from spring until late fall for deciduous plants and all year round for broadleaf evergreens and coniferous plants.

The next thing to remember is not as obvious – green is a color and has many variations in shade and tint. There are light greens such as those seen on the foliage of any of the *Scabiosa caucasica* (Pincushion Flower) cultivars or on *Hellelborus argutifolius* (foetidus); there are dark greens such as those found on the foliage of *Helleborus orientalis* or *Picea abies* 'Nidiformis' (Bird's Nest Spruce). Remember, too, that the shade of green will be affected by the texture of the foliage. One could also say that there is lime green, which is found on the leaves of that wonderful annual *Helichrysum petiolatum* 'Limelight' (Limelight False Licorice), but one could also characterize that color as yellow green or even as yellow, depending on the contrasting colors that surround it.

The botanical palette encompasses many beautiful examples of yellow-foliaged plants. Frequently used woodies are *Ligustrum x vicaryi* (Golden Vicary Privet), *Berberis thunbergii* 'Bonanza Gold' (Dwarf Golden Pygmy Barberry), and several cultivars of *Chamaecyparis obtusa*, *C.pisifera filifera* and *Juniperus* as well as many hybrids of *Spiraea*, most of which have the word gold in their names. A few trees, such as *Gleditisia tricanthos inermis* 'Sunburst' (Sunburst Honey Locust), also bear golden foliage.

Mention yellow foliage to someone in the perennial world and the plant that comes immediately to mind is *Hosta*. Now there are also yellow-foliaged Columbine (*Aquilegia vulgaris* 'Woodside Strain'), Gaura (*Gaura lindheimerii* 'Corrie's Gold') and Lambs Ears (*Stachys byzantina* 'Primrose Heron') that will add this hue to a landscape. There are also some grasses with yellow foliage such as *Carex morrowii 'Bowles Golden'* (Bowles Golden Sedge) and *Acorus gramineus 'Ogon'* (Golden Japanese Sweet Flag).

Gray-greens or silvers occur often in the plant world. An excellent small tree is *Pyrus salicifolia pendula 'Silver Frost'* (Silfrozam Pear); it is particularly effective if no suckers are allowed to interfere with the elegant weeping habit of this tree. Other shrubs that can also add gray-green/silver to a landscape include *Salix purpurea 'Nana'* (Dwarf Blue Arctic Willow) or *Salix p. 'Pendula'* (Weeping Blue Arctic Willow), which have the added attraction of purplish-red branches and are excellent in moist areas, *Salix repens v. 'Nitida'* (Silver Creeping Willow), which can be used as a tall groundcover, or any of the cultivars of *Caryopteris clandonensis* (Blue Mist Shrub).

Silver occurs most often in the perennial realm. The best-known silver-leaved perennial is probably *Lavandula angustifolia* (Lavender) and its cultivars 'Hidcote' and 'Munstead' but there are some new *Lavandula x intermedia* cultivars such as 'Dilly Dilly' and 'San Andreas' that are supposedly even more silver. Another widely known silver-leafed perennial is *Stachys byzantina* (Lambs Ears). The species itself has flowers that are silver and purple but if flowers are not desired, one can purchase the cultivar 'Silver Carpet'. All species of *Artemesia* except *lactiflora* have silver foliage. They vary in height and aggressiveness but, to my mind, the most beautiful is the hybrid 'Powis Castle', which is very lacy and grows only two feet high. Although supposedly a perennial, I frequently lose it due to poor drainage in my clay soil which, though amended, never seems to be amended enough for this one. However, I cannot live without this plant and repurchase it whenever it dies. The other perennial known for its silver foliage, which can also be characterized as a sub-shrub because it is quite woody, is *Perovskia atriplicifolia* (Russian Sage). There are enormous differences in the size and texture of the leaves of these perennials, from very delicate to large, and from lacy to furry.

Close to silver or gray is blue-green. Intensity of the color is somewhat responsible for classifying some plants as blue-green and others as silver or gray. Among the best-known woodies in this category are the conifers, particularly Spruce and Juniper. Who among us isn't acquainted with *Picea pungens* (Colorado Spruce)? The color is spectacular. I just wish more consideration would be given to the fact that its mature size is huge and that it should not be planted three feet out from the house but thirty feet away. As an alternative, one could substitute a smaller cultivar such as 'Montgomery'. There are innumerable *Juniperus* cultivars, both spreading and upright, that can be used to place this color in the landscape.

Take advantage of the variety of sizes of blue ornamental grasses. The smallest is *Festuca ovina glauca* (Blue Fescue) and its cultivars. Next on the size scale would be *Helictrotrichon sempervirens* (Blue Oat Grass), then *Schizachyrium scoparium* (Little Blue Stem), and finally one of the *Panicum virgatum* cultivars such as 'Heavy Metal', 'Prairie Sky' or 'Cloud Nine' or *Sorghastrum nutans* 'Sioux Blue' (Indian Grass). Both *Festuca* and *Helictotrichon* keep their blue color all year, but *Panicum* and *Sorghastrum* will turn yellow when temperatures dip in the fall.

Only a few perennials have blue foliage but the best known is definitely *Hosta*. The leaves can be tiny or huge, wavy or heavily quilted. Several cultivars of *Dianthus* (Pinks) have blue foliage. One of the best is *D. 'Bath's Pink'* because, unlike many *Dianthus*, it doesn't seem to mind humidity, but do explore the many other choices that are available.

So the next time you consider color in a landscape, think first of the expansive palette found with foliage. There are many benefits of using colored foliage in creative new ways, not the least of which is designing a landscape with an extended season of color.

The Foliage Palette:
Red and Purple

Colored foliage is an invaluable asset in the landscape. Some colors just deserve their own discussion, like red and purple. At their boldest, these colors have incredible impact in the garden and landscape. At their softest, they offer versatile coloring with a good range of differing shades. Many plants with red or purple coloring provide an evolving interest as they deepen or lessen in intensity as they mature, providing a changing look as the seasons progress.

Red foliage adds extraordinary vibrancy to the landscape. The one that first comes to my mind is *Imperata cylindrica* 'Red Baron', Japanese Blood Grass. Only twelve inches high and very slowly rhizomatous, this lovely ornamental grass becomes even more spectacular when it is positioned so that it can be backlit, making it look as though it is on fire. A taller red grass for the garden or landscape is *Panicum virgatum* 'Rotstrahlbusch' (Red Switch Grass). This grass will grow three to four feet at maturity. Its foliage is green with a red tinge that becomes more pronounced with cool autumn temperatures, and in late summer it sports a delicate pink inflorescence. A new *Panicum* cultivar named 'Shenandoah' is reputed to color up as early as June.

Which family of trees comes immediately to mind when the color red is mentioned? *Acer*, of course. It's probably a tie between *Acer palmatum* (Japanese Maple) and *Acer platanoides* 'Crimson King'. The Japanese Maples give us a wide range of choices of height and form, from the upright cultivars 'Bloodgood' and 'Trompenburg', which will grow fifteen feet high, to the myriad weeping cultivars, which can be kept at three to six feet in height but ten feet in width. The crimson-leaved cultivars of *Acer platanoides*, on the other hand, will grow at least twenty-five feet and up to forty feet. The other tree genus with some red-foliaged cultivars is *Malus* (Crabapple). Those cultivars are 'American Masterpiece', 'Brandywine', 'Red Barron' and 'Royal Sceptre'.

The best shrub genus for red foliage is *Berberis* (Barberry). *Berberis thunbergii atropurpurea* (Red Barberry) and its cultivars add red to the landscape from the time they foliate in spring until leaf drop in the fall. While the species grows five feet, the cultivars 'Nana' and 'Rose Glow' only reach two to three feet. Technically, *Berberis t.a.*'Rose Glow' is not red, merely shades of pink that are perceived as rosy red, but it fills the need for a subtler color in some designs.

Some perennials also have red or reddish foliage. Most of the red-flowered *Astilbe* have red stems and foliage with a reddish tinge. *Sedum spurium* 'Dragon's Blood' and 'Red Carpet' both have red-bronze foliage and are excellent groundcovers while the relatively new *Sedum* 'Matrona' has rosy-red stems and rose edging on the leaves.

Closely related to the color red is the color purple and I am sure that, to some eyes, the distinction is a fine one. Particularly on foliage, I think the differentiation is one of strength of color. The deeper it is, the more likely it is to be called purple. Several cultivars of *Fagus sylvatica* (European Beech) such as 'Purpurea Pendula', 'Riversii', 'Rohanii' and 'Spaethiana' have dark purple foliage. All of them except 'Purpurea Pendula' become very large trees. A smaller tree for the landscape is the Flowering Plum. Plums range in size from the seven-foot *Prunus x cistena* (Purple Sandcherry) to the fifteen-foot *Prunus x cerasifera* 'Newport' to the twenty-five-foot *Prunus cerasifera* 'Thundercloud'. *Prunus x cistena* is an overused small tree and is frequently inappropriately placed, rarely given enough space to grow naturally without pruning. There is also one Flowering Cherry with purple foliage, *Prunus serrulata* 'Royal Burgundy' that will become a good lawn tree at twenty to twenty-five feet.

My favorite purple-leaved shrub is *Cotinus coggyria* 'Velvet Cloak' (Purple Smoke Bush). Left alone, it will grow ten to fifteen feet high but since the best color is found in the foliage on new wood, I prune it down to two feet each spring, sacrificing the fluffy blooms. By the end of the summer, it is five to six feet tall again at the back of my purple and pink perennial border. Other candidates are *Sambucus nigra* 'Guincho Purple' or 'Black Beauty' (Purple Elderberry), which grow eight to ten feet tall, have purplish-tinged foliage that deepens in color in the fall and have purple berries as a bonus.

The best known purple-leaved perennial is *Heuchera 'Palace Purple'*, which was the Perennial Plant Association's Plant of the Year in 1991. Since then, Dan Heims of Terra Nova Nursery and others have been hybridizing and tissue-culturing innumerable new cultivars that are even better. Now there are *Heuchera* with ruffled foliage, with silvery overlays and with foliage that is more ruby than purple but all of them have flowers that are sprays of tiny bells.

Another front of the border perennial with purple foliage is *Penstemon digitalis 'Husker Red'*. Its leaves are lanceolate and the tubular flowers are similar to those of Foxglove. While the purple-leaved Heuchera are grown primarily for their foliage, this *Penstemon* is grown for both its flowers and its foliage.

When spring arrives, leaves will unfurl and the wonderful cycle of Mother Nature will begin anew. As it does, keep in mind all the colors that can be utilized to enhance the landscape.

Penstemon

The Foliage Palette:
Variegated Perennials and Grasses

The palette of plants with colored foliage is enormous. In previous articles, I have touched on specific colors but this time I want to concentrate on variegated foliage. Use variegated foliage to brighten a shady site or invigorate a sunny one. A favorite of mine is an ornamental grass called *Arrhenatherum bulbosum* 'Variegatum' (Bulbous Oat Grass). Its green- and white-variegated foliage only grows six to twelve inches high and thrives in well-drained loamy soil in either full sun or partial shade. It makes an excellent weaver among low, green-foliaged plants or as an edger.

A larger version of this grass is *Miscanthus sinensis* 'Gracillimus' (Gracillimus Maiden Grass), which is an improved version of *M.s.* 'Variegata'. This grass needs full sun and will grow five to six feet tall. Whereas the inflorescence of *Arrhenatherum* is small and early blooming (May/June), that of *Miscanthus* is quite showy when it appears in September and then remains throughout the winter. For a different look, try *Miscanthus sinensis* 'Strictus' (Zebra Grass), which is a more upright version of *M.s.* 'Zebrinus'. This grass is green and yellow and the striping is horizontal instead of vertical.

If you have space or a slope that cries out for a running grass, try *Phalaris arundinacea* (Ribbon Grass), which grows twelve to fifteen inches high. Sometimes it becomes ratty looking during midsummer at which time you can mow it or scythe it back and let it refoliate. It grows well in either full sun or partial shade.

The list of variegated foliage perennials is unbelievably long so I will only mention a few favorites. (You may find more on these in a brochure on foliage perennials that is published by the Perennial Plant Association.) I love *Ajuga* 'Burgundy Glow' for use under shade trees as an alternative groundcover for *Pachysandra* and *Vinca minor*. The pink, cream and green leaves give color to the landscape twelve months of the year and supply an additional wallop of blue when the *Ajuga* blooms in May. Only three inches high and eight when in bloom, it will grow in sun or partial shade and is very adaptable to dry shade.

Another favorite, but not well-known or used enough, is *Arabis caucasica* 'Variegata'. All Arabis are quickly spreading groundcovers and evergreen but this one has furry green and white leaves that are supplemented with white flowers in April and May. Only two inches high and five inches when in bloom, it too will grow in sun or partial shade. Once established, it is very drought tolerant. There is a similar *Arabis* that has tiny, non-furry leaves and is therefore useful as a spot planting in rock gardens. This is *Arabis ferdinandi-coburgi* 'Variegata'.

One of the most beautiful variegated perennials for the shade is *Brunnera macrophylla* 'Variegata' (Variegated Forget-Me-Not). The large heart-shaped leaves are green with an irregular wide white edge and stunning in a shade garden. Because it is difficult to propagate, this is an expensive plant but, in my mind, well worth it. There is another variegated cultivar called 'Langtrees', which has white spots, but I do not find it to be nearly as entrancing. Both have the charming blue flowers typical of Forget-Me-Nots.

Brunnera

Hosta, of course, supply an endless variety of variegated cultivars, ranging in size from tiny to huge. My all-time favorite is H. 'Frances Williams' with its huge, quilted blue leaves that are solidly edged in cream. A very popular new variegated *Hosta* is 'Patriot', which is deeply veined green with an irregular wide white edge. There are numerous other cultivars: some are mostly white with a green edge; some are blue with a cream center; some are yellow with a yellow edge – the possibilities are almost unlimited. Needless to say, partial shade is best for this genus.

There are also many variegated perennials for sun. Among the newest is *Phlox paniculata* 'Nora Leigh', which has cream and green foliage that grows thirty to thirty-six feet high and bears pink flowers during the summer. Many people like the contrast of the foliage with the flowers but I prefer it without the flowers. A similar plant, but one that I like better, is *Physostegia virginiana* 'Variegata'. Its flowers are pale purple. Unlike other *Physostegia*, I find this one to be a weak grower, so the fact that it is rhizomatous is actually a blessing. When judging these two perennials, take into account my bias in favor of green and white, rather than yellow and white variegation.

One of the newer *Sedum* is 'Frosty Morn'. It has succulent green leaves edged with white and flowers that can be either white or pale pink in late summer and early autumn. It grows about eighteen inches high and requires relatively dry soil. A useful creeping groundcover is *Sedum spurium* 'Tricolor', which has tiny leaves that have pink, white and green stripes. It blooms in early summer with small pink spurs. Periodically, this *Sedum* sports all green shoots that should be gently removed.

Don't forget about *Yucca*. These are stunningly dramatic plants that, as well as having variegated cultivars, are also evergreen. Two of the best are *Yucca filamentosa* 'Bright Edge', which has a yellow edge and 'Golden Sword', which has a yellow center. If you can find it, there is also 'Variegata', which has a white edge.

I intended this to be the last of the articles that are centered around the great interest that foliage lends to the landscape but as I wrote this article I realized that the group of plants that encompasses the palette of variegated foliage is so huge that I didn't even have space to include woodies in this article. Therefore, they will be the subject next time.

The Foliage Palette:
Variegated Shrubs

Plants with variegated foliage make quite an impact in the landscape, even more so when they are large. The few trees that fill this bill are, therefore, greatly treasured. *Acer palmatum 'Butterfly'* (Butterfly Japanese Maple) is a small tree for partial shade (only six to ten feet tall and four to five feet wide) but its green and white dissected foliage lends grace as well as light to the landscape. As the temperature drops in September, the white margins turn pink and then red, adding a tinge of fire to the autumn landscape. At the other end of the size scale is *Fagus sylvatica 'Roseomarginata'* (Rosepink European Beech) which will grow thirty feet tall and almost as wide. This tree makes an eye-catching lawn specimen if it gets a bit of shade to keep the irregular rose or rose-and-white edge from scorching. The primary color of the foliage is deep reddish-purple. This Beech is a more robust grower than *Fagus sylvatica 'Tricolor'*.

An intermediate sized deciduous tree with variegated foliage is *Cornus florida 'Cherokee Daybreak'*, which has green and creamy-white leaves that turn pink to deep red in the fall, or *'Cherokee Sunset'*, which has leaves with a broad irregular margin of yellow that also turn color in the fall. Both trees will grow fifteen to twenty feet tall. The Cherokee Series of Dogwoods has been bred for resistance to mildew and anthracnose. All of these trees are hardy to zone 5.

The only coniferous tree with variegated foliage of which I'm aware is *Pinus densiflora 'Oculis-draconis'* (Dragon's Eye Pine), which, over time, will become thirty-five feet tall. The needles have distinct yellow banding. This zone 4 tree is definitely a focal point because of its unusual coloration. However, be aware that the many people may think that it looks sickly. If you think you want to use it, be sure to see it in a nursery first.

There are several shrubs with variegated foliage. Not as well known as it should be is *Acanthopanax sieboldiana 'Variegata'* (Variegated Fiveleaf

Aralia). This five- to six-foot shrub will grow almost anywhere, being tolerant of adverse conditions such as cold (hardy to zone 3), drought and heavy shade as well as full sun. It makes an excellent specimen as well as a hedging barrier plant because of the prickles below each set of green and white leaves. Much better known are *Cornus alba 'Argenteo-marginata' also called 'Elegantissima'* (Silverblotch Dogwood) and *Cornus alba 'Ivory Halo'*. Both have red stems and white-edged green leaves. 'Ivory Halo' is somewhat more compact (five feet instead of eight to ten feet) and has more finely textured foliage than its cousin. This is a plant for full sun or partial shade and hardy to zone 4.

Hydrangea macrophylla 'Mariesii Variegata' has large, serrated leaves that are edged with white. Grow this three-foot plant solely for its lovely foliage because chances are good that it will not flower unless you garden in zone 7 or warmer. Although the plant itself is hardy to zone 5, the flower buds are not. Place in full sun or partial shade with adequate moisture. Flowering is never a problem with *Kerria japonica 'Picta'*, also known as *'Variegata'* (Variegated Kerria). Every spring, *Kerria* produces a flurry of bright yellow flowers but before and after bloom, this shrub claims a space in the sun or shade garden with its green and white foliage on evergreen stems. It is hardy to zone 5. Although the literature states that *Kerria j. 'Picta'* only grows three feet high and wide, I have seen it in gardens four to five feet high. Cutting it to the ground every few years will keep it at three feet.

Relatively new in the trade is *Salix integra 'Hakuru Nishiki'* (Hakuru Nishiki Willow). Hardy to zone 5, it should become five to eight high. I have only grown this Willow for three years; it is now three and a half feet high but receives minimal irrigation. It can be pruned quite low each year to keep it small and colorful. Its attraction is the striking pink and white new foliage, which becomes less pink and more green during the heat of summer. An old favorite is *Weigela florida 'Variegata'* which grows four to six high and wide. Hardy to zone 4, this ruby flowered shrub supplies color for the whole growing season with its creamy-edged foliage. Grown in full sun, this old-fashioned shrub will enhance the landscape for many years.

Chamaecyparis obtusa 'Snowkist' (Snowkist False Cypress) is an evergreen shrub that has creamy white variegated patches. Hardy to zone 5, it is a good rock garden or small garden plant that should become approximately three high and wide. *Tsuga canadensis 'Albospica'* is similar to *T.c. 'Gentsch White'* but is a more vigorous grower. Both have white tipped new growth and should, therefore, be pruned for good color and compactness. There are several other cultivars of these two genera, hardy to zone 4, which have variegated foliage, but they are usually only available at nurseries that specialize in conifers.

Naturally, there are many other variegated trees and shrubs, some common, some rare. I urge you to seek them out in order to make your landscapes more interesting.

A Botanical Veil:
Using See-Through Plants

As both an obsessed gardener and a landscape designer, I am always looking for opportunities to combine common and uncommon plants in unusual ways in order to excite the gardener as well as the visitor. As part of my design work, I frequently see gardens that feel static because plants are placed in a somewhat rigid manner, that is: short plants in the front, medium-sized plants in the middle and large or tall plants in the back. A less predictable arrangement makes the garden much more interesting because the variation in height placement adds a dimension of depth as well as surprise to the garden. One way to accomplish this, which I have observed in other gardens and use myself, is the placement of see-through plants, usually perennials, at the front or middle of a border.

So, how do I define a see-through plant? It is one that acts as a veil so that the viewer cannot see everything clearly at first but is impelled to come closer or to wander into the garden for a better look at what can be glimpsed through the veil. I try to create an atmosphere of adventure, mystery and romance in my gardens and find that the more layers and screens I have, the closer I come to accomplishing my goal.

Thus, not every plant that allows a view behind it is a see-through. An excellent example is *Allium giganteum* (Giant Allium), which has large heads through which one cannot see, but whose slim stems allow one to see perfectly the *Camassia*, *Nectarascordum* and *Fritillaria persica* immediately behind it.

A typical see-through plant has either delicate foliage and/or flowers with a loose growth habit or many stems and flowers that don't completely impede the view of plants behind them. Such plants typically have strong stems that do not flop or need to be staked. The other attribute is height. See-throughs need to be three feet or taller unless the viewer is a child; therefore, most see-through plants are summer or fall bloomers. The diameter of a see-through plant is basically irrelevant; it merely determines how many plants you will need to create your illusion.

I have not planted see-throughs in any particular pattern in my garden but have used them intermittently so that the viewer is invited to pause. Too many would make the garden seem cluttered. I do prefer "stuffed" gardens, but this should be balanced with an enticement to examine plants closely as well as a rhythmical flow for comfort. I rarely use see-throughs on corners because I think such placement negates the corner as being either a beginning or an end. My preference is to place the first see-throughs at least a few feet along a garden path so that the walk becomes a leisurely and exploring stroll. If the viewer can be induced to tarry, the garden designer will be all smiles.

Generally speaking, the use of see-through plants in the garden calls for large, splashy flowers or foliage behind the see-through because subtle plants will be lost in the veiling. Roses, *Clematis*, *Hemerocallis* (Daylily), *Phlox*, *Chrysanthemum superbum* (Shasta Daisy) – these all qualify as show-stoppers. So would yellow-foliaged *Hosta*. The color of "behind" plants can complement or contrast with the see-throughs depending entirely on the gardener's personal preferences. However, strong contrast is the most dramatic and easiest to see. If complementary colors are used, they should be very saturated. Old-fashioned roses, with their strong mauves and hot pinks, can be seen easily through perennials such as *Crambe*, *Phlox* or *Verbena bonariensis*.

One of the earliest blooming see-throughs in my garden is *Anthriscus sylvestris* 'Ravenswing', a black-leaved, ferny perennial. The basal foliage is only twelve inches high, but the white umbels are held on three-foot stems in mid-May and June. In my garden, I can see a large-flowered *Clematis* and an *Acer tataricum* (Tatarian Maple) through it. Planted just to the right of my *Anthriscus* is another relatively early bloomer, *Hesperis matrionalis* (Sweet Rocket), which has white or lavender flowers. The flowers are massed on the terminal head but sparser on side shoots. Although each plant sends up three or four stems, they are narrow enough that I can see *Scilla campanulata* (Wood Hyacinth) and *Pieris japonica* (Andromeda) behind them. Both the *Anthriscus* and the *Hesperis* will grow well in partial shade gardens.

A large, diaphanous, sun-loving perennial that I love to use for both its size and delicacy is the six-foot *Crambe cordifolia* (Giant Kale). Its airiness keeps it from being overwhelming, even when planted at the front of a border or, in my case, in the middle of a border but just at the top of the front slope. I can easily see a climbing *Rosa 'William Baffin'* through it from one angle and catch a peek of *Paeonia* and *Knautia* from another angle. *Knautia macedonica* and *Knautia arvensis* also act as see-through plants in the middle of my garden, even though they have very weak stems. I plant them closely so that they support one another. The casual stroller can see the climbing rose and *Salix integra 'Hakuru Nishiki'* (a relatively unknown Willow with pink, white and green variegated foliage) through the *Knautia*.

Another June bloomer is *Iris pseudacorus* (Yellow Flag Iris). The foliage is wide, providing a total screen, but the blossoms are far enough apart that one can peer through them to the roses behind. How can this unusual pairing of plants work? Their cultural needs are so different. The solution is to install them in two adjacent beds divided by stone walls as well as a small water bed. Masses of *Kniphofia uvaria* (Red Hot Poker), with its strappy foliage and very upright, brightly colored heads, make an excellent screen for an *Aruncus dioicus* (Goat's Beard) in the background. The above-mentioned combinations can be attributed to the design skills of Gertrude Jekyll and now to Rosamund Wallinger, the present owner, who has restored the gardens at Upton Grey in Hampshire.

Perennials with long spikes like *Kniphofia* or *Digitalis purpurea* (Common Foxglove), with their multi-tubed spires, allow us to see over the basal foliage, through the stems up to the blossoms and then between the blossoms themselves. This was exactly the case at Hadspen House in Somerset, where *Digitalis* veiled stone and water as I walked down the steps of the back garden. On closer examination, I beheld the large pond, which was bordered on one side by a high stone wall. Plantings flowed over the top and others had seeded into the wall.

Agastache cana (Mosquito Plant) – a terrible name for a beautiful plant – is another excellent example of a see-through plant. This drought-resistant perennial, with strong stems, narrow leaves and small tubular rosy-pink blooms, is airy enough that one can see through it to a mass of *Miscanthus sinensis 'Adagio'* in my garden. This *Agastache* is shorter than I specified above, but it is planted in my front garden at the top of a hill so that it is situated at eye level. *Verbena bonariensis* (a self-seeding annual in zone 6, where I live) blooms about the same time and also into the fall. This tall annual with stiffly narrow stems and pale purple dried-flower-like blossoms provides a perfect screen that can be as filmy or dense as you like, depending on how many you leave and how many you pull. I use it mainly on the same side of the garden as the *Knautia* and the *Crambe* to screen the *Phloxes*. In mid-July, when the *Crambe* has finished blooming, the *Verbena* comes into bloom and continues long after the *Knautia* has given up.

In a shaded, narrow bed on the east side of my property, I use *Cimicifuga racemosa* (Fairy Candles/Black Cohosh), a perennial I put into almost every shade garden I design. Its beautiful white spires of delicate blossoms rise from large screening foliage, making a thin veil behind which can easily be seen the blossoms or fluffy seedheads of *Clematis* '*General Sikorsky*' plus a small stand of *Lythrum virgatum* '*Morden's Pink*' (Purple Loosestrife), which has neither increased in size nor seeded in seventeen years. This ease of viewing is generally true with spiky perennials, e.g. *Digitalis* (Foxglove) and *Liatris* (Gayfeather).

Also useful in part shade or full sun is *Thalictrum*. The most useful species is *T. rochebrunianum* (Lavender Mist). Its cymes are so delicate that entire borders can be viewed through them. The other most commonly used *Thalictrum* are *T. aquilegifolium* and *T. glaucum*, but both of these have dense flower heads that one cannot see through. However, once the petals have fallen and only the seedheads are left, these plants become see-throughs.

Liatris

A late-blooming perennial that must not be omitted is *Perovskia atriplicifolia* (Russian Sage). Its narrow, gray-green foliage and spikes of pale lavender are an asset to any garden but enhance it even more if a boldly colored (white, magenta, yellow or orange) perennial or annual is planted behind it. Some choices that come to mind are *Helenium autumnale* (Sneezeweed), *Heliopsis helianthoides* (False Sunflower) and *Anemone japonica 'Alba'* (Japanese Anemone), or an annual such as *Cosmos bipinnatus 'Carmine'*.

The ornamental grasses are quintessential see-throughs. In addition, the grasses add two elements that most perennials do not. These are the linearity of the foliage and the ability of both the foliage and the inflorescences to sway in the wind and thus supply a changing picture. The first that comes to mind is *Pennisetum alopecuroides* (Fountain Grass) and its many cultivars. The delicate mounding habit of the foliage is delightful and provides great textural contrast to most other plants in the landscape. For my purpose, its bottlebrush inflorescences can provide a translucent screen behind which I can spy occasional bits of *Gaura lindheimeri*, itself a see-through plant. This is one of the few perennials that also waves in the wind.

Another useful grass is *Panicum virgatum* (Switch Grass), an American prairie native. I love the cultivars *'Rotstralbusch'* and *'Shenandoah'* with their reddish-tinged foliage that becomes even more brilliant in the fall. In September, they have an ethereal pink inflorescence which can provide a diaphanous veil in front of *Phlox paniculata 'David'* and *Phlox 'Speed Limit 45'*.

The easiest of the grasses to see through is *Molinia caerulea* (Moor Grass). This grass has foliage that usually grows one to two feet high, while the wispy inflorescences can be seven to eight feet high. This is especially true of the cultivars *'Windspiel'* and *'Skyracer'*.

At the front of the living room bed, I have planted my *Molinia 'Skyracer'*. This way I can see *Alcea rosea* (Hollyhock), *Cosmos bipinnatus* and *Nicotiana sylvestris* from inside or from the street. *Stipa gigantea* (Giant Needle Grass) is similar in appearance to *Molinia* (though more drought tolerant and hardy only to zone 6 instead of zone 4), but the multiple awns of its inflorescence give it more presence.

Although it is certainly not a grass, I would mention *Foeniculum vulgare* (Fennel) here. Both the species and the cultivar '*Rubrum*' (also sold as '*Purpurea*') make fine see-throughs. It is essentially a feathery foliage plant with very delicate umbels lending presence to the scene long after Poppies, with which it can be interplanted, are gone. Both the size of Poppies and their color make this a spectacular combination.

I am sure that you will compile your own list of see-through plants as you look anew at your gardens. In doing so, keep in mind that some woodies also make good see-throughs. But that list will have to wait for another day.

Conditions of Design: Site Situations and Seasons That Influence Design

The Sunny, Wet Garden:
A Golden Opportunity

How often have you heard someone complain about a particular site, "It's too wet to grow anything except weeds," or "I have to wear hip boots to get in there!" Expensive drain work would dry out a wetland, although that could be against environmental regulations and would probably destroy wildlife habitat. But there is another way of solving these "problems" that involves working with the site conditions provided by nature. If you are a landscape designer, you can create an innovative design and gain a reputation as someone who looks beyond the standard procedure to the exceptional solution. Knowledge of plants suitable to these site conditions is invaluable and can help turn so-called problems into golden opportunities.

There are many variations of wet sites, from wet meadow to emergent zone (marginal) to deep standing water. There are also distinct differences among marshes, swamps and bogs. Understanding these differences is crucial to the utilization of the plants that will thrive in those circumstances. So let's begin with some definitions. *

Wet meadow:
A site where the wetland grades into upland and regularly undergoes periods of wet and dry; may be dominated by emergent plants or shrubs and trees.

Emergent zone:
Adjacent to the wet meadow but lower; dominated by soft-stemmed herbaceous plants that grow partially in water (roots submerged but leaves and stems above water).

Deep water:
More than six inches, dominated by submersed aquatics and floating plants that are capable of photosynthesizing underwater.

Marsh:
Supports soft-stemmed herbaceous plants including grasses, reeds and sedges.

Swamp:
A closed canopy wetland dominated by woody flood-tolerant plants.

Bog:
Wetland characterized by high acidity, sphagnum mosses and peat.

Most homeowners who have problematic wet sites have either wet meadows or emergent zones. The wet meadows are commonly created by run-off from neighboring properties or steep grades on their own properties. These sites can be quite open and sunny or partially shaded by large trees. The amount of light is crucial when selecting the appropriate plant material. Many of our native woody plants grow naturally in wet habitats in either sun or partial shade. Among those that prefer sun are *Aronia arbutifolia* 'Brilliantissima' (Brilliant Red Chokeberry), *Cornus ammomum* (Silky Dogwood), *Cornus stolonifera* and *sericea* (Red-twig Dogwood), *Ilex verticillata* (Winterberry), *Rhododendron viscosum* (Swamp Azalea), *Rhododendron arborescens* (Sweet Azalea), *Rosa palustris* (Swamp Rose), *Salix discolor* (Pussy Willow), *Viburnum dentatum* (Arrowwood) and *Viburnum trilobum* (American Cranberrybush).

Some that prefer partial shade are *Cephalanthus occidentalis* (Buttonbush), *Clethra alnifolia* (Summersweet), *Fothergilla gardenii* (Dwarf Fothergilla), *Hamamelis virginiana* (Witchhazel), *Lindera benzoin* (Spicebush), *Rhododendron maximum* (Rosebay Rhododendron) and *Sambucus canadensis* (American Elderberry).

Let's not overlook the numerous perennials and ferns available to us. A few of my favorites are *Arisaema* (Jack-in-the-Pulpit) for their large foliage and unusual flowers, *Caltha palustris* (Marsh Marigold) for its bright yellow flowers, and *Camassia cusickii* (Camassia), which has tall blue spikes. For unusual August flowers, try *Chelone* (Turtlehead) or *Eupatorium maculatum* (Joe-Pye Weed), which towers over the meadow in August and September. Add to the list *Rudbeckia laciniata* (Cutleaf

Coneflower), which is as tall as Joe-Pye Weed, and *Vernonia noveboracensis* (Ironweed), whose purple flowers bloom at the same time and height as the previous two. All of these are native plants, but only the latter three prefer full sun.

Then consider the ferns and sedges that can be incorporated into your creative design. *Athyrium filix-femina* (Lady Fern), *Osmunda cinnamomea* (Cinnamon Fern), *Osmunda regalis* (Royal Fern) and *Thelypteris palustris* (Marsh Fern) are a few of those that thrive under these conditions. Many, but not all, of the sedges also thrive in wet sites, as will *Eriophorum* (Cottongrass).

If you need to create shade for these wet sites, trees such as *Acer rubrum* (Red Maple), *Amelanchier* (Serviceberry), *Betula nigra* (River Birch) and *Nyssa sylvatica* (Sour Gum) are among those that will serve well.

Most residential emergent zones will be contiguous with bodies of water such as natural or man-made ponds, lakes and rivers. If the design includes plants that grow on the edges of these bodies, they will be partially submerged. Thus you will need marginal plants such as *Hibiscus moscheutos* (Rose Mallow), which can be seen decorating the inlets of Long Island, *Iris versicolor* (Blue Flag), *Lobelia cardinalis* (Cardinal Flower), *Pontaderia cordate* (Pickerel Weed) and *Scirpus tabernaemontani* (Bullrush), among others.

To expand your knowledge of this subject matter, I would recommend some reading on the subject of wetlands before undertaking any extensive work and perhaps consulting a specialist. The paperback publication by the Brooklyn Botanic Garden called "The Natural Water Garden" is a good place to start.

I hope this essay prompts you to explore the possibilities and opportunities of a wet site. Like sunken treasure, you never know what jewels may emerge from the depths!

*Definitions were taken from "The Natural Water Garden," ed. Colston Bureell, Brooklyn Botanic Garden; Brooklyn, N.Y., 1997.

The Sunny, Dry Garden:
Another Golden Opportunity

Dilemma: What to do with a parched patch of land on which the sun beats down? Pretend you're in the Southwest and install such xeriscapic plants as *Fouquiera splendens* (Ocotillo), *Agave* and *Opuntia violacea* (Purple Prickly Pear)? Take a cue from Mother Nature by selecting hardy, desert-like plants such as *Opuntia basilaris*, *humifusa* or *imbricata* and *Yucca filimentosa*? Or take advantage of a third alternative. Use plants that can survive desert-like conditions but don't necessarily "look" like desert plants.

It is important to understand that sites with desert-like conditions usually have either a southern or western exposure, thus subjecting most plants to a great deal of stress as they try to cope with dehydration from both sun and wind. Such stress will curtail flowering and bleach out the blossoms that do appear. Therefore, picking plants that are long bloomers will help to ameliorate this problem. Choosing plants with short or strong stems will help where it is windy.

Several Mediterranean plants will survive in zones 5 and 6 as long as the soil is sandy, lean, well-drained and neutral to slightly alkaline. Many of the herbs, such as *Artemesia*, *Lavandula*, *Origanum*, *Santolina* and *Thymus* fit into this category, but check the species zone hardiness carefully because it does vary. It becomes quickly apparent that most of these plants have gray foliage, which is often hairy, and/or has small leaves – all characteristics that contribute to their drought tolerance. The hairs impart a woolly appearance, slow water evaporation and reflect sunlight from the leaves. The small, often narrow, nature of the foliage, typical of *Lavandula* and *Santolina*, minimizes exposure to the sun.

Most of these perennial herbs are grown for their foliage rather than their blooms, with *Lavandula* being a notable exception. Beautiful as they are, most lavenders do not survive well in Northeast Ohio. In fact, the only one that has survived in my garden is actually growing in a crevice in my asphalt driveway where it seeded. An excellent but different substitute is *Nepeta x faassennii* or *mussinii* (Catmint), which is hardy to zone 4, has gray-green foliage and is lax, rather than upright, in habit. It will bloom in flushes from May to October if it is pruned back after the flower spikes fade.

A second group of plants that thrive under sunny, dry conditions is the succulent family. *Sempervivum* (Hen-and-Chicks) and *Sedum* (Upright Stonecrop) are the best known and the only ones that are hardy in Northeast Ohio other than the above-mentioned cacti. They usually have shallow, fibrous root systems that extend horizontally to absorb infrequent rainfall as quickly as possible and thick waxy leaves that retain water for a long time and slow transpiration. The rosettes of *Sempervivum* are rarely taller than six inches, if that, while their flowers may reach twelve inches. After flowering, the mother plant usually dies but there are many "chicks" to replace her.

Other groups of applicable plants are *Echinops* (Thistle) and *Eryngium* (Sea Holly), which are frequently mistaken for each other. The thistles have larger heads that look like prickly metallic blue balls. *Echinops ritro* is hardy to zone 3 and *Eryngium amethystinum* even to zone 2. These perennials have prickly gray foliage on the stems although the basal foliage is often green. Their heads remain on the plants for a very long time, basically drying on the stems. If *Echinops* are pruned, lateral branches will bear additional blossoms. Most of these perennials vary in height from two to four feet. One outstanding exception is *Eryngium yuccifolium* (Rattlesnake Master), a native of the American plains, which can grow five to six feet tall and has small, creamy white, ball-like heads.

Some of the ornamental grasses, particularly those that are prairie natives, are very drought tolerant. One of my favorites is *Panicum virgatum* (Switch Grass). Its cultivars vary in color from metallic blue to maroon red during the growing season and then turn golden yellow or beige after heavy frost. Although the delicate inflorescences fall apart during the winter, the foliage holds up very well and extends the seasons of interest in the landscape. Other excellent prairie grasses are *Andropogon gerardii* (Big Bluestem) and *Schizachyrium scoparium* (Little Bluestem), which become very orange after a hard frost, and *Sorghastrum nutans* (Indian Grass), especially the cultivar *'Sioux Blue'*, which has very blue-green foliage until it dries in fall to an attractive burnt orange. Dry conditions will probably keep this grass to a height of three feet instead of five feet.

The list of perennials that will flourish in your "desert" is really quite long. Among them are the genera *Achillea* (Yarrow), *Anaphalis* (Pearly Everlasting), *Calamintha* (Calamint), *Dictamnus* (Gas Plant), *Knautia*, *Liatris* (Blazing Star), *Linaria* (Toadflax), *Lychnis* (Campion), *Oenothera* (Sundrops), *Perovskia* (Russian Sage) and *Verbascum* (Mullein).

Useful woodies include *Berberis* (Barberry), *Buddleia* (Butterfly Bush), *Callicarpa* (Beautyberry), *Caryopteris* (Bluebeard), *Cotoneaster*, *Cytisus* and *Genista* (Broom), *Hibiscus syriacus* (Rose-of-Sharon), *Juniperus* (Juniper), *Lespedeza* (Shrub Bushclover), *Potentilla fruticosa* (Shrubby Cinquefoil), *Rhus* (Sumac), *Rosa rugosa* and *Tamarix*.

Suffice it to say that there is a long list of plants that can be used where it is not feasible to amend the soil and add irrigation. Keep in mind, however, that some watering will be required for at least the first year until the plants are established. After that, they should be able to fend for themselves. So turn this dry dilemma into another golden opportunity.

Filling the Shadows with Light:
Perennials for the Shady Garden
Part I

How often do we have clients look at shady gardens as liabilities instead of assets? To their way of thinking, a dream garden is all about flowers, color and sun. When they discover that their designated garden area is not the sunniest of sites, they may be a little disappointed – because how much color can you find in the shade? But the truth is, there are hundreds of plants – both woody and herbaceous – that are great additions to the landscape but will not survive in the sun. These plants are colorful, thriving and beautiful. Most of the plants that I will discuss are herbaceous rather than woody, but all can be wonderful additions to the shady landscape. Most are hardy to zone 4, some even to zone 3.

The most important requirement for designing a shady garden is an exact knowledge of the amount of light available, be it morning sun followed by afternoon shade, morning shade followed by a few hours of afternoon sun, filtered light from tall trees overhead (as in a woodland setting), bright light on the north side of a building, or deep shade where only moss survives. The best way to obtain this knowledge is to create a light chart that lists the hours of the day from 9 a.m. to 4 p.m. vertically and the areas requiring landscaping, horizontally. This chart should be made three times: in April or May, in July and in September. This allows for variations in the angle of light, which changes with the ascent and descent of the sun above the equator.

The second most important requirement for designing a shady garden is determining the amount of soil moisture normally available in that area. Most plants that thrive in shade require the soil to be barely moist with excellent drainage all of the time. While some plants will tolerate less moisture, they will not thrive in such a situation. Others are quite happy in dry shade once they are established. Plants native to swampy habitats are quite happy in sites that never drain well, sites of which homeowners and landscapers frequently despair.

Planting under trees is a tricky business. Dry shade situations are usually created by the root systems of the trees that are creating the shade. These trees absorb most of the available moisture, and most have root systems that are composed mainly of tiny feeder roots near the surface. If too many of these roots are destroyed during soil preparation and subsequent installation, the tree will suffer serious damage and could even die. For this reason, I recommend never rototilling under such trees, and suggest using small plants that will mature but won't disturb the roots.

The other problem with planting under trees is changing the soil level. I understand wanting to improve the soil by amending it with organic matter, such as compost or leaf humus, but because the majority of roots are close to the surface of the soil, adding too much will suffocate the roots. Therefore, never add more than one to two inches of soil amendments at a time. You could probably add one or two inches per year as needed because the root system will subsequently invade the upper layers.

Although there is a great variety of long-blooming perennials, most do not bloom in the shade. There are exceptions, of course. One lovely example is *Stylophorum diphyllum* (Celandine Poppy, zone 4). Its bright yellow blossoms and lobed foliage enhance the woodland garden from May to June, and intermittently throughout the summer. Another is *Dicentra eximia* (formosa) (Everblooming Bleeding Heart, zone 3) with pink or white blossoms all summer long. It is important, therefore, to realize that the plant palette for shady gardens should include plants that have colorful foliage as well as, or instead of, colorful flowers.

Designing and working in shady sites requires an understanding of color. For whatever reason (as Mother Nature has yet to explain to me), color in the shade tends to be more subtle. It usually leans heavily on the cool palette: blue, pink and pale purple. Examples of this are the blossoms of *Brunnera macrophylla* (Heartleaf Brunnera), *Astilbe* and *Hosta*.

The other colors found frequently in the shade are white and silver. A very strong color, white can be easily seen, making it perfect for shady gardens as well as evening gardens. One white plant I love to use at the back of a shady perennial garden is *Aruncus dioicus* (Goat's Beard, zone 4).

Reaching six feet tall with an equal spread, this plant has great presence. It looks like a giant *Astilbe* with its large foliage and creamy white plumes that appear in early June. Another very useful white bloomer is *Actaea alba*, also known as *A.pachypoda* (White Baneberry, zone 3). This plant displays white-fringed flowers on long, terminal racemes in spring. It also has white berries that form on stalks in late summer and last well into fall.

If you install a group of white plants close together, you will notice that not all whites are the same. I have a walkway that is bordered by a large *Pieris japonica* (Japanese Pieris, zone 4 with some protection), featuring creamy white sprays of blooms in spring. Just a foot away is an area covered by *Arabis procurrens* (Rock Cress, zone 5) with glossy, evergreen foliage and bright white blossoms that bloom at the same time. Fortunately, they are separated by the foliage of *Echinacea purpurea* (Purple Coneflower, zone 3) and *Rosa* 'Meidomonac' ('Bonica'TM Meidiland Rose, zone 3).

Silver is one of my favorite colors to use in the shade because it gathers and reflects light. I frequently use *Athyrium niponicum* 'Pictum' (Japanese Painted Fern, zone 4) to illuminate an area of dim light. Because individual silver plants vary in coloration just a bit, try to hand-pick them. I also find myself using some of the newer *Pulmonaria* (Lungwort, zone 4) cultivars such as 'Excalibur', 'Majesté' and 'Silver Streamers' in addition to some of the ever expanding list of *Heuchera* (Alumroot, zone 4) cultivars like 'Pewter Veil' and 'Eco-Magnififolia'. All of these varieties feature very pretty, silvery foliage.

Another attribute of silver is its cooling effect. This comes into play most effectively in areas that receive some afternoon sun. On a hot summer day, people automatically head for shady spots. The next best alternative to a shady location is looking at something that feels cool. Silver plants can create such an effect. *Helictotrichon sempervirens* (Blue Oat Grass, zone 5) is a silver-blue beauty that prefers full sun, but for a few years will tolerate sites that only receive three to four hours of sun in the afternoon.

One of the most beautiful, silvery, shady corners I've ever seen was at the Conservatory Garden at Central Park Conservatory in New York City. In the front were *Helictotrichon* and *Astilbe chinensis var.taquetii*, formerly known as *A.taquettii* (Fall Astilbe, zone 5). The mid-ground featured *Anemone x hybrida* (Japanese Anemone, zone 4), the variegated grass, *Phalaris arundinacea* (Ribbon Grass, zone 4), *Achnatherum calamagrostis* (Silver Spike Grass, zone 6), and a blue-foliaged *Hosta*. The back-ground contained *Cornus alba* 'Argenteo-marginata', also known as 'Elegantissima' (Silverblotch Dogwood, zone 3), and a green woody that I didn't recognize. The repetition of silvers and blues, along with the use of variegated foliage, created a stunning composition.

Although the predominant blossom colors found in the shade belong to the cool palette, there are some shady plants that feature red or yellow flowers. One plant with red blossoms is *Lobelia cardinalis* (Cardinal Flower, zone 2), which requires moist shade and is very effective when planted near water. *Thalictrum flavum subsp. glaucum*, formerly known as *T.speciosis simum* (Dusty Meadow Rue, zone 5), has airy, bright-yellow panicles on three- to five-foot stalks that sport blue-green foliage. It is happiest in moist, light shade. Too much shade will cause the plants to lean and flop.

Black is an uncommon color that can add interest to a garden. Not many people would consider using black in a shady garden because it is difficult to see the color in the shade, but if used properly, the look can be striking. *Ophiopogon planiscapus* 'Nigrescens' (Black Mondo Grass, zone 6) is an ornamental grass that resembles a black Liriope and has similar blooms. Like purple, black must be carefully sited so that it doesn't get lost. I have seen it used very effectively in a Cleveland garden where the owner placed it in a mat of *Lysimachia nummularia* 'Aurea' (Golden Moneywort, zone 4). Be sure that the chosen site has enough light to keep the *Lysimachia* foliage yellow; too much shade will produce green foliage.

By expanding our knowledge of effective ways to work with shady sites, we can spread the knowledge that there are wonderful advantages to them. Let's elevate the lowly shade garden!

Filling the Shadows with Light:
Perennials for the Shady Garden
Part 2

A designer is constantly challenged to create a landscape that is interesting, ever-changing and beautiful. Most plants bloom for a relatively short period of time; therefore, the designer must keep in mind the image of the plant when it is not in bloom. It is here that foliage takes on a very important role with its own unique color, shape and texture.

The color green encompasses many beautiful shades and textures. Imagine the differences between the glossy, dark green of *Asarum europaeum* (European Ginger, zone 4), the matte, medium green of *A. canadense* (Canadian Wild Ginger, zone 2), and the hairy, light green of *Luzula nivea* (Snowy Woodrush, zone 5).

Variegated foliage also adds immeasurable interest to shady gardens. The multitudinous varieties of variegated *Hosta* look wonderful when planted with any number of other variegated, shade-loving plants such as *Symphytum grandiflorum* 'Goldsmith' (Gold-Edged Comfrey, zone 3), which has gold-edged foliage, *Ajuga* (Bugleweed, zone 3) cultivars such as *A.reptans* 'Burgundy Glow' or 'Silver Beauty', or one of the *Lamium maculatum* (Dead Nettle, zone 4) varieties.

There are many blue-green foliaged plants as well, including the ever-popular *Hosta* and *Alchemilla mollis* (Lady's Mantle, zone 4). Purple can be found in the foliage of several *Heuchera* selections, of which the best known is *Heuchera micrantha* 'Palace Purple' (Palace Purple Coral Bells, zone 4), and in *Sedum* cultivars such as 'Vera Jameson' and 'Mohrchen' (zone 3). The trick to using purple in the shade is to surround it with beige or green foliage, or use it in the front of the border, so its color doesn't get lost in the shade. An excellent foil would be *Carex buchananii* (Leatherleaf Sedge, zone 5), a bronzy ornamental grass. The biggest challenge in using this grass is explaining to your client that the plant is not dead or dying – bronze is its actual color.

Yellow foliage plants also abound, but care must be taken to avoid those varieties that lose their color in the shade and turn green. Although this won't happen with plants like *Lamium maculatum* 'Beedhams's White' (Spotted Dead Nettle, Zone 4), it will with others, such as *Lysimachia nummularia* 'Aurea'. An excellent yellow ornamental grass for the shade is *Hakonechloa macra* 'Aureola' (Golden Hakonechloa, zone 5). Its foliage is predominantly yellow with green striping, and the plant maintains its color as long as it gets some sun each day or high shade with sufficient light and lots of moisture.

All of the colors I have discussed so far have been those that are present during the growing season, but the advent of autumn adds new colors to the landscape. Who among us doesn't marvel at the oranges and reds of Sugar Maples and the pinky-reds of Dogwoods? Some perennials also change color in the fall. Many of the hardy geraniums, such as *Geranium macrorrhizum* (Bigroot Geranium, zone 4), become tinged with red as soon as the temperature drops. The foliage of *Platycodon* (Balloon Flower, zone 4) turns bright yellow, as does that of *Amsonia hubrichtii* (Arkansas Amsonia, zone 3).

The use of color echo will add power to color because repetition of a color reinforces it, thus making it stronger than it would be if only used in one type of plant. Under the canopy of an old Hawthorn, for example, I have grouped *Hydrangea arborescens* 'Annabelle' ('Annabelle' Smooth Hydrangea, zone 3), with its large, white panicles, beside *Calamagrostis x acutiflora* 'Overdam' ('Overdam' Feather Reed Grass, zone 5), which displays its green-and-white striped foliage. To the right of the *Calamagrostis* is *Hosta* 'Sugar and Cream' (zone 3), which sports white-edged leaves, and behind this, climbing on a fence, is *Clematis lanuginosa* 'Candida' (zone 6), which has large, white blossoms all summer. This area only receives filtered morning light and filtered afternoon sun; nevertheless, it is full of color all day long, from Spring through Autumn.

Traditionally, a designer searching for a shady groundcover would use *Hedera helix* (Ivy), *Pachysandra* (Spurge) or *Vinca minor* (Myrtle). But why restrict yourself to these three? How about using *Arabis caucasica* (Rock Cress, zone 4), which features gray-green, furry, ever-present foliage and white or rosy-pink, long-lasting spring blossoms? Or try one of my favorites, *Campanula poscharskyana* (Serbian Bellflower, zone 3). This plant has small, heart-shaped, evergreen foliage and starry, lilac blossoms that appear from early May to early July. *Arabis* thrives with a half day of sun, and *Campanula poscharskyana* loves shade, even dry shade.

A few semi-evergreen alternatives are *Symphytum grandiflorum* (Large-flowered Comfrey, zone 3), which spreads quickly and sports shiny, ovate leaves and a rhizomatous root system; *Geranium x cantabrigiense* (Cambridge Geranium, zone 5), with its unusual scalloped foliage and pink blossoms; or one of the *Epimedium* (Bishop's Hat, zone 5) selections, with their heart-shaped foliage that turns bronze during winter.

There are several species of *Epimedium*, each of which has a differently colored delicate blossom. Although short-lived, the blooms are beautiful. *Epimedium* is a suitable groundcover to use in a small but very noticeable area because it spreads very slowly. Be aware that this plant is very expensive due to the difficulty of propagation.

In areas where an evergreen groundcover is not needed, you could use *Chrysogonum virginianum* (Green and Gold, zone 5). This plant has dark green, triangular foliage and tiny, bright-yellow flowers that appear mainly in spring, but bloom intermittently throughout summer. *Ceratostigma plumbaginoides*, formerly known as *Plumbago larpentae* (Leadwort, zone 5), is also worth a try. This plant doesn't foliate until May, but it has beautiful bronze-tinged foliage and bright blue flowers in August and September.

A garden doesn't have to be sunny to possess color and beauty. With hundreds of woody and herbaceous plants to choose from, a shady garden can become an asset rather than a liability. By using these plants to liven up the shadiest of sites, your gardens won't be left in the dark.

Filling the Shadows with Light:
Spring

No matter what the season, herbaceous plants can light up shady sites and provide year-round beauty and texture to otherwise dull, dimly lit sites. Before we begin, remember that the shady garden is an asset rather than a liability. Let's look at some of the plant varieties that herald the arrival of spring and help bring light to a shady spot.

Technically, bulbs are not perceived as herbaceous plants, but many of them foliate, bloom, go dormant and rebloom the following year – the same cycle followed by herbaceous plants. Color in any garden can be extended through the use of bulbs, but this principle is particularly applicable to shady gardens. The majority of bulbs, with the exception of tulips and *Allium*, bloom and are in the process of dormancy before most trees foliate. Therefore, they receive enough sun to photosynthesize for rebloom the following year.

Eranthis hyemalis (Winter Aconite, zone 5) is a tiny bulb whose stem reaches only two inches tall. It sports bright yellow flowers and delicate, deeply cut foliage. The plant blooms in February or March, depending on the weather. For best results, soak the bulbs before planting them in a large mass of at least two hundred. A mass of five hundred produces an even better look. The slightly taller *Galanthus nivalis* (Snowdrop, zone 4) grows three to five inches tall and blooms in early March. This plant can poke its head up through the snow and still be seen because of the surrounding green foliage. It also looks striking against the bare ground if the snow has already melted. Like Winter Aconite, Snowdrop needs to be planted en masse. These two plants bring hope to our clients and us as they signify the eventual end of winter and lead us to the threshold of spring.

Following hard on their heels are *Crocus*. First comes *Crocus chrysanthus* (Snow Crocus, zone 4), a species of which I am particularly fond. Reaching two to four inches tall, this plant comes in single colors, as well as bi- and tri- colors, and withstands the vagaries of winter weather much better than its larger, later cousin. Another lovely crocus with strong colors is *Crocus vernus* (Dutch Crocus, zone 4), which grows four to six inches tall. Because this plant is larger than other bulbs, not many are required to create an impact. A grouping of ten beside or in front of a rock or step definitely catches the eye.

There are several small-flowered blue bulbs, all approximately four to six inches tall that work well in a shady garden. *Puschkinia scilloides var. libanotica*, formerly known as *P. libanotica* (Striped Squill, zone 5), has starry, pale blue-and-white clusters. *Chionodoxa* (Glory-of-the-Snow, zone 4) has small clusters of stars and varies in shades of blue, depending on the species. *Scilla sibirica* (Siberian Squill, zone 5), which is my favorite, naturalizes quickly and displays pure blue, starry bells. In my garden, I've planted Siberian Squill between the rosettes of *Hylotelephium spectabile* 'Autumn Joy', formerly known as *Sedum spectabile* 'Autumn Joy' (Autumn Joy Showy Stonecrop, zones 4 to 10), in a corner that is only touched with sun for a few hours in the afternoon. I also plant them in almost every client's garden.

One of the premier naturalizers is *Muscari armeniacum* (Grape Hyacinth, zone 4). I've had people ask me how to get rid of this plant, but I have never shared that sentiment. The blooms are an intense violet-blue that is quite striking. Unlike other bulbs, *M. armeniacum* foliates in fall. Some people might regard this as a disadvantage, but I see it as a bonus. It is so easy to forget exactly where you have planted daffodils or tulips, especially when you're in the garden, ready to plant new varieties. There is an easy way to remember without making a chart, however. Just plant *Muscari* on top of the bulbs that shouldn't be disturbed.

The lesser known *Muscari latifolium* (zone 4) is an unusual bi-color, blue on the top half and dark violet on the bottom half. I have planted this species between clumps of *Aconitum septentrionale*, formerly known as *A. lycotonum* (Wolfbane, zone 3) and *Lobelia siphilitica* (Big Blue Lobelia, zone 5), the foliage of which is only a few inches tall when the *Muscari* is in bloom. This way, I have added color to an area that would otherwise be only green.

There are so many wonderful classes and cultivars of *Narcissus* (Daffodil, zones 4 to 9) that it is difficult to choose among them. Most *Narcissus* want either a half-day of sun or filtered light all day, as well as excellent drainage. If you read bulb catalogs carefully, you can ascertain which *Narcissus* varieties are the best for shady situations. In his catalog, Brent Heath, owner of Brent and Becky's Bulbs (Gloucester, VA.), says *N. cyclamineus* (zone 6) seems to be more shade and moisture tolerant than other varieties. Two *Narcissus* cultivars that I have used extensively are 'February Gold', which is completely golden, and 'Jack Snipe', which features white petals and a soft-yellow cup. 'Ice Wings' is a triandus type, but the shade of an old Crabapple doesn't seem to hinder its rebloom. I have grouped this cultivar with *Primula* 'Pacific Giant Blue', *Muscari armeniacum* and *Helleborus foetidus* (Bearsfoot Hellebore, zone 5), all of which bloom at the same time.

One bulb that is not as well known and, therefore, underused is *Leucojum aestivum* (Summer Snowflake, zone 4), which requires shade and moisture. I first saw Summer Snowflake in a woodland setting with late-blooming *Narcissus* in a Cincinnati garden and then again in an old colonial cemetery in Charleston, S.C. The plant features bright white bells on twelve- to eighteen-inch stems. The cultivar 'Gravetye Giant', also known as 'Gravetye', reaches eighteen to twenty-four inches tall. In Cleveland, it blooms from the beginning of May into June, and its foliage does not go dormant until the end of summer. Therefore, the plant needs to be interplanted with something taller so that the foliage doesn't overwhelm its shorter neighbors. You could use one of the ornamental grasses like *Chasmanthium latifolium* or a tall perennial such as *Cimicifuga racemosa*, whose foliage emerges well above the base of the stem.

Another favorite of mine is *Hyacinthoides hispanica*, formerly known as *Scilla campanulata* and *S. hispanica* (Wood Hyacinth, zone 5). The soft lavender bells of this beauty rest on eight- to twelve-inch stems and cheer the shady garden in May. Using the principle of color echo, I have combined *Hyacinthoides hispanica* with the rosy- lavender *Allium christophii* (Star of Persia, zones 4-8), white *Arabis* (Rock Cress, zones 3 to 7), which is almost finished blooming in May, and *Astilbe* (False Spirea, zones 5 to 7) species that bloom later.

Many wildflowers work well in shady gardens because they, too, bloom and go dormant before most trees foliate. *Mertensia virginica* (Virginia Bluebells, zone 3) has large, ovate leaves and sprays of blue flowers in April and May. By June or July at the latest, the plant has completely disappeared, so you must interplant it with something that will fill the space it has vacated. A good candidate is a fern, which pushes up its fronds while *Mertensia* is in bloom and then proceeds to uncurl and spread out while *Mertensia* goes dormant.

Another candidate for the spring shady garden is one of the *Trillium* (zones 4 to 8) species. The most common is *T. grandiflorum* (White-Wake-Robin, zone 5), which displays white flowers, but there are other species with purple, red or yellow blossoms. The foliage on all of these persists until late summer if they do not dry out.

A more delicate wildflower is *Anemonella thalictroides* (True Anemone, zone 4). The foliage of this plant is slightly lobed like that of *Thalictrum*. An umbel of tiny white flowers is held a few inches above the foliage. *Anemonella thalictroides* begins blooming in May and continues well into June with sufficient moisture. It also goes dormant thereafter, so I suggest interplanting it with a dwarf *Platycodon* or *Ceratostigma plumbaginoides* (Plumbago, zone 5), which usually don't foliate until the beginning of May.

Polygonatum

Galax urceolata, formerly known as *G.aphylla* (Wandflower, zone 5), is another underused wildflower. Reaching six to twelve inches tall, this plant features round, shiny evergreen leaves that are often used for floral arranging. A wand of white emerges from the foliage in May and June, and moisture is essential.

Most spring wildflowers are short, but *Polygonatum odoratum* 'Variegatum' (Variegated Solomon's Seal, zone 4) is eighteen to twenty-four inches tall. Its tiny white bells dangle from arching stems in May, but the best feature of this wildflower is its white-edged foliage, which lights up shadowed sites. Its rhizomes slowly ramble outward to form a lovely mass. Related species are taller.

Although few herbs succeed in the shade, there are two exceptions for spring. *Galium odoratum* (Sweet Woodruff, zone 5) makes an excellent deciduous groundcover. It has delicately cut foliage and tiny white flowers that bloom in May for a few weeks. In Europe, these flowers are used to make wine. *Viola odorata* (Sweet Violet, zone 6) is the other herb that thrives in the shade. In fact, gardeners are continually evicting violets because they are so prolific. Few people know this plant is an herb, but violets have both medicinal and culinary properties. Violets range in color from purple and blue to pink and white, depending on the cultivar. Technically, *V.labradorica* (Labrador Violet, zone 3) is not an herb but a perennial, yet I love it for its purple-tinged foliage and mauve flowers.

When it comes to perennials, one of my favorites is the Hellebore. *Helleborus orientalis* (Lenten Rose, zone 5) is the best known and easiest to grow. This beauty displays wide, leathery leaves that are divided into several segments. Its flowers vary greatly in color, from purple to pink to cream. The bloom time of Lenten Rose depends not only on the region in which it's grown, but also where it is planted on the site. This is related to the theory of microclimates. I have one large clump growing on the north side of the house, at the base of a *Pieris japonica* (Japanese Pieris, zone 4) with some protection, where it receives a few hours of morning sun and shade the rest of the day. This clump usually does not bloom until May. I have another clump in a south facing garden under an old Crabapple where the soil is warmed by winter sun, but shaded once the tree foliates. This clump usually blooms in March or early April.

H.foetidus (Bearsfoot Hellebore, zones 5-9) is more delicate in appearance. Its paler evergreen foliage is deeply divided into narrow leaflets, and its flowers are light green and more clustered than those of *H.orientalis*. I have added this plant to the area under the Crabapple and the variety in leaf shape, leaf color and bloom color creates an excellent textural combination. Some recent hybrization has led to the creation of cultivars with very dark, almost black foliage. Most noteworthy, so far, is *H.'Wester Flisk'*.

H.argutifolius (Corsican Hellebore, zones 6-8) is the least hardy of the *Hellebores* and is easily identified by its thick, prickly tri-segmented foliage. Its flowers are very similar to those of *H.foetidus*. I have never grown *H.niger* (Christmas Rose, zone 3) because it requires limey soil, which I do not have. Although called Christmas Rose, the plant rarely blooms that early.

A bright yellow April bloomer is *Doronicum orientale*, formerly known as *D.caucasium* (Caucasian Leopard's Bane, zone 5). This perennial displays many-rayed, daisy-type blooms, which sit on one- to two-foot stems above kidney-shaped foliage. Its only drawback is early dormancy. The plant could easily be interplanted with small to medium sized Hosta to fill the space by June.

Another perennial with the same dormancy problem is *Dicentra spectabilis* (Common Bleeding Heart, zone 6). This is a plant that my grandparents grew and I have childhood memories of a large bush three to four feet tall, although perennial encyclopedias frequently say it only grows up to two feet. (Was I so short that two feet looked tall?) This species has deeply cut, compound leaves and pink, heart-shaped flowers with dangling inner petals on long, arching stems. There is also a white cultivar, 'Alba', which may not be as vigorous.

The time of dormancy for *D.spectabilis* is determined by the moisture level of the soil. The longer the soil remains moist, the later in the summer dormancy occurs. You might try planting *D. spectabilis* behind a somewhat tall fall bloomer such as *Tricyrtis hirta* (Toad Lily, zone 5) or behind an evergreen such as *Chamaecyparis pisifera filifera* 'Mops' to hide what would be an empty space once you cut it down.

A shorter perennial that is somewhat evergreen is *Bergenia cordifolia* (Heartleaf Bergenia, zone 3). Its leathery, cabbage-like leaves usually turn bronz during winter. In spring, twelve-inch shoots bearing small clusters of white, pink or rose flowers appear. This is a plant that needs to be massed to be effective and should be adjacent to a delicately foliated neighbor like a fern or perhaps *Corydalis lutea* (Yellow Corydalis, zone 6). Although it is touted as a wonderful plant for shade, the only places where I have seen it looking worthy of inclusion in the garden are the American Northwest,

Canada and England. It has never lived up to my expectations. Perhaps you'll have better luck than I.

Brunnera macrophylla (Heartleaf Brunnera, zone 3) is very happy in the shade. Its leaves emerge in April and are followed in May with sprays of delicate, light blue flowers. As the flowers fade, the leaves enlarge until they are finally three times the size of the April blooms. It is important to space this plant accordingly. If sited optimally, *B. macrophylla* will reseed and create nice colonies.

Many hardy geraniums prefer full sun, but there are several species that are quite satisfied in partial shade. Among these are *Geranium dalmaticum* (Dalmatian Cranesbill, zone 5), *G. x magnificum* (Showy Geranium, zone 5), *G.phaeum* (Mourning Widow, zone 5), *G.platypetalum* (Broad-petaled Geranium, zone 6), *G.psilostemon* (Armenian Geranium, zone 6) and *G.sylvaticum* (Wood Cranesbill, zone 4). Of these, I have grown *G.dalmaticum*, only four to six inches tall, at the front of a border that gets morning sun. If it received less light, the plant would probably still bloom, but on taller stems. *G.phaeum* thrives in filtered light under my *Acer palmatum 'Butterfly'*.

G.macrorrhizum (Bigroot Geranium, zone 4) thrives in dry, partial shade and quickly covers ground, so much so that it could be used as a groundcover. I can attest to this. Its attractive foliage is deeply cut and somewhat lobed. The purple-magenta blossoms of the species have calyces that are "inflated like little balloons," according to Dr. Allan Armitage in his book "Herbaceous Perennial Plants." Cultivar blossoms range from white to pale pink to clear magenta. Bigroot Geranium grows twelve to fifteen inches tall and blooms in May. Its other great asset is its reddish foliage in the fall and winter.

I have used several cultivars of *G.sanguineum* (Bloody Cranesbill, zone 5) in my garden, some in full sun and others in partial shade. The species is sited in an east-facing bed under a Crabapple and has been so vigorous that I have had to arrest its growth with a spade and dig out a few seedlings. Its foliage is more delicate and deeply cut than that of most geraniums, and the plant only grows nine to twelve inches tall. Blooms are bright magenta, a color that can be difficult to work with, yet I successfully used it with the blue of *Polemonium caeruleum* (Jacob's Ladder, zone 4) until the slugs ate it and the white of *Actaea pachypoda*, formerly known as *A. alba* (White Baneberry, zone 3). Several cultivars have been added to the palette: many other purple/magentas, '*Album*', and '*Striatum*', formerly known as '*Lancastriense*'.

How long hardy geraniums bloom depends on a combination of geography and weather. The farther north and the cooler the summer, the longer they will bloom. One of the great frustrations of a hardy-geranium lover is reading that the plants bloom all summer in England. But here in the U.S., with a few exceptions, they hate heat and stop blooming as soon as temperatures soar. When temperatures dip in fall, the hardy geraniums sometimes bear a blossom or two.

Iris are desired in the garden not only for their lovely flowers, but also for their mostly linear foliage, which adds a different form to the garden. The lovely little spring *Iris cristata* (Crested Iris, zone 4) is a North American native with vigorous rhizomes that quickly create sizable clumps of short, strappy foliage. The pale blue standards above yellow falls bloom in May on six- to nine-inch stems. They look wonderful drifted through a woodland garden and tolerate heavy shade.

In the middle of May, *Trollius* (Globeflower, zones 4 to 7) species and cultivars are ablaze with yellow or orange flowers that look like small roses. After the petals drop, a very attractive seedhead that resembles a bracted ball is left above the deeply divided, palmate foliage. If the foliage becomes ratty looking, cut it back and new leaves will emerge. *Trollius* requires cool, moist soil in either fall sun or partial shade.

The last two spring perennials I want to mention are *Aquilegia* (Columbine, zones 2 to 8) and *Corydalis*. *Aquilegia* is another old-fashioned perennial, but it has been hybridized extensively. Somewhere in your shady garden, there must be room for at least one grouping of this genus. Many of the older varieties discovered in clients' gardens have double blossoms without spurs. The old-fashioned Columbine varieties seed prolifically and do not seem to be as vulnerable to leaf miner damage as the hybrids.

The newer selections have one of the widest ranges of color of any perennial with which I am acquainted. There are dwarf ones like *A.flabellata* 'Nana' (Dwarf Blue Fan Columbine, zone 3), with blue-green foliage and six-inch wide, violet-blue and white flowers, all the way up to the three-foot-tall *A.chrysantha* (Golden Columbine, zone 3), which features deep yellow flowers.

A perennial with similar, but smaller, foliage is *Corydalis lutea*. Its blooms are clusters of thin, tubular segments held on wiry stems just above the foliage. You can start with one plant and, within a few years, it will randomly seed throughout your garden. This is one of the longest-blooming shade perennials I know. *C.lutea* prefers moist shade and spreads even more rapidly on that type of site, but mine seems to be perfectly content in dry shade. Its cousin, *C.ochroleuca* (Creamy Corydalis, zone 5), displays cream-colored blossoms and is the same in all other respects, except that it is much more difficult to obtain.

Three vines that bloom in partial shade are *Akebia quinata* (Fiveleaf Akebia, zone 5), some of the small-flowered *Clematis* and *Ampelopsis brevipedunculata* (Porcelainberry Vine, zone 5). *A.quinata* has very attractive, five-part foliage and is quite vigorous. In May, the plant boasts tiny purple flowers – so tiny that it is easy to miss them if you are not close. Mine have never fruited, although I have read that the blossoms are followed by purple pods. I also have *Akebia quinata* 'Alba' and I think this is even better for a shade site because the white flowers are much more visible. It is an extremely adaptable plant, taking full sun or shade, dry or moist soil. *Ampelopsis* has coarse foliage and unobtrusive green flowers; its great merit is its berries, which highlight the fall garden. It too is very adaptable and a vigorous grower.

There are three species of spring- flowering clematis: *C.alpina* (Alpine Clematis, zone 5), *C. macropetala* (Downy Clematis, zone 5) and *C.montana* (Anemone Clematis, zone 6). These bloom with a half day of sun or with all day filtered light. Only a few cultivars require full sun, and Raymond Evison's book, "Making the Most of Clematis," is the best authority I know. *C.alpina* and *C.macropetala* have bell-type blooms in blue, white or pink, while *C.montana* has small, flat blooms that are either white or shades of pink. Like *Akebia quinata*, they all bloom in May. They also have attractive seed heads.

As you can see, there are some old favorites as well as new species that welcome spring in a shady garden.

Filling the Shadows with Light:
Summer

No matter what the season, bulbs and perennials can light up shady sites and provide year-round beauty and texture to otherwise dull, dimly lit sites. It can't be said often enough that we need to change our way of thinking, to see the shady garden as an asset rather than a liability. Let's look at some of the plant varieties that put on a display during the summer season and help bring light to a shady spot.

I know that the calendar says summer doesn't arrive until June 21, but as far as I'm concerned, it arrives at the beginning of June. Few perennial bulbs fit this time period, but *Lilium* (Lily, zones 3 to 9) certainly does. When deeply planted, about eight inches, in well-drained soil and when heavily fertilized, lilies tolerate partial shade. There are so many types and cultivars, you can have them blooming in your garden from June to September. Plant heights range from two to six feet, and bloom colors include variations of white, yellow, red, orange and pink.

Another bulb that blooms during this time period is *Allium senescens* (Ornamental Onion, zone 5). Most people think of this plant as a perennial, but its root system is a tight cluster of small bulbs that can be carefully broken apart to create new plants. This species has lavender-pink, twelve-inch umbels in July. Unlike other *Allium* species, *A.senescens* is sterile. Its foliage is a two-inch-wide strap with rounded ends and always looks attractive. *A.s. var. glaucum* (Twisted Ornamental Onion, zone 5) is similar, although it is shorter and has twisted gray-green leaves. Both are perfectly happy in partial shade and tolerate dry shade.

Summer wildflowers best suited to a shady garden are *Hesperis matronalis* (Sweet Rocket or Dame's Rocket, zone 3), *Actaea* (Baneberry, zones 2 to 6) and *Lobelia cardinalis* (Cardinal Flower, zone 2). *Hesperis matronalis* is actually a self-seeding annual, but because it appears each year, the plant resembles a perennial. Its coarse leaves and two- to three-foot-tall habit make it a candidate for the middle or back of the border, but its fragrant white or purple flowers amply compensate, blooming in late May and continuing into June and July. In years with cool summers, *Hesperis* will continue to bloom sparsely into October, particularly if deadheaded.

Actaea rubra (Red Baneberry, zone 3) and *A.pachypoda* are two species of the Baneberry family that lend majesty to the shade garden with their large, compound foliage. Reaching two to four feet tall, the plants bear fringed, white blossoms on long racemes in April. During summer, their green stalks turn rosy red. In August and September, they develop oval, clustered berries that are very showy in the shade due to their strong colors. The berries of *A.rubra* are red, and those of *A. pachypoda* are white. Humusy, moist soil in shade is essential to the health of these North American woodland natives.

Lobelia can be classified as either wildflowers or perennials. *L.cardinalis* (Cardinal Flower, zones 2-9) and *L.siphilitica* (Big Blue Lobelia, zones 4-8) are two North American natives usually found near water. Both species like a constant source of moisture, but not boggy soil. They grow two to four feet tall and bloom in August on bracted racemes. Partial shade is necessary for their survival; in particular, *L.cardinalis* must receive afternoon shade. I have read that they are short-lived plants and should, therefore, be divided every few years.

There are some hybrids of *L.cardinalis* that have striking bronze or reddish foliage that is so bright, the plants are perceptible even from afar. The hybrid *L.x. gerardii* 'Vedrariensis' (zone 5) is very similar in appearance and culture to the others. A distinguishing feature is its glowing purple color, which I find entrancing. I have found that this species does not like as much moisture as *L.cardinalis*; in fact, too much moisture causes root rot.

Heuchera (Alumroot, Zone 4) is another American native that I find very useful in a shady garden. Most species, particularly *H.sanguinea* (Coralbells, Zone 6), have bright red and pink flowers that bloom for at least a month, usually beginning in mid to late May and going well into June. *H.s.*'Chatterbox', an old cultivar, has bloomed for me into July. The tiny, bell-like florets climb twelve- to eighteen-foot spires, which are held well above the scalloped, evergreen foliage. A newer cultivar, *'Raspberry Regal'*, is said to be another very strong bloomer.

H.americana (American Alumroot, Zone 4) and *H.micrantha* (Small Flowered Alumroot, Zone 5) are generally taller than other *Heuchera* species, reaching up to thirty inches tall, and have off-white flowers that are not nearly as attractive. Yet, these groups have been hybridized for their colored foliage. Some of the newer hybrids are now being bred for flower color as well, and pink is showing up again. These plants cry out for partial shade and humusy, well-drained soil.

Amsonia tabernaemontana (Willow Amsonia, Zone 3) is another native that works well in shady spots. Its pale-blue, starry florets only last for a few weeks, but its foliage

Heuchera

almost looks like an ornamental grass. It quickly forms an impenetrable mass so weeds will never invade it. *A. tabernaemontana* grows one foot to three feet tall, but you can prune it after it blooms to keep it shorter if desired. Moist soil and partial shade is ideal, but I find that the plant is also somewhat drought tolerant. Following my cool palette, I have planted it in combination with *Fragaria frei 'Pink Panda'* (Pink Panda Strawberry, zone 3), *Hosta plantaginea* (Fragrant Hosta, zone 3), *H.sieboldiana 'Frances Williams'* (Frances Williams Hosta, zone 3), *Filipendula vulgaris (hexapetala) 'Flore Pleno'* (Flore Pleno Double Dropwort, zone 3), *Rosa 'Climbing Iceberg'* and *Rosa rugosa 'Moje Hammerberg'*.

When sited correctly, *Aruncus* species, especially *A. dioicus* (zone 4), are special giants. Reaching six feet tall with an equal spread, *A. dioicus* features serrated, tri-pinnate foliage and long, creamy white plumes that create an imposing specimen. At the opposite end of the scale is *A.aethusifolius* (Dwarf Goatsbeard, zone 4), a delicate Lilliputian that reaches only eight to twelve inches tall. In between is the cultivar *A.dioicus 'Kneiffii'* (zone 3), which grows up to three feet. *Aruncus* (Goatsbeard, zone 3) must have a moist, shady site to thrive. Too much sun causes the leaves to burn and insufficient moisture browns the edges

Digitalis also grows well in partial shade, particularly at the edges of a woodland with high shade. The wonderfully tall, purple and pink spires of *D.purpurea* (Common Foxglove, zones 4 to 8) emerge through rosettes of large, hairy leaves. It is easy to forget how large the foliage grows and not leave enough space between the plants. This species is a biennial; if you plant it two years in a row you should have blooming plants every year thereafter. Less well-known and utilized are the truly perennial species such as *D.grandiflora*, formerly known as *D.ambigua* (Yellow Foxglove, zone 4), which has long sessile leaves, pale yellow florets and a height of two to three feet.

I don't know why *Astrantia major* (Greater Masterwort, zone 6) isn't planted more, but I would highly recommend using it. Its common name is no indication of its beauty. The plant actually resembles a strawflower but is generally more delicately colored, either greenish-white or pale pink. There is a cultivar, *A.m.'Lars'*, which is dark red, and a species, *A. carniolica 'Rubra'* (Lesser Masterwort, zone 6), which is maroon-red. There is also a spate of dark red cultivars coming on the market, many with the word ruby in their name. Two to three flowers on each stem are held well above the deeply divided, palmate foliage. Designing cutting gardens for shade is not easy, but the blooms of *Astrantia* last at least two weeks in a vase. I grow several cultivars in varying amounts of shade and all do quite well, although those that get the most moisture do the best.

Astilbe x arendsii (Astilbe Hybrid, zone 6) hybrids generally range in size from eighteen to thirty-six inches tall and wide and are available in varying shades of white, pink and red. The red-flowering hybrids are usually characterized by red stems, which add to their beauty in the garden. Some blooms are listed as purple, but most of them are really a lavender-pink. Catalogs list these plants as having different bloom times, but they usually bloom in June. Their deeply divided foliage is an asset to the garden at any time, as long as the plant has enough moisture. Like *Aruncus*, if *Astilbe x arendsii* hybrids are allowed to dry out, the edges brown and crisp.

A.chinensis (Chinese Astilbe, zone 5) is a small plant that blooms later in the season. The smallest variety is *A.c.'Pumila'*, which reaches only eight to twelve inches tall. The largest, *A.c.'King Albert'*, is a new introduction I have only read about. It supposedly grows to thirty-six inches. Most *A.chinensis* cultivars are fifteen to eighteen inches tall. Unlike other *Astilbe* species, *A.chinensis* is not a clumper, but spreads slowly and colonizes. Its spikes are stiffer and thicker than those of *A.x arendsii*. The species holds color for about a month, but can be a presence in the garden for much longer if you don't cut off the spikes after they turn beige.

Astilbe simplicifolia (Star Astilbe, zone 4) has shinier leaves than any other species. It, too, tends to be on the small side, reaching anywhere from ten to sixteen inches tall. *A.s.'Sprite'* displays arching, pale-pink plumes over delicate, dark-green foliage and was the Perennial Plant Association's Perennial Plant of the Year in 1994. *A. thunbergii* (zone 4) is a larger species, usually growing three feet to four feet tall. This plant features distinctive drooping plumes. *A.t.'Ostrich Plume'*, also known as 'Straussenfeder', is probably the best-known cultivar of this species, but my favorite is *A.t.'Professor Van der Wielen'*, which boasts bright white plumes that bloom in June and July.

One of the longest blooming perennials for the summer shade garden is *Dicentra eximia* (Fringed Bleeding-Heart, zone 3). Only twelve inches tall, its delicate foliage has a ferny appearance that complements the heart-shaped flowers held above it. This perennial has been hybridized to produce varying shades of red and pink flowers, as well as white ones. I love the cultivar *D.e.'Langtrees'*, which boasts white flowers and blue-green foliage. All *Dicentra* species perform well throughout the summer as long as they have rich, moist soil. Soil that is too moist, however, causes the plants to rot.

Another long bloomer is *Campanula persicifolia* (Peachleaf Bellflower, zone 3). It has the typical cup-shaped blooms all the way up its two- to three-foot stem and can be found in various shades of blue and white. The only drawback to this plant is the need to constantly pinch off the faded blossoms, which really detract from its beauty.

Is there anyone who hasn't used *Hemerocallis* (Daylily, zones 3 to 9) in the shade garden? Although any color except blue is available, two in particular are suited for a shady spot: white and red. White not only shows up well in a shady site, it seems to add light to the dimness. One of the best white daylily cultivars is *'Ice Carnival'* but there are others that also work well. Red daylilies benefit from being sited in afternoon shade because the shade prevents the color from fading. Although daylilies will bloom in the shade, they will not bloom as prolifically as when sited in full sun. Try to give them at least a full morning of sun.

My signature plant in shady gardens is *Cimicifuga racemosa* (Fairy Candles, zone 4). This impressive perennial grows five feet tall and doesn't need staking until after it blooms, when the heavy seed pods sometimes pull it down. Its large, divided foliage begins partway up the stem. In July, a tall spire covered with white buttons appears, and gradually the buttons open to become tiny flowers not unlike those of *Veronica*.

Cimicifuga stays in bloom for at least a month. Its imposing presence remains, however, until it is blackened by frost. Even though *Cimicifuga* is a large plant, it looks best if planted in a group of at least five. At Chanticleer, an old estate garden in the Philadelphia area, I saw a long border (at least 200 feet) of *C. ramosa* (Branched Bugbane, zone 3) against a stone wall. It was absolutely breathtaking. *C. ramosa* is a species that has three selections distinguished by their purple-tinged foliage: *C.r. var.atropurpurea*, *C.r.'Brunette'* and *C.r.'Hillside Black Beauty'*.

Hosta, of course, is an integral part of the shade garden. The choices are mind-boggling in terms of color, texture, shape and size. The only problem I have encountered with *Hosta* is the ubiquitous slug. Instead of attempting to kill the pests, it is easier to choose *Hosta* that are not as tempting to them, i.e. *Hosta* with thick foliage.

You may not think of *Rudbeckia* (Coneflower, zones 3 to 7) as a shade perennial, but it grows almost anywhere. Everyone is familiar with *Rudbeckia fulgida var. sullivantii* 'Goldsturm' (Goldsturm Coneflower, zone 4), but what about *R.triloba* (Brown-eyed Susan, Zone 5)? This is a plant worth knowing. This native is a biennial that grows two to three feet tall. It is multibranched and blooms at the same time as 'Goldsturm' but *R. triloba* has a softer look because the flowers are smaller.

I love *Platycodon* (Balloon Flower, zone 4) and use the tall species in my sunny garden but I think the dwarf varieties are better suited to the shade garden because the taller ones flop in the shade. It's difficult to flop if you're only fifteen to eighteen inches tall like the cultivars 'Hime Murasaki', which is lavender-blue, and 'Misato Purple'. *Platycodon* appreciates a half-day of sun. It is very long-lived and rarely needs division. The flowers bloom in August and September and look like balloons before they open; upon opening, they become cup-shaped. Like *Campanula persicifolia*, *Platycodon* looks best if the faded blossoms are pinched off. Because *Platycodon* foliates very late, you might want to mark the space in some way so that you don't accidentally dig the plant up in early spring.

Platycodon

The last summer perennial I want to mention is *Aconitum carmichaelii* (Azure Monkshood, zone 3). Its two- to three-foot spires of violet-blue grace the garden in August and September. The foliage is deeply divided and quite beautiful. This species grows in either full sun or partial shade with adequate moisture. Again, too much moisture causes rot. Although I love *A. carmichaelii* and couldn't live without it, I have found it difficult to find a site where the plant gets the exact amount of moisture needed for optimal growth.

Ornamental grasses add a loose texture to the shady garden that few other plants can match. *Luzula nivea* (Snowy Woodrush, zone 5) is one of my favorites. Its narrow, evergreen foliage is covered with white hairs that give it its name. In June, showy spikes of white flowers rise high above a twelve-inch mound of foliage and gradually fade to beige. I usually cut off the spikes in early August when virtually only the stalk is left. I have successfully grown *L.nivea* in midday sun and in partial shade.

Another outstanding grass is *Chasmanthium latifolium* (Northern Sea Oats, zone 4). This is a larger plant, growing three to four feet tall if moist and only two to three feet if dry; it demands partial shade. Its foliage is wider than that of *L.nivea* and becomes coppery in fall and brown in winter. The oat-like inflorescensces appear in July and make me feel like I'm in the country or at the beach. Later in fall, when the oats dry and turn brown, they rattle in the wind. If you're searching for an unorthodox plant for a foundation grouping, I'd suggest trying *Chasmanthium*. It will need to be pruned to the ground in early spring before new growth emerges, but if you front it with *Narcissus*, it comes to life while the *Narcissus* are going into dormancy.

A third grass to try is *Deschampsia caespitosa* (Tufted Hair Grass, zone 5). Very narrow leaves and pale-green, airy panicles in June turn pale gold shortly after emerging, giving this one- to three-foot-tall grass a very delicate character. It looks best when massed and backlit by early morning or late afternoon sun. *Deschampsia* needs rich, moist soil and light or high shade.

A more adaptable grass is *Liriope* (Lilyturf, zones 4 to 8). It is aptly named, particularly *L.spicata* (Creeping Lilyturf, zone 4), which is a creeper rather than a clumper, like *L. muscari* (Big Blue Lily-Turf, zone 6). The flowers of *L.spicata* do not rise above the foliage and are thus not easily seen, but the mat of evergreen is worth that drawback. *L.muscari* has several cultivars that have variegated foliage, larger flowers or white flowers, such as *L.m.'Monroe's White'*. Both species tolerate heavy shade.

Among the best flowering vines for the shade are *Clematis*. Many of the large-flowered Clematis bloom well with only a half-day of sun or good light all day. I have grown several cultivars, including C. 'Silver Moon', which glows in the shade as it encircles an old stump. Less well-known are the small-flowered Clematis species, which are fairly adaptable to varying amounts of sun. C.x triternata 'Rubro-marginata' (zone 6) features tiny, open stars that are a maroon-white bicolor on very lacy foliage. It is covered with hundreds of blossoms in July. Other Clematis species to consider are C.viticella (Italian Clematis, zone 6) and C.texensis (Scarlet Clematis, zone 5).

Only a few herbs can be used in the shade in summer. One is Mentha suaveolens 'Variegata' (Pineapple Mint, zone 6), which I have seen used very effectively as a border at the Chicago Botanic Garden. This is one to grow for its beautiful foliage rather than its flowers, which are fluffy, somewhat weedy-looking spikes. All of the mints thrive in moist, partial shade, but Pineapple Mint is the prettiest. They all benefit from frequent cutting and division to keep them compact. An herb that is grown for its stature, and its unusual maroon flowers is Angelica gigas (Purple-stem Angelica, zone 4), a four-foot-tall plant with huge, palmate leaves. This bi-ennial blooms in July and August and reseeds freely.

There are many possibilities and opportunities for turning the shady summer garden into a place of both excitement and refuge. When the temperatures and humidity drive us toward the shady spots in our garden, let's enjoy the creative atmosphere we have designed through the use of these plants.

Next, we will look to the fall and winter season plants for shady gardens.

Filling the Shadows with Light:
Fall and Winter

As discussed in the previous articles, no matter what the season, herbaceous plants can light up shady sites and provide year-round beauty and texture to otherwise dull, dimly lit sites. Fall and winter gardens have the poor reputation of being dull or just plain dead. But this simply isn't the case. Let's look at some of the plants that add life, movement and color to the fall and winter months.

Rarely seen, but so much fun to plant, are the fall-blooming Crocus *speciosus* (Showy Crocus, zones 5 to 7) and *Colchicum* (Autumn Crocus, zones 4 to 8). Most people don't even know that these plants exist, so when they see a flower that looks like a crocus, they are completely puzzled. Showy Crocus are four to six inches tall and come in shades of white, lavender-blue and rich blue with bright orange stigma. I have some that pop up between parsley plants, but they can be planted in between any other relatively small perennial or an ornamental grass like *Carex* (Sedge, zones 3 to 9).

Colchicum, although the same size as Autumn Crocus, is showier, particularly the cultivar '*Waterlily*', one of several doubles. The plant blooms anytime from September to October in shades of white, pink and purple, although there is one yellow species, *C.luteum*. Similar to the habit of *Arum italicum* '*Pictum*', its large, strappy leaves appear in spring and then go dormant. It is never dug up by critters because it is poisonous. Perhaps we see *Colchicum* so seldom because of its expense. It does, however, naturalize in rich, well-drained soil in partial shade. *Colchicum*, like *Crocus speciosus*, benefits from being planted between perennials that will hold the blooms up since they tend to flop, particularly after rain.

A few years ago, a friend brought me some seedlings of *Solidago caesia* (Shade or Wreath Goldenrod, zone 4). The plant only grows two feet tall and, with its linear leaves and tiny golden flowers, has a very delicate appearance, unlike that of any other Goldenrod. Those few seedlings have turned into a large colony. If you don't want it to reseed, you have to cut *S.caesia* down as soon as it finishes flowering in September and October. My plants have thrived with only filtered light and fairly dry soil.

The other wildflower I would highly recommend for the fall shade garden is *Aster divaricatus* (White Wood Aster, zone 4). As an American woodland native, it is perfectly happy in partial shade but will also grow in full sun. It is a well-branched plant with very nice heart-shaped leaves and only grows eighteen to twenty-four inches tall. In September, hundreds of tiny white daisies appear and last well into October. The seed heads and the branching structure are also attractive. I do not cut this perennial down until early spring.

The queen of the fall shade garden is *Anemone x. hybrida* (Hybrid Anemone, zone 4) and its related species, *A. vitifolia* 'Robustissima' (Grapeleaf Anemone, zone 5) and *A. hupehensis var. japonica* (Japanese Anemone, zone 6). There is a great deal of confu-sion about which ones are which, but for our purposes, it is irrelevant. Their habits are very similar, and they feature large, divided or lobed foliage. All grow two to three feet tall, which makes them an excellent background for whatever is planted in front of them. Blooms appear in late August to early September in singles or doubles, and in shades of white and pink, according to the chosen cultivar. *A. hupehensis* 'September Charm' (September Charm

Anemone

Anemone, zone 4) displays rosy-pink blossoms that are darker on the outside than the inside, giving the impression of a bicolor. My experience is that this cultivar grows under almost any circumstances, including a great deal of shade.

A fall-blooming perennial that would be lovely adjacent to or near *Anemone* varieties is *Tricyrtis* (Japanese Toad Lily). Again, I have found a great deal of confusion among the experts as to the differences between two species, *T. hirta* and *T. formosana*, which is also known as *T. stolonifera* (Formosa Toad Lily, zone 5). Supposedly, the most important difference is that *T. hirta* is a clumper and *T. formosana* is stoloniferous. If this is true, most of the plants I have were mislabeled. I thought I purchased *T. hirta* but what I have is stoloniferous and formed a beautiful mass with pale purple flowers dotted with darker purple spots (sounds like *T. formosana* to me). Despite the mixup, I love what I have and look forward to its blossoms each year.

Both species are Asian woodland natives. Their foliage is somewhat linear, but whorled around the two- to three-foot-tall, slightly arching stems. The small, orchid-like blossoms emerge at the tips of the stems and in the axils of the leaves. Blossom color varies from white to pale purple, with different colored spots depending on the cultivar and species. One cultivar, 'Albo-marginata' has white-edged margins, which is always a bonus in the shade.

An unusual fall perennial is *Arum italicum* 'Pictum' (Italian Arum, zone 5), a European woodland native. This plant boasts spectacular foliage for a shady spot, featuring arrow-shaped leaves with large white spots. These leaves emerge in spring and go dormant in midsummer. In their place, in late summer, springs up a twelve- to eighteen-inch stalk of large, orange-red berries that are so bright, they can be seen even in deep shade. Massed, this plant is absolutely incredible.

We talked about *Hosta* earlier, but now I want to bring a few late bloomers to your attention. Both *Hosta tardiva* (zone 3) and *H. tardiflora* (Tardiflora Hosta, zone 3) delay their bloom until September. Both are small plants. *H. tardiva* has small, heart-shaped leaves that form a mound only fifteen inches tall with violet scapes. *H. tardiflora* has shiny, dark-green leaves on ten-inch mounds and blue-suffused white flower scapes. Either species would work well as an edger. Breeders are also developing reblooming *Hosta*. In 1995, I saw one called '*Snow Flakes*' at the Trompenberg Arboretum in Rotterdam. It had pure white flowers that resembled a small *H.plantaginea* blossom.

I love *Cimicifuga* in the summer garden. Happily, there is a fall-blooming species, *C.simplex* (Kamchatka Bugbane, zone 3), not quite as tall at four feet, which has arching rather than upright spires of white flowers. This species, however, does not bloom until October, meaning it may not bloom before frost blackens it. In addition, *C.ramosa* (Black-Leaved Snakeroot) and its cultivars bloom in late September and early October and are fragrant as well. '*Hillside Black Beauty*' is probably the darkest of the cultivars but all of them add a color to the fall garden that is usually missing.

Most *Calamagrostis* (Feather Reed Grass, zone 5) are early summer bloomers, but *C.arundinacea var.brachytricha* (Fall-blooming Reed Grass, zone 5) doesn't bloom until September or October. It has feathery flower spikes that emerge green and are blushed with pink. They turn beige in late fall and look silvery if backlit. The foliage is a rich green until frost, when it turns beige. This is a clumper that grows three to four feet tall in full sun or partial shade in moist or slightly dry soil. This is the tallest of the grasses that do really well in the shade.

There are some fall-blooming *Clematis* species that work well in the fall garden. The best-known is *C.terniflora*, formerly known as *C.maximowicziana* (Sweet Autumn Clematis, zone 6). Its small, white, fragrant, starry blossoms are not quite so prolific in the shade, but it does still bloom and produce silvery seed heads afterward. When mine was competing with Hawthorn roots in a very dry, narrow site, the bloom was sparse. As soon as the tree was felled by a heavy November snow, the *Clematis* bloom was increased immeasurably. Be prepared to have this vine grow twenty to thirty feet tall.

Very different in form are the flowers of *C.tangutica* (Golden Clematis, zone 5) and *C.orientalis* (Oriental Clematis, zone 6). The down-facing, bell-shaped flowers of *C.orientalis* are nearly closed while those of *C.tangutica* are open. Both have lovely whorled seed heads.

Ampelopsis brevipedunculata has coarse foliage and unobtrusive green flowers; its great merit is its berries, which highlight the fall garden. I love to watch the berries' transformation from a green, so pale it's almost white, to turquoise. Their unusual color is a joy to see on a weathered fence in the shade of a Hawthorn or Crabapple. In my garden, *Ampelopsis* gets only filtered light in the morning and very little light in the afternoon. The cultivar *'Elegans'* has leaves that are streaked with white, a desirable attribute in the shade. Other vines with outstanding berries for fall shady sites are *A.acontifolia* (Monks Hood Vine, zone 4) and *Celastrus scandens* (American Bittersweet, zone 4). Be prepared to keep *C.scandens* under control (heavy pruning in the spring) and remember that it is primarily dioecious.

Color in the shade is an attainable objective with myriad choices to help you get there. My list of suggestions is far from inclusive, although I have discussed what must seem like hundreds of plants. It's important to experiment, because conditions vary so greatly across this country and what doesn't work for me may work for you. Despite different regions and microclimates, working with shady spots remains the same. By choosing the right plants, you can turn any dim landscape into a world of color, texture and light.

Tables of Plants by Season

SPRING

BOTANICAL NAME	COMMON NAME
Akebia quinata	Fiveleaf Akebia
Ampelopsis brevipedunculata	Porcelain Vine
Anemonella thalictroides	Rue Anemone
Aquilegia	Columbine
Aquilegia chrysantha	Golden Columbine
Aquilegia flabellata 'Nana'	Dwarf Fan Columbine
Bergenia cordifolia	Heartleaf Bergenia
Brunnera macrophylla	Heartleaf Forget-Me-Not
Chionodoxa	Glory-of-the-Snow
Clematis alpina	Alpine Cclematis
Clematis macropetala	Downy Clematis
Clematis montana	Anemone Clematis
Corydalis lutea	Yellow Corydalis
Corydalis ochroleuca	Creamy Corydalis
Crocus chrysanthus	Snow Crocus
Crocus vernus	Dutch Crocus
Dicenta spectabllis	Common Bleeding Heart
Dicentra spectabllis 'Alba'	Common Bleeding Heart
Doronicum orientale	Caucasian Leopard's Bane
(Formerly known as *D.caucasicum*)	
Eranthis hyemalis	Winter Aconite
Galanthus nivalis	Snow Drop
Galax urceolata	Wandflower
(Formerly known as *G.aphylla*)	
Galium odoratum	Sweet Woodruff
Geranium dalmaticum	Dalmation Cranesbill
Geranium macrorrhizum	Bigroot Geranium
Geranium phaeum	Mourning Widow
Geranium platypetalum	Broad-petaled Geranium
Geranium psilostemon	Armenian Geranium
Geranium sanguineum	Bloody Cranesbill
Geranium sylvaticum	Wood Cranesbill
Geranium x magnificum	Showy Geranium
Helleboros argutifolius	Corsican Hellebore
Helleborus foetidus	Bear's Foot Hellebore

SPRING (cont'd.)

BOTANICAL NAME	COMMON NAME
Helleborus niger	Christmas Rose
Helleborus orientalis	Lenten Rose
Hyacinthoides hispanica	Wood Hyacinth
(Formerly *Scilla campanulata* and *S.hispanica*)	
Iris cristata	Crested Iris
Leucojum aestivum	Summer Snowflake
Leucojum aestivum 'Gravetye Giant'	Gravetye Giant Summer Snowflake
Mertensia virginica	Virginia Bluebells
Muscari armeniacum	Grape Hyacinth
Muscari latifolium	
Narcissus	Daffodil
Narcissus 'February Gold'	February Gold Daffodil
Narcissus 'Ice Wings'	Ice Wings Daffodil
Narcissus 'Jack Snipe'	Jack Snipe Daffodil
Narcissus cyclamineus	
Polygonatum odoratum 'Variegatum'	Variegated Solomon's Seal
Puschkinia scilloides var. Libanotica	Striped Squill
(Formerly known as *P.libanotica*)	
Scilla siberica	Siberian Squill
Trillium	
Trillium grandiflorum	White Wake-Robin
Trollius	Globeflower
Viola labradorica	Labrador Violet
Viola odorata	Sweet Violet

SUMMER

BOTANICAL NAME	COMMON NAME
Aconitum carmichaelii	Azure Monkshood
Actaea pachypoda (alba)	White Baneberry
Actaea rubra	Red Baneberry
Allium senescens	Ornamental Onion
Allium senescens var. glaucum	Twisted Ornamental Onion
Amsonia tabernaemontana	Willow Amsonia
Angelica gigas	Purple-stem Angelica
Aruncus aethusifolius	Dwarf Goat's Beard
Aruncus dioicus	Goat's Beard
Aruncus dioicus 'Kneffii'	
Astilbe chinensis	Chinese Astilbe

SUMMER (cont'd.)

BOTANICAL NAME **COMMON NAME**

Astilbe chinensis 'Pumila'
Astilbe simplicifolia 'Sprite'
Astilbe thunbergii – 'Ostrich Plume' (also known as 'Straussenfeder')
Astilbe thunbergii – Professor Van de Wielen'
Astilbe x arendsii ....Astilbe hybrid
Astrantia carniolica 'Rubra' ....Lesser Masterwort
Astrantia major ....Greater Masterwort
Astrantia major 'Lars'
Campanula persicifolia ....Peachleaf Bellflower
Chasmanthium latifolium.....................Northern Sea Oats
Cimicifuga racemosa.............................Fairy Candles
Cimicifuga ramosa.................................Branched Bugbane
Cimicifuga ramosa 'Brunette'
Cimicifuga ramosa var.atropurpurea
Clematis 'Silver Moon'
Clematis texensis ....Scarlet Clematis
Clematis viticella ....Italian Clematis
Clematis x triternata 'Rubro-marginata'
Deschampsia caespitosa ....Tufted Hair Grass
Dicentra eximia ....Fringed Bleeding Heart
Dicentra eximia 'Langtrees'
Digitalis
Digitalis grandiflora ....Yellow Foxglove
   (Formerly known as D.ambigua)
Digitalis purpurea ....Common Fxglove
Hemerocallis...Daylily
Hemerocallis 'Ice Carnival'
Hesperis matronalis...............................Sweet or Dame's Rocket
Heuchera americana...............................American Alumroot
Heuchera micrantha ....Small Flowered Alumroot
Heuchera sanguinea ....Coralbells
Heuchera sanguinea 'Chatterbox'
Hosta ....Plantain Lily
Lilium..Lily
Liriope muscari......................................Big Blue Lilyturf
Liriope muscari 'Monroe's White'
Liriope spicata ....Creeping Lilyturf
Lobelia cardinalis..................................Cardinal Flower
Lobelia siphilltica ....Big Blue Lobelia

Lobelia x gerardii 'Vedrarensis' ....Hybrid Purple Lobelia
Luzula nivea.......................................Snowy Woodrush
Mentha suaveolens 'Variegata' ....Pineapple Mint
Platycodon...Balloon Flower
Platycodon 'Hime Murasaki'
Platycodon 'Misato Purple'
Rudbeckia...Coneflower
   Rudbeckia fulgida var.sullvantii 'Goldsturm'
Rudbeckia triloba ....Brown-eyed Susan

FALL

BOTANICAL NAME   COMMON NAME

Ampelopsis aconitifolia.........................Monks Hood Vine
Ampelopsis brevipedunculata ....Porcelainberry Vine
Anemone hupehensis ....September Charm
   'September Charm' ....Anemone
Anemone hupehensis var. ....Japanese Anemone
   japonica
Anemone vitifolia ....Robustissima Grape-Leaf Anemone
   'Robustissima'
Anenome x hybrida...............................Japanese Anemone
Arum italicum 'Pictum' ....Italian Arum
Aster divaricatus.................................White Wood Aster
Calamagrostis arundinacea ....Fall Blooming
   var. brachytricha..............................Reed Grass
Celastrus scandens...............................American Bittersweet
Cimicifuga simplex...............................Karnchatka Bgbane
Clematis orientalis ....Oriental Clematis
Clematis tangutica ....Golden Clematis
Clematis terniflora ....Sweet Autumn Clematis
   (Formerly known as C.maximowicziana)
Colchicum ....Autumn Crocus
Crocus speciosus ....Fall-Blooming Crocus
Hosta 'Snow Flakes'
Hosta tardiflora ....Tardiflora Hosta
Hosta tardiva......................................Late-Blooming Hosta
Solidago caesia....................................Shade Goldenrod
Tricytis 'Albo-marginata'
Tricytis formosana................................Formosa Toad Lily
   (also known as T.stolonifera)
Tricytis hirta ....Japanese Toad Lily

Filling the Shadows with Light: Woody Ornamentals for the Shady Garden

Although I am not alone in obsessing about perennials and ornamental grasses, I want to stress how important the woody ornamentals are. They provide the "bones" and background of our landscapes, whether sunny or shady. There are too many woody ornamentals that bloom in the shade to mention them all, but I will suggest some of my favorites, which all have more than one season of interest.

The first is *Fothergilla gardenii* (Dwarf Fothergilla, zones 5-8). Because this plant is only two to three feet tall, it is an excellent candidate for small gardens. Its other virtues include blue-green foliage, which looks brilliant in fall if the plant receives some sun, and fragrant, white, bottlebrush-type flowers in April or May. For a larger space, *Fothergilla major* (Large Fothergilla), which grows six to ten feet tall, could be used. For maximum flowering and fall color, site this plant where it will receive morning sun. Fothergilla is a native to the Southeastern United States but will flourish in Ohio if supplied with moist, well-drained, acid to neutral soil.

Another woody with similar flowers is *Clethra alnifolia* (Summersweet, zones 4-9). This plant features mildly fragrant blooms in July that are either white or pink. Fall foliage is a soft golden-yellow. Recently, we have been blessed with a new cultivar called *'Ruby Spice'*, which has rosy pink racemes, a vast improvement on the pale pink of *Clethra a.'Rosea'*. The genus usually grows four to five feet tall, but the dwarf cultivar *C.a.'Hummingbird'* is only two to three feet tall, yet it still has all of the assets of the species. This woody is native to the eastern half of the country. It is naturally found in wet sites but will grow well in any irrigated garden.

Hydrangea arborescens 'Annabelle' (Smooth Hydrangea, zones 3 [with protection] to 9) is a four-season plant that grows three to five feet tall with an equal spread. It begins blooming in June and continues to send out new, large panicles during the summer. They emerge apple-green and become white shortly thereafter. Later in the summer, they fade to pink, and then turn beige in the fall and remain on the plant until the following spring if not cut off for arrangements. The upright stalks make an architectural statement even if the winter wind blows away some of the panicles. This *Hydrangea* flowers on new wood; therefore, cut it to the ground each year in early spring. Because the flower heads are so large and heavy, they tend to drag the branches to the ground. If an upright habit is desired, place a grow-through grid over the plant just after spring pruning and let the new growth come up through the grid, raising the grid as the stems elongate. *Hydrangea arborescens 'Annabelle'* is a superior selection from the species, which is native to the eastern United States. Give it plenty of moisture or it will droop.

H.quercifolia (Oakleaf Hydrangea, zones 5-9) is another outstanding Hydrangea for the shady garden. This one takes its name from the shape of its foliage, which becomes tinged with maroon in the fall. Large, white panicles appear in late June and eventually fade to pink and then beige, similar to those of *'Annabelle'*. *H.quercifolia* will grow five to eight feet tall. Older stems have russet brown, exfoliating bark, adding to its value in the landscape. Prune after flowering only for the purpose of removing dead wood or to shape. There are now several cultivars including *'Snowflake'*, which has multiple bracts creating a double-flowered effect. *'Alice'* is much larger at twelve feet and more sun tolerant. The cultivar *'Sikes Dwarf'* grows just three feet tall by four feet wide. As a general rule, give this native of the Southeastern United States moist, fertile, well-drained soil. I have, however, grown this plant in less than ideal conditions (i.e. moisture only when it rains) and it has rewarded me nonetheless with a multiplicity of blossoms.

The latest-blooming Hydrangea is *H.paniculata 'Tardiva'* (Late Panicle Hydrangea, zones 3-8), a native of Japan. Its panicles do not appear until August or September. This woody can be grown as a small tree (ten feet tall) unless it is cut to the ground annually in late winter or early spring, in which case it will only grow three to five feet tall as a fountain-shaped mound. Older bark is gray and peeling. Like the other Hydrangea, this one also needs adequate moisture and partial shade although it will grow in full sun as long as it does not dry out.

If you really want to liven up a shady spot, try *Kerria japonica* (Japanese Kerria, zones 4b-9). Featuring bright yellow flowers in May, both the species and its cultivar, *K.j.'Pleniflora'*, grow approximately six feet tall and wide. I prefer the flower of the species to the multi-petaled *'Pleniflora'* simply because I have a personal bias against double flowers – they look artificial to me. In addition, the flower of the species is a clear yellow whereas that of *'Pleniflora'* is an orangey-yellow, not one of my favorite tones. Another *K.japonica* cultivar that I use frequently is *'Picta'*, which is also sold as *'Variegata'*. This variety is smaller than the others – supposedly only three feet in height – but it has grown four to five feet tall in some of my clients' gardens. The variegated foliage is very attractive and contributes to the landscape long after the flowers have faded.

While the branches of *Kerria* remain evergreen throughout the winter, some of them will die back and need spring pruning. I have grown this genus in several different situations: under Privet "trees," where they've only received filtered light, at a site that only receives morning sun, and at a full-sun site. Its only drawback is its tendency to sport all-green reversions that must be removed. Grow in well-drained soil and do not overwater. Too much moisture will contribute to excessively large plants.

Mahonia aquifolium (Oregon Grape-Holly, zones 4-7) is another excellent plant for the shade. Its shiny holly-like leaves make an excellent background for its bright-yellow, spring flowers and blue berries that appear in late summer and fall. As the temperature drops, the foliage turns purple and remains that color until the following spring. It can grow to nine feet but is easy to keep smaller with judicious pruning a few times a year. A smaller relative, *M. repens* (Creeping Mahonia,), can be used as a groundcover or as a short foundation planting. Both Mahonia are native to the Northwestern United States and prefer moist, acid, well-drained soil.

Pieris japonica (zones 4b-7), which has small, glossy foliage and Lily-of-the-Valley-type creamy white flowers in spring is another evergreen to try. An outstanding feature of *Pieris* is its bronze-red new growth. Many cultivars have been bred from this Oriental native for more intense foliage color or for pink or red blossoms. *P.j.'Variegata'* (Variegated Japanese Pieris, zone 6) has foliage with white margins and is especially useful for dark shady nooks. I was quite impressed by a mass planting of this plant at the Parc André-Citroën in Paris. Old *Pieris* can become as tall as twelve feet but growth is slow.

Viburnums are highly valued for their contribution to the shady garden. Many varieties of this genus have white flowers in one form or another and feature red berries. Since *Viburnum carlesii* (Korean Spice Viburnum, zones 4-8) has very fragrant blooms in April, it should be near a walkway; after they fade, the plant is relatively unprepossessing. *V. x carlcephalum* (Fragrant Snowball, zones 5-8) is a bit larger at six to ten feet tall and displays similar, fragrant blooms in May. Its foliage turns burgundy in the fall. Neither *V.carlesii* nor *V.carlcephalum* has berries. If you are looking for excellent berry color, try *V.plicatum var. tomentosum* (Doublefile Viburnum, zones 5-8). The horizontal branching of this plant lends an unusual architectural element to the garden. The flat blooms undulate across the branches and are followed by bright red peduncles that hold pendent, bright red fruit. Even after the berries have been eaten by birds, the peduncles remain for brilliant winter color. This species has many virtues among which is its dark maroon fall foliage. The height of Viburnums varies from six to ten feet tall, depending on the cultivar.

V.rhytidophyllum (Leatherleaf Viburnum, zones 5-7), with creamy white blossoms and red berries that turn black later in the fall, grows up to fifteen feet tall. Its greatest asset is that it blooms in dense shade. Another Viburnum is *V.setigerum* (Tea Viburnum, zones 5-7), which quickly grows twelve feet tall and appears leggier than the other Viburnum varieties. What makes this plant worthy of recommendation is its stunning bright red berry clusters. In fact, Michael A. Dirr says in his book, "Manual of Woody Landscape Plants," that this plant is "possibly the most handsome fruiter among the Viburnum." Its flowers are undistinguished white cymes and its fall foliage color is inconsistent, varying from orange to reddish-purple. This is one to use at the back of a shrub or perennial border. All of the Viburnum that I have mentioned are native to the Orient. The most important cultural requirement for them is well-drained soil.

One of my favorite woodies for the shade has no flowers, but its structure and foliage color far outweigh the loss of flowers. *Acer palmatum* (Japanese Maple, zone 5), especially the weeping, dissected types, adds so much interest to the landscape. The maroon-red foliage of most of the cultivars blends well with almost any color scheme, but you need to choose the cultivar carefully because some lose their color when the temperature rises in summer.

The color transformation of *A.palmatum var.dissectum* 'Viridis' (Green Cutleaf Japanese Maple, zone 5) never ceases to amaze me. The new growth is reddish in spring; then in summer it turns green; and finally, in fall, it becomes a fiery orange. Winter is the time to fully appreciate its intricate branched form. There are also upright red Japanese Maples and related species such as *A.japonicum* 'Aureum' (zone 5), which has yellow foliage. All of them are best sited in moist, organic, well-drained soil and dappled shade.

The range of plants that we can use to fill our shadows with light is nearly infinite. What fun we can have as we find the perfect plant to turn our supposed liabilities into illuminated assets.

The Fall Garden

By the time October and November arrive, many people have given up on their gardens when it is actually a time to glory in the garden. The air is crisp, sunny days are interspersed with rainy ones (finally) and Indian Summer has come and gone. The fall perennial garden, although not lush like the summer garden, is still a thing of beauty, particularly if shrub roses, subshrubs, vines and woody ornamentals that berry have been incorporated. There is an extensive range of plants that add color, structure and interest to the fall garden. Giving attention to the fall season in our designs will provide an uplifting and exciting landscape. Let's discuss some exceptional plants that should be part of it.

The list of fall-blooming perennials is quite long: among these are *Aconitum* (Monkshood), *Anemone japonica* (Japanese Anemone), *Boltonia* (Bolton's Aster), *Eupatorium fistulosum* (Joe Pye Weed), *Sedum* 'Autumn Joy' and 'Matrona', and *Tricyrtis* (Japanese Toad Lily).

Other perennials for the fall garden are Asters, *Allium tuberosum* (Garlic Chives), *Eupatorium rugosum* 'Chocolate', *Geranium* 'Dilys', *Physostegia virginiana* (Obedient Plant) and the very late blooming but extremely hardy Chrysanthemums such as *Dendrathema* 'Sheffield Pink' and 'Mei-Kyo'.

I'm sure that many of you are familiar with the New England Asters such as *Aster novae-angliae* 'Hella Lacy' (purple) and 'Alma Potschke' (hot pink) but the old, yet underused *Aster tataricus* 'Jin Dai' (Tatarian Aster) is another one to look for. The species is a bit tall at six feet but the cultivar 'Jin Dai' will only grow three to five feet tall. Its uniqueness lies in the fact that it does not even begin blooming until mid to late October and thus is still at its prime in early November. Both drought and heat tolerant, it is somewhat invasive but this trait can be controlled by annual division. Like most Asters, this one requires full sun.

This is the second year that I've grown *Eupatorium rugosum* 'Chocolate' (Chocolate Snakeroot). As of mid-October, it had been in bloom for two weeks and was still going strong. In fact, the fuzzy white flowers had not yet begun to fade. This not a short plant either; it will grow three to four feet and is distinguished earlier in the year by its dark stems and foliage. Give it full sun or partial shade but be aware that the foliage will be greener in the sun.

I love *Allium tuberosum*. These Chives have the typical grassy foliage but do not bloom until mid-September and carry their blooms into mid-October. By November, the seedheads begin to lend interest to the garden. The only drawback to this wonderful plant is its prolific seeding. This can be avoided, however, by assiduous deadheading at the expense of the beauty of the heads during the winter. Like other *Allium*, give this one full sun.

Most hardy Geraniums bloom in the spring and early summer but *Geranium 'Dilys'* starts blooming in midsummer and doesn't quit until frost. Its small magenta blossoms on loosely weaving stems are quite welcome in October and November. This is a plant to use at the front of the sunny border, either by itself or in between a low clumping perennial such as one of the dwarf Balloon Flowers like *Platycodon 'Sentimental Blue'*.

I rarely plant Chrysanthemums because few of them seem to be hardy. However, there are a few very old cultivars that are reliably hardy. *Dendrathema 'Sheffield Pink'* has pink buds but peachy-apricot blossoms which do not even begin blooming until the middle of October. In full sun, it will grow two to three feet tall and wide. It is quite lovely and a favorite of mine. I planted *Dendrathema 'Mei Kyo'* last year. It blooms even later (late October) than *'Sheffield Pink'* and is more of a rosy-pink pompom-type bloom while *'Sheffield Pink'* is a quill type. If unpinched, it will grow to four feet, but if pinched early, will only be eighteen inches.

Most of the ornamental grasses are at their prime in October and November. They vary in height, foliage color and inflorescence color. *Miscanthus sinensis* (Maiden Grass) can be three to six feet tall with white or rosy feathers; *Panicum virgatum* (Switch Grass) can be four to six feet tall with pale yellow or rose panicles, and the foliage can be blue (yellow after frost) or red. *Schizachyrium scoparius* (Little Bluestem) and

Andropogon gerardii (Big Bluestem) not only bloom in the fall but their foliage becomes bright orange. These are all grasses for the sun. For shade, the best fall bloomer is *Calamagrostis arundinacea* 'Brachytricha' (Fall-Blooming Reed Grass), which has dark bottle-brush type inflorescences, at its best when backlit. This grass will grow three to four feet tall.

Although technically not perennials, subshrubs such as *Buddleia davidii* (Butterfly Bush), *Caryopteris x clandonensis* (Blue Mist Shrub) and *Lespedeza thunbergii* (Bush Clover) should be an integral part of the fall garden. *Buddleia* will begin blooming in midsummer, *Caryopteris* in August and *Lespedeza* in late August/early September. All will continue to bloom until frost.

There are other options to bring interest into the fall garden. Among them are shrub roses for their low maintenance requirements and their long bloom. The Carpet series of roses is particularly floriferous as are the Meidillands; their massed color in the fall landscape is particularly vibrant. Some vines, such as *Lonicera* (Honeysuckle) and *Ampelopsis* (Porcelainberry), have beautiful berries in the fall. And don't forget to use woodies such as Viburnums, *Malus* (Crabapple) and *Crataegus* (Hawthorn), to mention a few, as background for the perennials.

With all of these suggestions, the fall garden can be a beautiful and exciting experience.

The Fall Garden Revisited:
Foliage

When the days are golden and the nights are nippy, wonderful changes are occurring in the landscape. Most of us marvel at the explosion of color on the leaves of deciduous trees and shrubs such as *Nyssa sylvatica* (Sour Gum), *Oxydendron arboreum* (Sourwood), *Cornus florida* (Florida Dogwood), *Euonymus alatus* (Burning Bush) and *Aronia arbutifolia* 'Brilliantissima' (Brilliant Red Chokeberry). But how many people see the new colors in perennial foliage or notice the extraordinary array of seedheads and pods?

The most obvious changes are seen on the ornamental grasses but I have discussed their transformation at great length in other articles. Therefore, I will concentrate on the foliage and seedheads of herbaceous plants.

Amsonia (Blue Star Flower) is a genus that is rarely planted, much less recognized, but it is a worthy addition to the perennial garden for its June-blooming pale blue flowers on two- to three-foot stems, willow-like foliage, and its undemanding character; in other words, it is disease and insect resistant and requires very little maintenance. But its strongest point is its overnight metamorphosis from "a nice green plant" during the summer to an eye-catching golden yellow in the fall. This is particularly true of *Amsonia hubrictii* (Arkansas Amsonia), which, unfortunately, is hardy only to zone 6. *Amsonia tabernaemontana* (Blue Star) is much hardier (to zone 3) but in my garden, it never turned yellow although the books say it should. Both will grow in full sun or partial shade, but if grown in shade, they should be cut in half after blooming to prevent flopping.

Another perennial with golden foliage in the fall is *Platycodon grandiflorus* (Balloon Flower). When the foliage turns to gold, the plant stops blooming but just becomes colorful in another mode. What never ceases to amaze me is that I can have plants that are still green and blooming right next to ones that have turned yellow with no blooms. The juxtaposition of the blue flowers next to the yellow foliage is really quite lovely.

Hosta, of course, are available in many colors. When fall comes, the yellow ones stay yellow but the rest of them turn yellow, usually in mid to late October. *Polygonatum* species (Solomon's Seal), a group of woodland perennials, have strong stems with alternate leaves that persist until frost. Cool temperatures stop the flow of chlorophyll and the leaves turn yellow.

The foliage of many of the hardy Geranium reddens with the advent of fall. *Geranium macrorrhizum* (Bigroot Geranium), an excellent choice for the shade garden, comes immediately to mind. The foliage looks as though an artist had wandered through the garden, brushing strokes of red onto the leaves. Some of the foliage of *C.cantabrigiense* 'Biokovo' and *Biokovo* 'Karmina' stays evergreen and some turns a purply-red. Ask not why only some of it turns because I have no answer. Not well known, but a worthy acquaintance is *G.wlassovianum*, which does not produce its flowers (purplish-violet with a white eye) until late summer and has foliage that becomes fiery red in late October.

Last, but not least, I want to mention three groundcovers and vines that add immeasurably to the fall landscape. *Ceratostigma plumbaginoides* (Leadwort) gives us a hint of the future when it foliates in the spring. At that time, its leaves are slightly tinged with bronze. Then in the fall, the leaves become bronze-red, a beautiful contrast with its sky-blue flowers that appeared in August. *Parthenocissus tricuspidata* (Boston Ivy) will climb on anything and before you know it, buildings disappear under a blanket that is green until October when it becomes enflamed. *Vitis coignetiae* (Crimson Glory Vine) has leaves that are similar in shape to those of Boston Ivy but these leaves are much larger. This rampant climber, which needs severe annual pruning, turns bright scarlet in the cool days of Autumn, even in partial shade.

Enjoy the glory days of autumn and remember to incorporate some of Mother Nature's paint brushed creations in your landscapes.

The Fall Garden Revisited:
Seedheads

As fall progresses, some perennials and sub-shrubs are still blooming in my garden, and the bright red berries of *Ilex verticillata* gladden my spirits. But there is also a more intriguing joy in my garden – induced by the subtle colors of foliage and seedheads as well as their interesting shapes when enhanced by backlight.

Astilbe bloomed months ago but I am still enjoying their plumes, which will persist through the winter long after the foliage disappears. These plumes of ascending arms thrust strongly above the foliage, appearing to reach for the sky. The fullest and strongest plumes are found on cultivars of *Astilbe chinensis* such as 'Pumila', 'Späthsommer' and 'Visions'. The plumes of other *Astilbe* species are sparser or do not have such stalwart stems.

Echinops

If deadheaded, *Echinacea purpurea* (Coneflower) fills the garden with rosy pink or white daisy-type flowers from July to October. But as the bloom season ends, I stop deadheading and leave the bronzy stems and golden brown cones for their slightly pyramidal shapes and as a source of food for the birds. Similarly, I leave some of the black cones of *Rudbeckia* for the birds, though I would not advise leaving all of them unless I were growing the *Rudbeckia* in a fairly wild area where it could seed wantonly.

Eryngium (False Sea Holly), with its mass of small, blue prickly flowers from July to September, becomes a sea of silvery-brown, small rounded cones atop a surround of narrow petal-like bracts. *Echinops* (Sea Holly) has larger blue flowers but the effect is similar. Both genera impart a sense of drama to the garden because of their unusual shapes.

Cimicifuga (Snakeroot) is totally different in form from any of these. *Cimicifuga racemosa* blooms in July, but the five-foot stems remain fairly erect well into the fall, and its spires of green "buttons" do not turn brown until the first frost. Only after a heavy frost do the stems blacken and fall apart. *Cimicifuga ramosa* does not bloom until September and continues well into October. Its white blooms, apparently unaffected by very chilly nights, show to great effect against the purple stems and foliage.

Likewise, *Allium tuberosum* (Garlic Chives) do not bloom until September, when their cheerful white heads are most welcome. I have interplanted them with *Iris siberica* in order to wrest two seasons of bloom from the same space. The black seeds keep their hold until well into the winter when the winds disperse them into the garden, leaving the beige open pods to stand bravely above the snow until they finally fall over in early spring. The only drawback is having to dig the seedlings in the spring as they become too numerous. If a low-maintenance garden is desired, plant *Allium tuberosum* in a position where it can seed at will.

Don't forget the beauty of *Clematis* seedheads, which last a very long time. These seedheads are delicate, fuzzy pinwheels that remain well into the winter, long after the leaves have browned.

I frequently include shrub roses in my perennial designs, particularly those of *Rosa rugosa* heritage because most of them have large, brightly colored hips that appear only if the rose is not deadheaded. While the bright orange hips might not seem to fit into a blue/purple/pink color-schemed garden, they are characteristic of the fall palette and provide a bit of spicy excitement.

This array of seedheads is an indication of nature's diversity as well as a reiteration of variety as a design principle. All of these wonderful seedheads remain as a reminder throughout the winter that the garden is not dead but merely dormant and that the cycle of life will begin again in the spring. Next year, be sure to include perennials with seedheads on stems that will remain after the bloom period has ended.

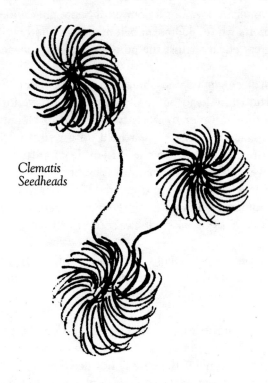

Clematis
Seedheads

The Garden in Winter

On a typical winter day, when the sky is gloomy gray and the wind whirls through the trees, what is there to see that will renew the soul? Is there any color? Any movement? Anything to catch the eye? In most landscapes, the most that can be hoped for is something evergreen, usually an overgrown *Taxus* or *Rhododendron*. But it doesn't have to be that way. Good design creates a landscape that never stops giving inspiration and energy to the viewer. There are so many elements that can be included in a landscape or garden for winter interest. Consider incorporating trees and shrubs with colored and/or exfoliating bark, ones with unusual structure to be utilized as architectural tools. Conifers (other than *Taxus*) may be green but may also be blue or yellow or tipped with white or cream and have different textures. Perennials that remain evergreen, have imposing structure or have pods can also add winter interest. Don't overlook ornamental grasses that retain their inflorescence for all or most of the winter, and woody ornamentals that have bright berries.

A well-designed landscape is always interesting and always changing. That requires a thoughtful mix of evergreens, deciduous woodies and perennials. The more avid gardener would also include bulbs and annuals in this mix. The true test of the "bones" of a landscape is its appearance in the winter. It should appear unified while flowing easily from one area to another. Winter is a good time to evaluate a neighboring landscape from your viewpoint, since it may not be visible when plants are foliated. When the leaves have dropped, what do you see?

As a prelude to the creation of a design, it is crucial that the winter landscape be viewed from indoors, that being the place where most of us spend our winter. This viewing should be made with an eye to locating not only specimen botanical elements but also hardscaping elements such as walls, pergolas, arches, trellises, statuary and paths. Evaluate the areas where we (or our guests) walk when approaching and entering the house.

Give attention to the walkway leading to the door and the surrounding area. Does it guide and welcome visitors? All of this should be visualized twice: when the ground is bare and when the ground and all other elements are covered with snow.

Frequently, the winter landscape can be improved with better use of existing plant material. Overgrown trees and shrubs can be thinned and pruned to emphasize their architecture and artistry. Hedges such as *Buxus* (Boxwood) or *Berberis* (Barberry), which delineate beds, will be more effective "bones" if are carefully clipped to control their aggrandizing tendencies. The only perennials that should be cut to the ground after a heavy frost are those that it blackens. The others lend presence and even appeal. As winter advances, some perennials become ragged and can then be cut down, but others such as *Sedum 'Autumn Joy'* still look good even as the new rosettes appear in early spring. Only then is it necessary to carefully cut down the stalks.

Another frequently overlooked aspect of the winter landscape should be night lighting. Darkness envelopes us so early during the winter that we feel starved of light. Therefore, a house and landscape that are well lit feel welcoming and warm. Lighting, which is generally regarded as a method of emphasizing focal points, thus provides an additional benefit. When designing lighting, remember that the specimen being lit may be viewed from inside as well as outside. This knowledge will affect the placement and type of lights. Lighting is much more effective if it is subtle and if the source is unseen. While most lighting is for emphasis, the use of "fairy lights" can create a totally different effect. I'll never forget my first visit (in a long ago February) to the Tavern on the Green in New York's Central Park. All of the deciduous trees were lit with strands of tiny clear lights wound through their branches. It was like being in a magical fantasyland. This concept could be easily achieved in our landscapes.

The sun (when it does appear) offers us another aspect of lighting – shadows! Study the landscape during the winter to see where and when shadows are or can be cast on the ground or on significant walls and then pick plant material that will allow this feature to be employed.

Conditions of Design

I would like to elaborate now on some of the types of plant material to which I alluded to at the beginning of this article. The emphasis on sight in the landscape is so strong that sound as a facet of the landscape is often forgotten. Ornamental grasses are one of the best ways to integrate sound into the winter landscape. When the wind whips through them, their foliage, and sometimes their inflorescences, rustle loudly. This is true also of perennials such as *Baptisia* (Wild Indigo), which has large black pods that rattle. Oak trees, which often retain their leaves until spring, also provide a welcome rustle.

Ornamental grasses can also contribute color to the winter landscape. Some of them like *Festuca* (Blue Fescue) and *Helictotrichon sempervirens* (Blue Oat Grass) are steely blue year round. *Miscanthus sinensis 'Purpurascens'* (Flame Grass) turns bright orange or red when the temperature drops and remains that way until cut down in spring. *Schizachyrium scoparium* (Little Bluestem), which has blue-green foliage during the summer, also becomes bright orange in the fall and winter. *Imperata cylindrica 'Red Baron'* (Japanese Blood Grass) keeps its ruby red color all year. The last three grasses, if positioned so as to be backlit, look as if they are on fire.

Both broadleaf and needled evergreens are an integral part of the winter landscape. Let's discuss a few members of the large palette of evergreens that are available. The traditional broadleaf evergreens such as *Rhododendron*, *Azalea* (technically *Rhododendron*) and *Ilex* (particularly the Meserve hybrids) must be carefully sited so that winter sun and wind do not desiccate them. A position on the east side of a building is the most efficacious. On the other hand, *Pieris japonica* and *Euonymus* don't seem to mind western winds or southern sun. *Mahonia aquifolium*, (Oregon Grape-Holly) has glossy green leaves that become a purple bronze during the winter and add another color to the winter spectrum.

Needled evergreens occupy a sizeable portion of any book describing woody plants. The *Juniperus* and *Picea* (Spruce) genera include plants with foliage that can be steely blue, silvery blue, yellow or bi-colored in addition to green. The forms of this entire conifer family vary enormously, from pyramidal to mounded, from nested to prostrate and from arching or weeping to columnar. Some have a dense compact form while others have a more open structure. They possess many diverse textures: soft, stiff, feathery, to name a few. Size also varies enormously and mature growth is always an important factor to consider when selecting the appropriate conifer. Many conifers are now available in a wide range of sizes, including dwarf to small (relatively speaking) cultivars.

Several genera offer berries for winter interest, but knowledge of specific cultivars is crucial because some drop their fruit very early. Many articles published in horticultural journals compare the length of time berries remain on their respective trees. You want to be particularly aware of this characteristic when considering *Malus* (Crabapple) and *Crataegus* (Hawthorn). Most *Viburnums* have berries but some are blue-black, which are not easily seen, while others have a more eye-catching orange- red, scarlet-red or yellow berry. *Aronia arbutifolia 'Brilliantissima'* (Brilliant Red Chokeberry) is an under-utilized woody with brilliant, multiple red berries that last all winter.

Many buildings, whether residential or commercial, have large containers planted frequently with colorful annuals during summer and fall. Instead of being empty during the winter, fill them with prunings from conifers, broadleaf evergreens and berried woodies. Or the containers could be filled initially with ornamental grasses or conifers of unusual forms for year-round interest.

One last element of the winter landscape is wildlife. Deer are generally not considered desirable visitors. There are an infinite number of lists and publications about their eating habits, but they are merely guidelines. None are foolproof; moreover, the extremity of the winter is also a factor in these habits. What they might not normally eat may become a delicacy if other food is not available. Birds, on the other hand, are a delight to watch. Many types of feeders are on the market, some of which are touted to be squirrel-proof. The feeders range from utilitarian to beautiful.

I hope that this article will change your outlook on winter. Instead of regarding it as a dreaded event, think of it now as an opportunity to beautify the landscape.

Putting the Perennial Garden to Bed

Once November arrives and it's too late to plant any more perennials, we should discuss getting the perennial garden ready for winter. Ready, set, go! Just cut everything to the ground and rake out all the leaves. Right? WRONG!!!

For starters, I have never understood the obsession with raking leaves out of beds. Of course, they must be raked or blown out of groundcover to prevent rot. However, where they fall between perennials, if left alone, they will decompose eventually and contribute to the organic content of the soil. It also follows that when spring comes, you may still leave them in the beds, where they will soon be covered by the new foliage of bulbs and/or perennials. Since organic matter decomposes and thus eventually disappears, we should add one to two inches of humus to the garden annually. It is much easier to do it in the fall when most of the perennials have been cut back and we have a bit more time than we do in the spring. The humus can easily be laid as a mulch over the leaves.

Perennials that are blackened by frost or become very limp should always be cut to the ground, but perennials that lend structure and architectural interest to the garden should be left standing until early spring. Examples of these perennials include upright *Sedum*, *Aster divaricatus* (White Wood Aster) and *Polygonum affine* (Himalayan Fleeceflower). Another perennial that I do not cut down until spring is the common *Chrysanthemum*. Leaving the heads and stems up means that snow will collect in them and add insulation to the crowns. Few mums survive the winter, especially if they are not planted until fall, but some old cultivars such as 'Pink Grandchild' seem impervious to winter's vagaries.

Some perennials have seedpods that they retain throughout the winter to provide interest in the garden. *Iris siberica*, for instance, develops lovely seedpods on strong stems if all the stalks are not cut down in June after they finish blooming.   Leave only one-third of the stalks in order to sustain rebloom the following year. In late fall, these pods open to reveal dark seeds that are a strong contrast to the foliage, which turns bronzy-orange. There is no need to ever cut back the foliage, as it will be covered by new green foliage in the spring.

Two other examples are *Baptisia australis* (False Blue Indigo), a June bloomer that has large, black pods, and *Allium tuberosum* (Garlic Chives), which doesn't even bloom until September and then retains its seedheads well into winter. The only drawback to the *Allium* seedheads is that these seeds do germinate readily and should thus be confined to an area where they are free to do so unless you are willing to dig them out when they appear where they are unwanted.

Dried *Astilbe* blossoms, particularly those of the *chinensis* species, which are thicker than those of the *Arendsii* hybrids, can be left on the plants through the winter to provide additional interest.

Another group of plants that should be left up for winter interest are the sub-shrubs such as *Lavandula* (Lavender), *Perovskia* (Russian Sage), *Caryopteris* (Blue Mist Shrub) and *Buddleia* (Butterfly Bush). All of these have strong architectural features but die back almost to their woody bases during the winter. If you prune them back in the fall, they are liable to die all the way back. Instead, wait until mid to late spring, when you can see the new foliation, before pruning back to just above it. In a mild winter, these plants may only die back halfway, and unless you prune back further, they will be taller than normal for that year.

What you do with *Coreopsis verticillata* (Threadleaf Tickseed) is a toss-up. You could take the time to cut it back to the ground, or you could let Mother Nature knock it down gradually during the winter and just wait for the new foliage to cover it up. This allows you to add organic matter to your garden without paying for it – just another way of letting the cycles of nature assist in your garden.

Naturally, those perennials that are evergreen are left alone in order to let us know that the garden is merely resting. As with the big three of groundcovers (*Pachysandra*, *Ivy* and *Vinca*), it is necessary to remove fall leaves from all groundcovers, including *Arabis*, *Aubrieta*, *Armeria*, *Campanula poscharkyana*, *Phlox subulata* and those hardy geraniums that remain green. If they are spreading more than is desired, the best time to prune them back is immediately after they flower in the spring.

Technically, roses are shrubs, not perennials, but I mention them here because they are frequently used in the perennial garden, the taller ones as background and the shorter ones in the mid-ground or foreground. On many roses, if the dead flowers are not pruned off after August, hips will develop. They look a lot like cherry tomatoes and provide wonderful visual interest. Especially beautiful are varieties of *Rosa rugosa*, some of which are bright orange and others are very red.

One of the greatest attributes of ornamental grasses is their beauty and visual impact during the fall and winter, when most perennials are dormant and invisible. It is for this reason that they should not be cut back in the fall. Their inflorescences vary in density and thus in ability to withstand shattering, but the mass of foliage still stands as a sentinel in the winter landscape. Few plants are as breathtaking as a grouping of snow-covered *Miscanthus* (Maiden Grass) swaying in the gale force of a blizzard.

Now I hope that you will take this information and put it into practice so that all perennial gardens will have reminders of the previous seasons and portents of seasons to come.

Reflections
on
Design

Mary, Mary, Quite Contrary, How Does Your Garden Grow? A Treatise on Plant Habit

Knowledge about the culture of plants, such as light and moisture requirements as well as various aspects like color of bloom, time of bloom, and size and texture of foliage, are all very important. If, however, that knowledge does not include growth habit, a design that looks great upon being installed will look like a jungle in no time flat.

I love *Lysimachia clethroides* (Gooseneck), but it can be very invasive since its root system consists of long rhizomes that will run as far as the site allows. Plant it in rich, moist soil and watch it mow down everything in its path. Plant it in dry soil beneath an old Crabapple and it will stay exactly where you planted it. Or, plant it next to another aggressive perennial such as *Rudbeckia fulgida* 'Goldsturm' and let them fight it out. This is just as true for woodies like *Cornus alba* 'Sibirica' (Red Twig Dogwood) and *Sorbaria sorbifolia* (False Spirea) as it is for perennials. The growth habit of virtually any aggressive plant will be affected by such site factors.

Clumping plants, on the other hand, will never take over a site. This is not to say that the clumps will not increase in size; they will. The really important factor here is allowing enough space initially for that growth. In the effort to produce instant landscapes for impatient clients, it is tempting to reduce the amount of space needed because the newly installed landscape looks very sparse. Ornamental grasses are an excellent case in point. Most of the *Miscanthus sinensis* (Maiden Grass) cultivars will ultimately grow almost as large in diameter as they grow tall. This means spacing them approximately five feet apart. If sufficient space is not left, the landscape will look overcrowded within five to ten years. Then it becomes necessary to remove some of them. And to you I say, "Good luck!" Ornamental grasses have incredibly thick, fibrous root systems that require a backhoe to dig them out after a few years. Once a landscape has been installed, there is frequently no room to maneuver such machinery.

In addition, the client will have spent more money on plant material and its installation than necessary.

The answer to this problem is twofold. One, client education is crucial. Show pictures of landscapes when newly installed, one year later, two years later, and five years later. This pictorial illustration will have infinitely more impact than anything you can say. Second, suggest planting annuals for the first few years until the landscape starts to fill out. This gives you the opportunity to provide your clients with additional services, and your company with additional income. As the landscape becomes mature, fewer annuals will be needed but they will always add extra color.

The height of mature plants is crucial in their selection. Let me modify the meaning of mature to take reality into account. A tree that would be eighty feet when mature in the wild will probably mature to fifty to sixty feet in the landscape. And then the question becomes, "How long will that take?" What is the growth rate: slow, medium or fast? This is a problem that each of us must struggle with. I usually show the canopy of a deciduous tree as 2/3 the size of its mature landscape diameter. This means that the owner of the building should not have problems for at least twenty-five years and perhaps fifty. We can disagree on whether this is too many but my basic philosophy is to not create trouble for present or future owners.

How often do we fail to see houses because they are totally hidden by woodies that were planted too close to the house or because they are no longer pruned? In older landscapes, plant material was frequently chosen without regard to ultimate size because gardeners were plentiful and cheap. Today, we repeatedly hear from our clients that they want low maintenance. Part of low maintenance is choosing plants that will not need to be pruned, but the tradeoff is looking small initially. If, for instance, a *Taxus* (Yew) is desired for placement under a three-foot-high windowsill, why select *Taxus x media* 'Brownii', which will grow six feet high when *Taxus x media* 'Wardii', which will only grow to three feet, would be more appropriate? Again, probably because of client impatience coupled with the availability of larger immediate size with the 'Brownii'.

A totally different aspect of plant habit is plant patterns. As landscape architects, designers and contractors, we tend to design plant groupings as lines or triangles, sometimes as curves and drifts. What we rarely recall is nature's way of clustering plants but then feathering them out on the ends. The other element we forget is that nature doesn't plant everything in a grouping at the same time; therefore, the individual plants in a cluster have varying heights. We tend to order the same size material for each selection in a design.

I have tried to raise some questions about how our "gardens" will grow – as a naturally unfolding creation that will delight our clients – or as an overgrown jungle that will infuriate them in years to come. Think about it!

A 67 > 10 yrs   2015
77 > 20 yrs.
87 > 30 yrs.
97

Lavender Envy

I'm a sucker for any blue or purple flowers, especially *Campanula* and *Scabiosa*, *Stokesia* and *Perovskia*. But Lavender and *Delphinium* haven't survived the three-strike rule. I'll try any plant three times but if it dies all three times, I say, "Que sera, que sera" (although what I really want to say is not so philosophical or printable).

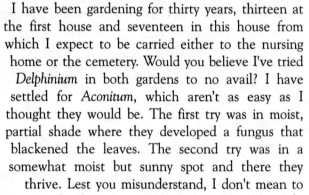

I have been gardening for thirty years, thirteen at the first house and seventeen in this house from which I expect to be carried either to the nursing home or the cemetery. Would you believe I've tried *Delphinium* in both gardens to no avail? I have settled for *Aconitum*, which aren't as easy as I thought they would be. The first try was in moist, partial shade where they developed a fungus that blackened the leaves. The second try was in a somewhat moist but sunny spot and there they thrive. Lest you misunderstand, I don't mean to imply that *Aconitum* are less desirable than *Delphinium*. They are quite beautiful, but I too look at the glossy photographs of *Delphinium* and lust after them.

Delphinium

I've always liked Lavender but after seeing the long border at Wakehurst Place in England (only two hundred feet long!), I came away with a severe case of Lavender envy. Now, mind you, I don't even have space for a border that long, but I wanted at least a drift of Lavender. I've tried three different cultivars of *Lavandula angustifolia* as well as *Lavandin* and *Lavandula 'Grosso'* but all of them bit the dust (or the clay, so to speak).

Recently, I spent three days in Provence. One of those days, I drove with my husband on the Routes de la Lavande, through two areas called

Le Vaucluse and Les Alpes de Haute-Provence. We saw field after field of Lavender, always growing in rows for ease of harvesting. Most of the time, the color was an intense purple but sometimes lighter where a different cultivar was being grown. Even though it was an extremely warm July day, we rolled the windows down so that we could inhale the breathtaking fragrance.

Lavender

The soil seen between the rows was most enlightening – actually small pieces of rock. We were in the mountains, after all, and most of the fields were naturally sloped. I, of course, was trying to grow it in Cleveland where the indigenous soil is heavy clay. Now, don't get me wrong; I didn't just dig a hole and plant Lavender. I really do know better! I rototilled the soil and then added copious amounts of leaf humus to improve the drainage. And my Lavender plants did last for a few years. But even if I had double dug, I suspect they would still have died from too much care and wet feet.

I have, however, finally discovered a way to grow it. Plant it in the garden near a concrete or asphalt driveway that is cracked. The garden Lavender will seed into the cracks and thus ensure its succession nearby when it succumbs to winter rot. I dread the day the city inspector comes to tell us that the driveway must be resurfaced. I wonder if I can get a variance for the crack where my Lavender grows?

Musings of a Frenzied Plant Junkie

What a contradiction of terms! How can a frenzied plant junkie possibly have time for musings? There is one way – in retrospect. First let me explain that I am a landscape designer who has been gardening and collecting plants for thirty years. Besides the fact that I am a confirmed, obsessed plant nerd, I also hesitate to include plants in my designs that I have not trialed first in my own garden. After all, plants can't read and therefore they frequently do not follow their zone designations or cultural requirements. Second, I work out of my house and my gardens are my showcase. I invite clients to my gardens to show them plants "in the flesh," so to speak – so much more effective than showing pictures in books. Third, particularly in the spring, I am pressed for time. Not only am I trying to maintain my gardens, but I am also designing and ordering plant material for my clients.

So when I see that first box of goodies on my doorstep, I think, "Oh ye-e-e-s-s-s!" And then I think, "Oh n-o-o-o-o!" It's already two o'clock and I have another appointment at four. How will I ever be able to get everything planted?

Let me backtrack a bit to those dreary winter months of December, January and February when our mailboxes fill with multiple catalogs that break the mailman's back but give us gardeners dreams of plant heaven. The biggest problem, of course, is curbing the desire to have everything. The next problem is finding a way to organize our dreams. Some of you may have unlimited space, but I suspect that most of you, like me, have relatively small spaces. My gardens are so crowded that if I order something new, I have to take out something old.

Therefore, I use legal pads to organize my desires. I write the name of the catalog at the top of the page; under it, I list every plant that sounds wonderful to me, along with the pertinent information needed to find a home for it: height, time and color of bloom, type of foliage, cultural requirement, etc. I do this for every catalog I receive. Then I look at the charts of the gardens. I make these charts on tracing paper. To paraphrase the Big Bad Wolf, "All the better to erase you with my dear". Each year, I make a copy of the trace as it was for the previous year and thus have a record for each year. Then I erase the plants I'm taking out or those that have died.

Next, I look at my notes from my garden notebook to help determine what can be added and what should be removed. What hasn't come up to my expectations? What died? What should be moved? What has particular design needs that aren't being satisfied by the plants around it?

Then I'm back to the wish lists and begin a kind of internal thought process. If I order this one, where will it go? I like *Centranthus ruber*, for instance; it's reliable and blooms for a long time but I'd really like to grow *Achillea millefolium* 'Summerwine'. I saw it in Germany in 1995 and was very impressed with its beautiful color and the fact that the faded color is still attractive, not true for many of the other cultivars. It would also echo the color of the foliage of *Panicum virgatum* 'Rehbraun' that is nearby. This process includes plant knowledge, incorporates particular needs of the garden that year, and continually readjusts one's vision of the ideal garden.

Achillea

All this takes place during the winter and then we have that brief period of calm before the first box of goodies arrives, pitching me right back into a frenzied state. Putting in the new plants is never a quick process. The first thing I do is make permanent plant labels so that they can be put in the ground the minute the plant is installed. Otherwise, I never get around to it. Then I look through my notes to see where each plant is supposed to go, but I become so involved in the decision process that in some instances, I forgot to write down the location. Then I pray that I noted the location on one of the garden charts. Thank goodness I did (most of the time)! Next I have to dig out and pot up the old plant to sell or give away. And then I often notice that I forgot to prune the plant next to it so out come the pruning shears.

If I have no indication where the new plant was supposed to go, I walk around the gardens with plant and spade in hand, pondering where it will look good and survive. That ritual really lengthens the planting process! Time is short and I know that the next box is going to come just as I am getting ready to do something else.

I really love spring but the days are never long enough, not even with the slight advantage of Daylight Savings Time. But I absolutely love what I do. That's why I'm a frenzied plant junkie.

Biography

Bobbie Schwartz is the owner of Bobbie's Green Thumb, a fulltime business focusing on landscape design, consultation, installation and maintenance, lecturing and writing.

Most of Bobbie's designs are for residential properties, but she has also designed for industrial sites, corporations, a hospital and the City of Brecksville, a Cleveland suburb. Her landscape signature is the use of perennials, flowering shrubs and ornamental grasses to facilitate color and interest throughout the year.

An obsessed gardener for thirty years and a landscape designer for twenty years, she is continually learning from seminars and conventions of the trade associations to which she belongs. Her extensive travels to gardens and nurseries have contributed greatly to her knowledge of design and new plants.

Bobbie is actively involved in several industry organizations, including the Perennial Plant Association and the Association of Professional Landscape Designers, of which she is a certified member. She is currently serving on the APLD board as Certification Committee Chair. Over the past fifteen years, she has been a board member, a committee chair or a committee member of the Ohio Nursery and Landscape Association in addition to serving as president of the Design Network, a Cleveland-area group of women working in various aspects of horticulture.

She is a member of the Ohio Landscapers Association and writes a monthly column about perennials and grasses for its publication, "The Growing Concern." The column is also published periodically by the Northern Ohio Perennial Society, of which she is a member. In addition, she writes a quarterly column on design for "The Buckeye," the publication of the Ohio and Nursery Landscape Association. Bobbie has also written articles for "American Nurseryman," "WaterShapes" and "Fine Gardening," and has contributed to "The Cleveland Garden Handbook," "Great Garden Shortcuts" and "Easy-Care Perennial

Gardens." She has recently written and published "The Design Puzzle: Putting the Pieces Together," a book about the elements of design and designing with plant material.

Bobbie has received several design awards from the Perennial Plant Association, the Ohio Nursery and Landscape Association, the Ohio Landscapers Association and the Cleveland Botanical Garden/ASLA for residential, commercial and institutional designs.

Since 1988, Bobbie has been lecturing locally at Cleveland Botanical Garden, the Holden Arboretum and nationally for botanical gardens and landscape associations on various aspects of design and perennial and ornamental grass gardening.

Notes

Notes